KU-711-963

RUSSIA

RAINE

OLDOVA

RUSSIA

TURKEY

KAZAKHSTAN

MONGOLIA

CYPRUS

GEORGIA
ARM
AZER
UZBEK
KIRGIZ

TURKEY

TURKMEN
TAJIK

SYRIA
IRAQ
IRAN
AFGH

CHINA

N. KOREA
S. KOREA
JAPAN

LEB
ISR
JOR
KUWAIT
BAH
QATAR
UAE

PAKISTAN

NEPAL
BHU

BYA

EGYPT

SAUDI
ARABIA

OMAN

B'DESH

INDIA

MYANMAR
LAOS

HONG
KONG
MACAO

TAIWAN

HAD

SUDAN

ERITREA
DJIB
YEMEN

THAILAND
VIETNAM
CAMBODIA

PHILIPPINES

CAR

ETHIOPIA

SOMALIA

SRI
LANKA

BRUNEI

NGO-BRAZ
CONGO

UGAN
DA
KENYA

TANZANIA

MALAYSIA
SING

PAPUA
NEW GUINEA

OLA
ZAMBIA
MALAWI

INDONESIA

FIJI

BIA

ZIMB
BOT
MOZ
MADAGASCAR
MAURITIUS

AUSTRALIA

SWAZ

SOUTH
AFRICA
LESOTHO

NEW ZEALAND

POCKET WORLD IN FIGURES
2010 EDITION

OTHER ECONOMIST BOOKS

Guide to Analysing Companies
Guide to Business Modelling
Guide to Business Planning
Guide to Economic Indicators
Guide to the European Union
Guide to Financial Management
Guide to Financial Markets
Guide to Investment Strategy
Guide to Management Ideas and Gurus
Guide to Organisation Design
Guide to Project Management
Guide to Supply Chain Management
Numbers Guide
Style Guide

Book of Obituaries
Brands and Branding
Business Consulting
Business Miscellany
Coaching and Mentoring
Dealing with Financial Risk
Economics
Emerging Markets
The Future of Technology
Headhunters and How to Use Them
Mapping the Markets
Marketing
Successful Strategy Execution
The City

Directors: an A–Z Guide
Economics: an A–Z Guide
Investment: an A–Z Guide
Negotiation: an A–Z Guide

The
Economist

Pocket
World in
Figures

2010 Edition

THE ECONOMIST IN ASSOCIATION WITH
PROFILE BOOKS LTD

Published by Profile Books Ltd,
3A Exmouth House, Pine Street, London EC1R OJH

This edition published by Profile Books in association with
The Economist, 2009

Copyright © The Economist Newspaper Ltd, 1991, 1992,
1993, 1994, 1995, 1996, 1997, 1998, 1999, 2000, 2001, 2002, 2003,
2004, 2005, 2006, 2007, 2008, 2009

Material researched and compiled by
Sophie Brown, Andrea Burgess, Ulrika Davies, Mark Doyle,
Ian Emery, Andrew Gilbert, Conrad Heine, Carol Howard,
Stella Jones, David McKelvey, Roxana Willis, Simon Wright

All rights reserved. Without limiting the rights under copyright
reserved above, no part of this publication may be reproduced,
stored in or introduced into a retrieval system, or transmitted, in any
form or by any means (electronic, mechanical, photocopying,
recording or otherwise), without the prior written permission of
both the copyright owner and the above publisher of this book.

The greatest care has been taken in compiling this book. However,
no responsibility can be accepted by the publishers or compilers
for the accuracy of the information presented.

Typeset in Officina by MacGuru Ltd
info@macguru.org.uk

Printed in Italy by
Graphicom

A CIP catalogue record for this book is available
from the British Library

ISBN 978 1 84668 136 3

Contents

CONTENTS

Biggest users of clean energy   Lowest access to improved
sanitation facilities for urban and rural populations
Lowest access to improved water source for rural population

Notes

This 2010 edition of *The Economist Pocket World in Figures*
includes new rankings on such things as demographics,
company market capitalisations, stockmarket falls,
universities, broadband, leisure time and activities, police
forces, household sizes, champagne drinking and various
environmental measures. The world rankings consider 189
countries; all those with a population of at least 1m or a GDP
of at least $1bn; they are listed on pages 250–54. The country
profiles cover 67 major countries. Also included are profiles of
the euro area and the world. The extent and quality of the
statistics available varies from country to country. Every care
has been taken to specify the broad definitions on which the
data are based and to indicate cases where data quality or
technical difficulties are such that interpretation of the
figures is likely to be seriously affected. Nevertheless, figures
from individual countries may differ from standard
international statistical definitions. The term "country" can
also refer to territories or economic entities.

Some country definitions
Macedonia is officially known as the Former Yugoslav Republic
of Macedonia. Data for Cyprus normally refer to Greek Cyprus
only. Data for China do not include Hong Kong or Macau. For
countries such as Morocco they exclude disputed areas.
Congo-Kinshasa refers to the Democratic Republic of Congo,
formerly known as Zaire. Congo-Brazzaville refers to the other
Congo. Data for the EU refer to the 27 members as at
January 1 2007, unless otherwise noted. Euro area data
normally refer to the 13 members that had adopted the euro
as at December 31 2007: Austria, Belgium, France, Finland,
Germany, Greece, Ireland, Italy, Luxembourg, Netherlands,
Portugal, Slovenia and Spain. For more information about the
EU and the euro area see page 248.

Statistical basis
The all-important factor in a book of this kind is to be able to
make reliable comparisons between countries. Although this
is never quite possible for the reasons stated above, the best
route, which this book takes, is to compare data for the same
year or period and to use actual, not estimated, figures
wherever possible. Where a country's data is excessively out of
date, it is excluded. The research for this edition of *The
Economist Pocket World in Figures* was carried out in 2009

using the latest available sources that present data on an internationally comparable basis.

Data in the country profiles, unless otherwise indicated, refer to the year ending December 31 2007. Life expectancy , crude birth, death and fertility rates are based on 2005–10 averages; human development indices and energy data are for 2006; marriage and divorce, employment, health and education data refer to the latest year for which figures are available; internet hosts are as at January 2009.

Other definitions

Data shown in country profiles may not always be consistent with those shown in the world rankings because the definitions or years covered can differ.

Statistics for principal exports and principal imports are normally based on customs statistics. These are generally compiled on different definitions to the visible exports and imports figures shown in the balance of payments section.

Definitions of the statistics shown are given on the relevant page or in the glossary on page 248. Figures may not add exactly to totals, or percentages to 100, because of rounding or, in the case of GDP, statistical adjustment. Sums of money have generally been converted to US dollars at the official exchange rate ruling at the time to which the figures refer.

Energy consumption data are not always reliable, particularly for the major oil producing countries; consumption per head data may therefore be higher than in reality. Energy exports can exceed production and imports can exceed consumption if transit operations distort trade data or oil is imported for refining and re-exported.

Abbreviations

bn	billion (one thousand million)	m	million
EU	European Union	PPP	Purchasing power parity
kg	kilogram	TOE	tonnes of oil equivalent
km	kilometre	trn	trillion (one thousand billion)
GDP	Gross domestic product	...	not available
ha	hectare		

World rankings

Countries: natural facts

Countries: *the largest*[a]

'000 sq km

1	Russia	17,075		31	Tanzania	945
2	Canada	9,971		32	Nigeria	924
3	China	9,561		33	Venezuela	912
4	United States	9,373		34	Namibia	824
5	Brazil	8,512		35	Pakistan	804
6	Australia	7,682		36	Mozambique	799
7	India	3,287		37	Turkey	779
8	Argentina	2,767		38	Chile	757
9	Kazakhstan	2,717		39	Zambia	753
10	Sudan	2,506		40	Myanmar	677
11	Algeria	2,382		41	Afghanistan	652
12	Congo	2,345		42	Somalia	638
13	Saudi Arabia	2,200		43	Central African Rep	622
14	Greenland	2,176		44	Ukraine	604
15	Mexico	1,973		45	Madagascar	587
16	Indonesia	1,904		46	Kenya	583
17	Libya	1,760		47	Botswana	581
18	Iran	1,648		48	France	544
19	Mongolia	1,565		49	Yemen	528
20	Peru	1,285		50	Thailand	513
21	Chad	1,284		51	Spain	505
22	Niger	1,267		52	Turkmenistan	488
23	Angola	1,247		53	Cameroon	475
24	Mali	1,240		54	Papua New Guinea	463
25	South Africa	1,226		55	Sweden	450
26	Colombia	1,142		56	Morocco	447
27	Ethiopia	1,134			Uzbekistan	447
28	Bolivia	1,099		58	Iraq	438
29	Mauritania	1,031		59	Paraguay	407
30	Egypt	1,000		60	Zimbabwe	391

Mountains: *the highest*[b]

	Name	Location	Height (m)
1	Everest	Nepal-China	8,848
2	K2 (Godwin Austen)	Pakistan	8,611
3	Kangchenjunga	Nepal-Sikkim	8,586
4	Lhotse	Nepal-China	8,516
5	Makalu	Nepal-China	8,463
6	Cho Oyu	Nepal-China	8,201
7	Dhaulagiri	Nepal	8,167
8	Manaslu	Nepal	8,163
9	Nanga Parbat	Pakistan	8,126
10	Annapurna I	Nepal	8,091
11	Gasherbrum I	Pakistan-China	8,068
12	Broad Peak	Pakistan-China	8,047
13	Gasherbrum II	Pakistan-China	8,035
14	Xixabangma Feng	China	8,012

a Includes freshwater.
b Includes separate peaks which are part of the same massif.

Rivers: *the longest*

	Name	Location	Length (km)
1	Nile	Africa	6,695
2	Amazon	South America	6,516
3	Yangtze	Asia	6,380
4	Mississippi-Missouri system	North America	5,959
5	Ob'-Irtysh	Asia	5,568
6	Yenisey-Angara-Selanga	Asia	5,550
7	Huang He (Yellow)	Asia	5,464
8	Congo	Africa	4,667
9	Rio de la Plata-Paraná	South America	4,500
10	Irtysh	Asia	4,440

Deserts: *the largest*

	Name	Location	Area ('000 sq km)
1	Sahara	Northern Africa	8,600
2	Arabia	SW Asia	2,300
3	Gobi	Mongolia/China	1,166
4	Patagonian	Argentina	673
5	Great Victoria	W and S Australia	647
6	Great Basin	SW United States	492
7	Chihuahuan	N Mexico	450
8	Great Sandy	W Australia	400

Lakes: *the largest*

	Name	Location	Area ('000 sq km)
1	Caspian Sea	Central Asia	371
2	Superior	Canada/US	82
3	Victoria	E Africa	69
4	Huron	Canada/US	60
5	Michigan	US	58
6	Tanganyika	E Africa	33
7	Baikal	Russia	31
	Great Bear	Canada	31

Islands: *the largest*

	Name	Location	Area ('000 sq km)
1	Greenland	North Atlantic Ocean	2,176
2	New Guinea	South-west Pacific Ocean	809
3	Borneo	Western Pacific Ocean	746
4	Madagascar	Indian Ocean	587
5	Baffin	North Atlantic Ocean	507
6	Sumatra	North-east Indian Ocean	474
7	Honshu	Sea of Japan-Pacific Ocean	227
8	Great Britain	Off coast of north-west Europe	218

Notes: Estimates of the lengths of rivers vary widely depending on eg, the path to take through a delta. The definition of a desert is normally a mean annual precipitation value equal to 250ml or less. Australia (7.69 sq km) is defined as a continent rather than an island.

Population: size and growth

Largest populations
Millions, 2007

1	China	1,331.4	34	Kenya	36.0
2	India	1,135.6	35	Algeria	33.9
3	United States	303.9	36	Canada	32.9
4	Indonesia	228.1	37	Morocco	32.4
5	Brazil	191.3	38	Afghanistan	32.3
6	Pakistan	164.6	39	Uganda	30.9
7	Bangladesh	147.1	40	Iraq	30.3
8	Russia	141.9	41	Peru	28.8
9	Nigeria	137.2	42	Nepal	28.2
10	Japan	128.3	43	Venezuela	27.7
11	Mexico	109.6	44	Uzbekistan	27.4
12	Vietnam	86.4	45	Malaysia	26.2
13	Philippines	85.9	46	Saudi Arabia	25.8
14	Germany	82.7	47	Ghana	23.0
15	Ethiopia	81.2	48	Taiwan	22.9
16	Egypt	76.9	49	North Korea	22.7
17	Turkey	75.2	50	Yemen	22.3
18	Iran	71.2	51	Romania	21.5
19	Thailand	65.3	52	Sri Lanka	21.1
20	Congo-Kinshasa	61.2	53	Australia	20.6
21	France	60.9	54	Mozambique	20.5
22	United Kingdom	60.0	55	Syria	20.0
23	Italy	58.2	56	Madagascar	19.6
24	Myanmar	51.5	57	Côte d'Ivoire	18.8
25	South Korea	48.1	58	Angola	16.9
26	South Africa	47.7		Cameroon	16.9
27	Colombia	47.0	60	Chile	16.6
28	Ukraine	45.5	61	Netherlands	16.4
29	Spain	43.6	62	Niger	14.9
30	Tanzania	39.7	63	Kazakhstan	14.8
31	Argentina	39.5	64	Cambodia	14.6
32	Poland	38.5	65	Mali	14.3
33	Sudan	37.8	66	Burkina Faso	14.0

Largest populations
Millions, 2025

1	China	1,453.1	15	Vietnam	102.1
2	India	1,431.3	16	Congo-Kinshasa	98.1
3	United States	358.7	17	Turkey	87.4
4	Indonesia	263.3	18	Iran	87.1
5	Pakistan	246.3	19	Germany	79.3
6	Brazil	213.8	20	Tanzania	72.6
7	Nigeria	210.1		Thailand	72.6
8	Bangladesh	195.0	22	United Kingdom	66.6
9	Russia	132.3	23	France	65.8
10	Mexico	123.4	24	Italy	60.0
11	Japan	120.8	25	Kenya	57.6
12	Ethiopia	119.8		Myanmar	57.6
13	Philippines	117.3	27	Sudan	56.7
14	Egypt	105.0	28	Colombia	54.9

Fastest growing populations
Average annual % change, 2010–15

1	Niger	3.73		Zambia	2.44
2	Timor-Leste	3.35	26	Guatemala	2.42
3	Afghanistan	3.25	27	Equatorial Guinea	2.37
4	Uganda	3.23	28	Mali	2.36
5	Burkina Faso	3.10	29	Congo-Brazzaville	2.34
6	Tanzania	2.92	30	Sierra Leone	2.33
7	Benin	2.90	31	Côte d'Ivoire	2.31
8	West Bank and Gaza	2.87	32	Guinea-Bissau	2.30
9	Eritrea	2.80		Togo	2.30
10	Guinea	2.75	34	Papua New Guinea	2.17
11	Malawi	2.74	35	Pakistan	2.13
	Somalia	2.74	36	Nigeria	2.12
	Yemen	2.74	37	Cameroon	2.10
14	Rwanda	2.67	38	Zimbabwe	2.08
15	Angola	2.66	39	Mauritania	2.07
16	Congo-Kinshasa	2.65		Mozambique	2.07
17	Iraq	2.63	41	Kuwait	2.04
18	Chad	2.62	42	Ghana	2.03
19	Liberia	2.57	43	Burundi	2.00
20	Kenya	2.56		Sudan	2.00
21	Gambia, The	2.52	45	United Arab Emirates	1.97
	Madagascar	2.52	46	Saudi Arabia	1.95
23	Ethiopia	2.49	47	Honduras	1.93
24	Senegal	2.44	48	Oman	1.92

Slowest growing populations
Average annual % change, 2010–15

1	Lithuania	-0.70	24	Portugal	0.10
2	Georgia	-0.65	25	Channel Islands	0.12
3	Moldova	-0.64		Taiwan	0.12
4	Bulgaria	-0.63	27	Greece	0.14
5	Ukraine	-0.57	28	Bermuda	0.15
6	Belarus	-0.49		Denmark	0.15
7	Latvia	-0.39	30	Italy	0.17
8	Romania	-0.38	31	Austria	0.19
9	Russia	-0.34		Czech Republic	0.19
10	Virgin Islands (US)	-0.26		Slovenia	0.19
11	Hungary	-0.20	34	Barbados	0.24
12	Japan	-0.19	35	Martinique	0.26
13	Croatia	-0.18	36	South Korea	0.27
14	Bosnia	-0.17	37	Netherlands	0.31
	Germany	-0.17	38	Armenia	0.32
16	Poland	-0.13		Finland	0.32
17	Serbia	-0.06	40	Belgium	0.33
18	Estonia	-0.03		Malta	0.33
19	Cuba	0.02	42	Aruba	0.34
	Greenland	0.02		North Korea	0.34
	Macedonia	0.02		Uruguay	0.34
22	Montenegro	0.04	45	Trinidad & Tobago	0.35
23	Slovakia	0.09	46	Switzerland	0.37

Population: matters of breeding

Fertility rates, 2010–15

Highest av. no. of children per woman		Lowest av. no. of children per woman	
1 Niger	6.86	1 Hong Kong	1.01
2 Afghanistan	6.25	Macau	1.01
3 Somalia	6.17	3 Bosnia	1.24
4 Timor-Leste	6.00	4 South Korea	1.26
5 Uganda	5.91	5 Japan	1.27
6 Chad	5.78	6 Belarus	1.29
7 Burkina Faso	5.55	Malta	1.29
8 Congo-Kinshasa	5.52	Poland	1.29
9 Guinea-Bissau	5.43	Singapore	1.29
10 Zambia	5.34	10 Germany	1.34
11 Angola	5.33	11 Romania	1.35
12 Tanzania	5.30	Slovakia	1.35
13 Mali	5.17	13 Portugal	1.39
14 Malawi	5.12	14 Austria	1.41
15 Benin	5.09	Greece	1.41
16 Equatorial Guinea	5.08	Italy	1.41
17 Rwanda	5.05	17 Channel Islands	1.42
18 Guinea	5.01	Hungary	1.42
19 Sierra Leone	4.97	19 Lithuania	1.43
20 Ethiopia	4.80	20 Russia	1.46

Crude birth rates

Births per 1,000 population, 2008

Highest		Lowest	
1 Guinea-Bissau	50	1 Austria	9
Liberia	50	Bosnia	9
3 Malawi	48	Croatia	9
Mali	48	Germany	9
Sierra Leone	48	Italy	9
Uganda	48	Japan	9
7 Afghanistan	47	Macau	9
Angola	47	Taiwan	9
9 Burundi	46	9 Andorra	10
Niger	46	Bulgaria	10
Somalia	46	Cuba	10
12 Burkina Faso	45	Greece	10
13 Chad	44	Hong Kong	10
Congo-Kinshasa	44	Hungary	10
15 Nigeria	43	Latvia	10
Rwanda	43	Lithuania	10
Zambia	43	Malta	10
18 Benin	42	Poland	10
Guinea	42	Portugal	10
Timor-Leste	42	Romania	10
21 Mozambique	41	Serbia	10
Yemen	41	Slovakia	10
23 Eritrea	40	Slovenia	10
Ethiopia	40	South Korea	10
Kenya	40	Switzerland	10
		Ukraine	10

Women[a] who use modern methods of contraception[b]

2007, highest, %		2007, lowest, %	
1 China	90.2	1 Chad	2.8
2 Hong Kong	86.2	2 Sierra Leone	5.3
3 Switzerland	82.0	3 Angola	6.2
United Kingdom	82.0	4 Liberia	6.4
5 France	81.8	5 Guinea-Bissau	7.6
6 South Korea	80.5	Sudan	7.6
7 Costa Rica	80.0	7 Somalia	7.9
8 Netherlands	78.5	8 Eritrea	8.0
Vietnam	78.5	Mauritania	8.0
10 Belgium	78.4	10 Mali	8.1
11 Colombia	78.2	11 Guinea	9.1
12 Denmark	78.0	12 Gambia, The	9.6
13 Puerto Rico	77.7	13 Timor-Leste	10.0
14 Finland	77.4	14 Afghanistan	10.3
Hungary	77.4	15 Niger	11.2
16 Uruguay	77.0	16 Senegal	11.8
17 Brazil	76.7	17 Nigeria	12.6
18 Mauritius	75.9	18 Macedonia	13.5
19 Sweden	75.2	19 Burkina Faso	13.8
20 Albania	75.1	20 Ethiopia	14.7
21 Canada	74.7	21 Côte d'Ivoire	15.0
22 New Zealand	74.1	22 Mozambique	16.5
23 Slovakia	74.0	23 Rwanda	17.4
24 Cuba	73.8	24 Benin	18.6
Iran	73.8	25 Burundi	19.7
Norway	73.8	26 Yemen	23.1
Slovenia	73.3	27 Oman	23.7
28 Paraguay	72.8	Uganda	23.7
United States	72.8	29 Ghana	25.2
30 Ecuador	72.7	30 Togo	25.7

Sex ratio, males per 100 females, 2009

Highest		Lowest	
1 Qatar	307	1 Latvia	85
2 United Arab Emirates	205	2 Estonia	86
3 Kuwait	147	Russia	86
4 Bahrain	135	Ukraine	86
5 Oman	129	5 Armenia	87
6 Saudi Arabia	121	Belarus	87
7 Greenland	113	Netherlands Antilles	87
8 Bhutan	112	8 Lithuania	88
9 Andorra	110	Martinique	88
10 China	108	10 El Salvador	89
11 Afghanistan	107	Georgia	89
Brunei	107	12 Hong Kong	90
Faroe Islands	107	Hungary	90
India	107	Moldova	90
Libya	107	Virgin Islands (US)	90

a Married women aged 15–49.
b Excludes traditional methods of contraception, such as the rhythm method.

Population: age

Median age[a]

Highest, 2009		*Lowest, 2009*	
1 Japan	44.4	1 Niger	15.1
2 Germany	43.9	2 Uganda	15.5
3 Italy	43.0	3 Congo-Kinshasa	16.5
4 Finland	41.8	4 Burkina Faso	16.7
5 Channel Islands	41.7	5 Afghanistan	16.8
6 Switzerland	41.6	Malawi	16.8
7 Bulgaria	41.5	Zambia	16.8
8 Austria	41.4	8 Chad	17.0
Slovenia	41.4	9 Timor-Leste	17.2
10 Croatia	41.3	10 Angola	17.3
Greece	41.3	11 West Bank and Gaza	17.4
Hong Kong	41.3	12 Tanzania	17.5
13 Belgium	41.1	13 Mali	17.6
14 Sweden	40.7	Somalia	17.6
15 Portugal	40.6	Yemen	17.6
16 Denmark	40.5	16 Ethiopia	17.9
Netherlands	40.5	Mozambique	17.9
18 Bermuda	40.0	Senegal	17.9
Singapore	40.0	19 Benin	18.3
20 France	39.9	Kenya	18.3
Latvia	39.9	Madagascar	18.3
Spain	39.9	Sierra Leone	18.3
23 Hungary	39.7	23 Guinea	18.4
United Kingdom	39.7	Liberia	18.4
25 Canada	39.6	25 Nigeria	18.5
26 Estonia	39.5	Rwanda	18.5
27 Czech Republic	39.4	27 Guatemala	18.7
Lithuania	39.4	Guinea-Bissau	18.7
Ukraine	39.4	29 Gambia, The	18.8
30 Luxembourg	39.1	30 Zimbabwe	18.9
31 Andorra	39.0	31 Eritrea	19.0
32 Bosnia	38.9	32 Cameroon	19.1
33 Malta	38.7	Equatorial Guinea	19.1
Norway	38.7	Swaziland	19.1
35 Martinique	38.3	35 Iraq	19.2
36 Aruba	38.2	36 Central African Rep	19.4
37 Romania	38.1	Congo-Brazzaville	19.4
Virgin Islands (US)	38.1	Côte d'Ivoire	19.4
39 Belarus	38.0	39 Lesotho	19.6
40 Macau	37.9	Togo	19.6
Netherlands Antilles	37.9	41 Burundi	19.9
Poland	37.9	Mauritania	19.9
Russia	37.9	Papua New Guinea	19.9
44 Cuba	37.7	44 Sudan	20.1
45 Australia	37.5	45 Ghana	20.4
46 Serbia	37.4	Laos	20.4
47 Barbados	37.3	Tajikistan	20.4
South Korea	37.3	48 Honduras	20.7
49 Georgia	37.2	49 Namibia	20.8

a Age at which there are an equal number of people above and below.

Population aged 0–14
%, 2009

1	Niger	49.9	19	Sierra Leone	43.4
2	Uganda	48.9	20	Benin	43.1
3	Congo-Kinshasa	46.7	21	Madagascar	42.9
4	Burkina Faso	46.3	22	Guinea	42.8
5	Malawi	46.2		Kenya	42.8
6	Zambia	46.2	24	Liberia	42.7
7	Afghanistan	46.1	25	Guinea-Bissau	42.6
8	Chad	45.7	26	Nigeria	42.5
9	Angola	45.0	27	Gambia, The	42.3
	Timor-Leste	45.0		Rwanda	42.3
11	Somalia	44.9	29	Guatemala	41.9
	West Bank and Gaza	44.9	30	Eritrea	41.5
13	Tanzania	44.7	31	Iraq	41.1
14	Mali	44.2	32	Equatorial Guinea	41.0
15	Mozambique	44.0	33	Cameroon	40.9
16	Yemen	43.8	34	Central African Rep	40.6
17	Senegal	43.6		Côte d'Ivoire	40.6
18	Ethiopia	43.5	36	Congo-Brazzaville	40.5

Population aged 60 and over
%, 2009

1	Japan	29.7	19	Hungary	22.1
2	Italy	26.4	20	Slovenia	21.9
3	Germany	25.7	21	Channel Islands	21.8
4	Sweden	24.7		Czech Republic	21.8
5	Bulgaria	24.2	23	Netherlands	21.4
6	Finland	24.0	24	Lithuania	21.3
	Greece	24.0	25	Malta	21.2
8	Portugal	23.3	26	Norway	20.8
9	Croatia	23.1		Ukraine	20.8
10	Belgium	23.0	28	Virgin Islands (US)	20.2
	Denmark	23.0	29	Romania	20.0
	Switzerland	23.0	30	Bermuda	19.9
13	Austria	22.9		Faroe Islands	19.9
14	France	22.7	32	Canada	19.5
15	Latvia	22.5	33	Serbia	19.4
16	Estonia	22.4	34	Australia	19.1
	United Kingdom	22.4		Puerto Rico	19.1
18	Spain	22.2	36	Martinique	19.0

Population aged 80 and over
%, 2009

1	Japan	6.1	9	Austria	4.7
2	Italy	5.8		United Kingdom	4.7
3	Sweden	5.4	11	Finland	4.5
4	France	5.3		Norway	4.5
5	Germany	5.0	13	Portugal	4.4
6	Belgium	4.9	14	Denmark	4.2
	Spain	4.9	15	Estonia	4.0
	Switzerland	4.9		Guadeloupe	4.0

City living

Biggest cities[a]
Population m, 2007

1	Tokyo, Japan	35.7
2	Mexico City, Mexico	19.0
	Mumbai, India	19.0
	New York, US	19.0
5	São Paulo, Brazil	18.8
6	Delhi, India	15.9
7	Shanghai, China	15.0
8	Kolkata, India	14.8
9	Dhaka, Bangladesh	13.5
10	Buenos Aires, Argentina	12.8
11	Los Angeles, US	12.5
12	Karachi, Pakistan	12.1
13	Cairo, Egypt	11.9
14	Rio de Janeiro, Brazil	11.7
15	Osaka, Japan	11.3
16	Beijing, China	11.1
	Manila, Philippines	11.1
18	Moscow, Russia	10.5
19	Istanbul, Turkey	10.1
20	Paris, France	9.9
21	Seoul, South Korea	9.8
22	Lagos, Nigeria	9.5
23	Jakarta, Indonesia	9.1
24	Chicago, United States	9.0
25	Guangzhou, China	8.8
26	London, UK	8.6
27	Lima, Peru	8.0
28	Tehran, Iran	7.9
29	Bogotá, Colombia	7.8
	Kinshasa, Congo-Kins.	7.8
31	Shenzhen, China	7.6
32	Chennai, India	7.2
	Hong Kong	7.2
	Tianjin, China	7.2
	Wuhan, China	7.2
36	Bangalore, India	6.8
37	Bangkok, Thailand	6.7
38	Lahore, Pakistan	6.6
39	Chongqing, China	6.5
40	Hyderabad, India	6.4
41	Santiago, Chile	5.7
42	Belo Horizonte, Brazil	5.6
	Madrid, Spain	5.6
	Miami, United States	5.6
45	Philadelphia, US	5.5
46	Ahmadabad, India	5.4
47	Ho Chi Minh City, Viet.	5.3
48	Toronto, Canada	5.2

49	Baghdad, Iraq	5.1
50	Barcelona, Spain	4.9
51	Dallas, United States	4.8
	Khartoum, Sudan	4.8
	Shenyang, China	4.8
54	Pune, India	4.7
55	Saint Petersburg, Russia	4.6
56	Atlanta, United States	4.5
	Boston, United States	4.5
	Chittagong, Bangladesh	4.5
	Dongguan, China	4.5
	Houston, United States	4.5
	Riyadh, Saudi Arabia	4.5
62	Hanoi, Vietnam	4.4
	Singapore	4.4
64	Sydney, Australia	4.3
	Washington, DC, US	4.3
66	Alexandria, Egypt	4.2
	Guadalajara, Mexico	4.2
68	Chengdu, China	4.1
	Detroit, United States	4.1
	Yangon, Myanmar	4.1
71	Luanda, Angola	4.0
	Xian, China	4.0
73	Pôrto Alegre, Brazil	3.9
74	Abidjan, Côte d'Ivoire	3.8
	Surat, India	3.8
76	Ankara, Turkey	3.7
	Guiyang, China	3.7
	Melbourne, Australia	3.7
	Monterrey, Mexico	3.7
	Montréal, Canada	3.7
	Nanjing, China	3.7
	Recife, Brazil	3.7
83	Brasília, Brazil	3.6
	Harbin, China	3.6
	Phoenix, United States	3.6
86	Busan, South Korea	3.5
	Salvador, Brazil	3.5
	San Francisco, US	3.5
89	Algiers, Algeria	3.4
	Berlin, Germany	3.4
	Fortaleza, Brazil	3.4
	Johannesburg, S. Africa	3.4
93	Kabul, Afghanistan	3.3
	Medellín, Colombia	3.3
	Pyongyang, North Korea	3.3
	Rome, Italy	3.3

a Urban agglomerations. Data may change from year-to-year based on reassessments of agglomeration boundaries.

Fastest growing cities[a]

Average annual growth, 2005–10, %

1	Abuja, Nigeria	8.3	24	Addis Ababa, Ethiopia	3.5
2	Luanda, Angola	6.0		Douala, Cameroon	3.5
3	Sana'a, Yemen	5.3		Dubai, UAE	3.5
4	Kinshasa, Congo-Kins.	4.8	27	Ghaziabad, India	3.4
	Lomé, Togo	4.8	28	Antananarivo, Madag.	3.3
	Ouagadougou, Burkina F.	4.8		Brasília, Brazil	3.3
7	Kabul, Afghanistan	4.6		Dhaka, Bangladesh	3.3
	Mbuji-Mayi, Congo-Kins.	4.6		Nanchang, China	3.3
9	Bamako, Mali	4.4	32	Abidjan, Côte d'Ivoire	3.2
10	Brazzaville, Congo-Braz.	4.3		Accra, Ghana	3.2
	Dar es Salaam, Tanzania	4.3		Dakar, Senegal	3.2
	Lubumbashi, Congo-Kins.	4.3		Jinxi, China	3.2
13	Florianópolis, Brazil	4.0		Mosul, Iraq	3.2
	Kuwait City, Kuwait	4.0		Port-au-Prince, Haiti	3.2
15	Maputo, Mozambique	3.9		Santa Cruz, Bolivia	3.2
16	Kampala, Uganda	3.8		Shantou, China	3.2
	Nairobi, Kenya	3.8		Surat, India	3.2
	Phnom Penh, Cambodia	3.8	41	Conakry, Guinea	3.1
19	Karaj, Iran	3.7		Faridabad, India	3.1
	Kumasi, Ghana	3.7		Medina, Saudi Arabia	3.1
	Lagos, Nigeria	3.7		Xuzhou, China	3.1
22	Chittagong, Bangladesh	3.6	45	Khulna, Bangladesh	3.0
	Yaoundé, Cameroon	3.6		Quito, Ecuador	3.0

Slowest growing cities[a]

Average annual growth, 2005–10, %

1	Ufa, Russia	-0.7		Hiroshima, Japan	0.0
2	Busan, South Korea	-0.6		Kyoto, Japan	0.0
3	Budapest, Hungary	-0.4		Manchester, UK	0.0
	St Petersburg, Russia	-0.4		Yerevan, Armenia	0.0
5	Havana, Cuba	-0.3	28	Birmingham, UK	0.1
	Montevideo, Uruguay	-0.3		Bucharest, Romania	0.1
	Nizhniy Nov., Russia	-0.3		Glasgow, UK	0.1
	Novosibirsk, Russia	-0.3		Kazan, Russia	0.1
	Samara, Russia	-0.3		Naples, Italy	0.1
10	Belgrade, Serbia	-0.2		Osaka, Japan	0.1
	Dnipropetrovs'k, Ukraine	-0.2	34	Athens, Greece	0.2
	Omsk, Russia	-0.2		Berlin, Germany	0.2
	Rostov-on-Don, Russia	-0.2		London, UK	0.2
	Turin, Italy	-0.2		Moscow, Russia	0.2
15	Chelyabinsk, Russia	-0.1		Paris, France	0.2
	Daegu, South Korea	-0.1		Sapporo, Japan	0.2
	Kharkiv, Ukraine	-0.1		Yekaterinburg, Russia	0.2
	Milan, Italy	-0.1	41	Fukuoka, Japan	0.3
	Prague, Czech Republic	-0.1		Rotterdam, Netherlands	0.3
	Rome, Italy	-0.1		Taipei, Taiwan	0.3
	Seoul, South Korea	-0.1		Tbilisi, Georgia	0.3
22	Brussels, Belgium	0.0		Zurich, Switzerland	0.3
	Copenhagen, Denmark	0.0			

a With populations over 750,000.

Urban population
Highest, %, 2007

1	Bermuda	100.0		Réunion	93.1
	Cayman Islands	100.0		Venezuela	93.1
	Hong Kong	100.0	17	Netherlands Antilles	92.5
	Macau	100.0	18	Iceland	92.2
	Singapore	100.0		Uruguay	92.2
6	Guadeloupe	98.3	20	Argentina	91.8
	Kuwait	98.3	21	Israel	91.7
8	Puerto Rico	98.2	22	United Kingdom	89.9
9	Martinique	98.0	23	Andorra	89.3
10	Belgium	97.3	24	Australia	88.6
11	Qatar	95.6	25	Bahrain	88.5
12	Virgin Islands (US)	94.7	26	Chile	88.2
13	Malta	94.1	27	Lebanon	86.8
14	Guam	93.1			

Urban population
Lowest, %, 2007

1	Burundi	10.1	14	Kenya	21.3
2	Papua New Guinea	12.5	15	Afghanistan	23.6
3	Uganda	12.8	16	Swaziland	24.6
4	Trinidad & Tobago	12.9	17	Lesotho	24.7
5	Sri Lanka	15.1	18	Tanzania	25.0
6	Niger	16.4	19	Chad	26.1
7	Ethiopia	16.6	20	Tajikistan	26.4
8	Nepal	16.7	21	Bangladesh	26.6
9	Rwanda	18.2	22	Timor-Leste	26.9
10	Malawi	18.3	23	Vietnam	27.3
11	Burkina Faso	19.1	24	Madagascar	29.1
12	Eritrea	20.2	25	India	29.2
13	Cambodia	20.9			

Quality of living index[a]
New York = 100

1	Vienna, Austria	108.6		Ottawa, Canada	105.0
2	Zurich, Switzerland	108.0	18	Melbourne, Australia	104.8
3	Geneva, Switzerland	107.9	19	Luxembourg	104.6
4	Auckland, New Zealand	107.4	20	Stockholm, Sweden	104.5
	Vancouver, Canada	107.4	21	Perth, Australia	104.3
6	Dusseldorf, Germany	107.2	22	Montreal, Canada	104.2
7	Munich, Germany	107.0	23	Nuremberg, Germany	104.1
8	Frankfurt, Germany	106.8	24	Oslo, Norway	103.7
9	Bern, Switzerland	106.5	25	Dublin, Ireland	103.6
10	Sydney, Australia	106.3	26	Calgary, Canada	103.5
11	Copenhagen, Denmark	106.2		Singapore	103.5
12	Wellington, N. Zealand	105.9	28	Hamburg, Germany	103.4
13	Amsterdam, Neths.	105.7	29	Honolulu, US	103.1
14	Brussels, Belgium	105.4	30	Adelaide, Australia	103.0
15	Toronto, Canada	105.3		Helsinki, Finland	103.0
16	Berlin, Germany	105.0		San Francisco, US	103.0

a Based on 39 factors, ranging from political stability to natural environment.

Refugees[a] and asylum seekers

Largest refugee[a] nationalities
'000, 2007

1	Afghanistan	3,057.7	11	Eritrea	208.7
2	Iraq	2,309.2	12	Myanmar	191.3
3	Colombia	551.7	13	Angola	186.2
4	Sudan	523.0	14	Serbia	165.6
5	Somalia	457.4	15	China	149.1
6	Burundi	375.7	16	Sri Lanka	135.0
7	Congo-Kinshasa	370.4	17	Bhutan	110.6
8	West Bank and Gaza	341.2	18	Croatia	100.4
9	Vietnam	327.8	19	Central African Rep	98.1
10	Turkey	221.9	20	Russia	93.2

Countries with largest refugee[a] populations
'000, 2007

1	Pakistan	2,035.0	11	Kenya	265.7
2	Syria	1,503.8	12	Ecuador	264.9
3	Iran	963.5	13	Saudi Arabia	240.7
4	Germany	578.9	14	Uganda	228.7
5	Jordan	500.3	15	Sudan	222.7
6	Tanzania	435.6	16	Venezuela	200.9
7	China	301.1	17	Congo-Kinshasa	177.4
8	United Kingdom	299.7	18	Canada	175.7
9	Chad	294.0	19	India	161.6
10	United States	281.2	20	France	151.8

Asylum applications in industrialised countries
'000, 2007

1	United States	50.7	11	Switzerland	10.8
2	Sweden	36.4	12	Spain	7.7
3	France	29.4		Turkey	7.7
4	Canada	28.3	14	Poland	7.2
	United Kingdom	28.3	15	Netherlands	7.1
6	Greece	25.1	16	Cyprus	6.8
7	Germany	19.2	17	Norway	6.5
8	Italy	14.1	18	Australia	4.4
9	Austria	11.9	19	Ireland	4.0
10	Belgium	11.1			

Origin of asylum applications to indust. countries
'000, 2007

1	Iraq	45.1	10	Iran	8.7
2	Russia	18.8	11	Nigeria	8.0
3	China	17.2	12	Sri Lanka	7.8
4	Serbia	16.1	13	Turkey	7.2
5	Pakistan	14.4	14	Colombia	6.6
6	Somalia	12.3		Haiti	6.6
7	Afghanistan	10.0	16	Bangladesh	6.1
8	Mexico	9.6	17	Syria	5.6
9	Eritrea	9.2	18	India	5.0

a According to UNHCR. Includes people in "refugee-like situations".

The world economy

Biggest economies

GDP, $bn, 2007

1	United States	13,751		24	Saudi Arabia	383
2	Japan	4,384			Taiwan	383
3	Germany	3,317		26	Austria	373
4	China	3,206		27	Greece	313
5	United Kingdom	2,772		28	Denmark	312
6	France[a]	2,590		29	Iran	286
7	Italy	2,102		30	South Africa	283
8	Spain	1,436		31	Argentina	262
9	Canada	1,330		32	Ireland	259
10	Brazil	1,313		33	Finland	245
11	Russia	1,290			Thailand	245
12	India	1,177		35	Venezuela	228
13	Mexico	1,023		36	Portugal	223
14	South Korea	970		37	Colombia	208
15	Australia	821		38	Hong Kong	207
16	Netherlands	766		39	United Arab Emirates	199
17	Turkey	656		40	Malaysia	187
18	Sweden	464		41	Czech Republic	175
19	Belgium	453		42	Romania	166
20	Indonesia	433		43	Nigeria	165
21	Switzerland	424		44	Chile	164
22	Poland	422			Israel	164
23	Norway	388		46	Singapore	161

Biggest economies by purchasing power

GDP PPP, $bn, 2007

1	United States	13,751		23	Argentina	523
2	China	7,097		24	Thailand	519
3	Japan	4,297		25	South Africa	467
4	India	3,097		26	Pakistan	406
5	Germany	2,830		27	Egypt	404
6	United Kingdom	2,143		28	Colombia	378
7	Russia	2,087		29	Belgium	371
8	France	2,078		30	Malaysia	359
9	Brazil	1,833		31	Sweden	336
10	Italy	1,802		32	Venezuela	334
11	Mexico	1,485		33	Ukraine	322
12	Spain	1,416		34	Greece	319
13	South Korea	1,202		35	Austria	311
14	Canada	1,181		36	Switzerland	307
15	Turkey	957		37	Philippines	299
16	Indonesia	838		38	Hong Kong	293
17	Taiwan	784		39	Nigeria	291
18	Iran	778		40	Romania	267
19	Australia	734		41	Algeria	262
20	Netherlands	634		42	Norway	252
21	Poland	609		43	Czech Republic	250
22	Saudi Arabia	554		44	Portugal	241

Note: For a list of 189 countries with their GDPs, see pages 250–254.

a Includes overseas departments.

Regional GDP

$bn, 2008		*% annual growth 2003–08*	
World	60,690	World	4.6
Advanced economies	42,100	Advanced economies	2.5
G7	32,221	G7	2.1
Euro area (16)	13,633	Euro area (16)	2.1
Asia[a]	7,239	Asia[a]	9.1
Latin America	4,210	Latin America	5.3
Eastern Europe[b]	4,049	Eastern Europe[b]	6.7
Middle East	1,814	Middle East	5.9
Africa	1,278	Africa	6.0

Regional purchasing power

GDP, % of total, 2008		*$ per head, 2008*	
World	100.0	World	10,220
Advanced economies	55.3	Advanced economies	36,900
G7	42.1	G7	38,720
Euro area (16)	15.7	Euro area (16)	32,110
Asia[a]	21.0	Asia[a]	4,070
Latin America	8.6	Latin America	10,430
Eastern Europe[b]	8.1	Eastern Europe[b]	12,090
Middle East	3.9	Middle East	10,760
Africa	3.1	Africa	2,460

Regional population

% of total (6.8bn), 2008		*No. of countries[c], 2008*	
Advanced economies	15.3	Advanced economies	33
G7	11.1	G7	7
Euro area (16)	5.0	Euro area (16)	16
Asia[a]	52.9	Asia[a]	23
Latin America	8.5	Latin America	32
Eastern Europe[b]	6.8	Eastern Europe[b]	24
Middle East	3.7	Middle East	13
Africa	12.9	Africa	47

Regional international trade

Exports of goods & services *% of total, 2008*		*Current account balances* *$bn, 2008*	
Advanced economies	65.1	Advanced economies	-465
G7	36.5	G7	-435
Euro area (16)	28.6	Euro area (16)	-96
Asia[a]	13.8	Asia[a]	422
Latin America	5.1	Latin America	-28
Eastern Europe[b]	7.6	Eastern Europe[b]	-34
Middle East	5.6	Middle East	342
Africa	2.7	Africa	12

a Excludes Hong Kong, Japan, Singapore, South Korea and Taiwan.
b Includes Russia, other CIS and Turkey.
c IMF definition.

Living standards

Highest GDP per head
$, 2007

1	Luxembourg	103,040	36	Cyprus	24,900
2	Bermuda	91,490	37	Slovenia	23,380
3	Norway	82,480	38	Israel	22,840
4	Channel Islands	77,170	39	Aruba[bc]	22,580
5	Iceland	64,190	40	Bahrain[a]	21,420
	Qatar[a]	64,190	41	Portugal	21,000
7	Ireland	59,320	42	South Korea	20,010
8	Denmark	57,050	43	Bahamas	19,840
9	Switzerland	56,210	44	Equatorial Guinea	19,550
10	Sweden	49,660	45	Puerto Rico[b]	19,350
11	Netherlands	46,750	46	Malta	18,200
12	Finland	46,260	47	Czech Republic	16,930
13	United States	45,590	48	French Polynesia[bd]	16,910
14	United Kingdom	45,440	49	Taiwan	16,740
15	Andorra[b]	45,190	50	French Guiana[a]	16,060
16	Austria	44,880	51	Oman[a]	16,040
17	Belgium	42,610	52	Réunion[a]	15,830
18	Kuwait	42,100	53	Saudi Arabia	15,800
19	France	41,970	54	Trinidad & Tobago	15,670
20	United Arab Emirates	41,460	55	Estonia	15,580
21	Cayman Islands[bd]	41,260	56	Guam[bc]	14,370
22	Canada	40,330	57	Virgin Islands (US)[bd]	14,340
23	Germany	40,320	58	New Caledonia[be]	14,230
24	Australia	39,070	59	Slovakia	13,890
25	Faroe Islands[c]	35,420	60	Hungary	13,770
26	Italy	35,400	61	Netherlands Ant.[bd]	12,500
27	Singapore	35,160	62	Latvia	11,930
28	Japan	34,310	63	Croatia	11,560
29	New Zealand	32,090	64	Lithuania	11,360
30	Spain	32,020	65	Poland	11,070
31	Brunei[a]	30,030	66	Barbados[c]	10,430
32	Hong Kong	29,910	67	Chile	9,880
33	Macau[a]	29,740	68	Guadeloupe[a]	9,780
34	Greenland[bc]	29,310	69	Mexico	9,720
35	Greece	28,000	70	Martinique[a]	9,590

Lowest GDP per head
$, 2007

1	Burundi	120	11	Niger	290
2	Congo-Kinshasa	140	12	Somalia[b]	290
3	Liberia	200	13	Rwanda	340
4	Guinea-Bissau	210	14	Mozambique	360
5	Ethiopia	250	15	Nepal	370
6	Malawi	260	16	Timor-Leste	370
7	Zimbabwe[c]	260	17	Gambia, The	380
8	Afghanistan[a]	260	18	Madagascar	380
9	Eritrea	280	19	Togo	380
10	Sierra Leone	280	20	Uganda	380

a 2006 b Estimate. c 2005 d 2004 e 2003

Highest purchasing power
GDP per head in PPP (USA = 100), 2007

1	Luxembourg	174.3	36	Bahamas[b]	62.1
2	Qatar[a]	155.1	37	Bahrain[a]	61.6
3	Bermuda[bc]	153.3	38	New Zealand	60.0
4	Norway	117.2	39	Slovenia	58.7
5	United Arab Emirates[d]	116.7	40	Israel	57.7
6	Brunei	110.1	41	Cyprus	54.4
7	Channel Islands[b]	109.2		South Korea	54.4
8	Singapore	109.0	43	Czech Republic	53.0
9	Kuwait[d]	102.2	44	Trinidad & Tobago	51.6
10	United States	100.0	45	Malta	50.6
11	Ireland	97.9	46	Saudi Arabia	50.3
12	Macau[d]	96.7	47	Portugal	49.9
13	Cayman Islands[bc]	96.1	48	Martinique[d]	48.8
14	Andorra[b]	93.2	49	Oman[d]	48.7
15	Hong Kong	92.8	50	Aruba[bc]	47.8
16	Switzerland	89.2	51	Estonia	44.7
17	Netherlands	84.9	52	Guadeloupe	44.6
18	Austria	82.0	53	Slovakia	44.0
19	Sweden	80.5	54	Greenland	43.9
20	Denmark	79.2	55	Hungary	41.1
21	Canada	78.5	56	Réunion	40.2
22	Iceland	78.4	57	Puerto Rico[b]	40.1
23	United Kingdom	77.1	58	French Polynesia[bc]	39.5
24	Australia	76.6	59	Lithuania	38.5
	Belgium	76.6	60	Barbados[a]	37.2
26	Finland	75.7	61	Latvia	35.9
27	Germany	75.5	62	Croatia	35.2
28	Taiwan	75.4	63	Netherlands Antilles[bc]	35.1
29	France	73.9		Poland	35.1
30	Japan	73.8	65	Gabon	33.3
31	Spain	69.2	66	Guam[ab]	32.9
32	Faroe Islands	68.0		New Caledonia[be]	32.9
33	Equatorial Guinea	67.2	68	Russia	32.2
34	Italy	66.6	69	French Guiana	31.9
35	Greece	62.5	70	Virgin Islands (US)[bc]	31.8

Lowest purchasing power
GDP per head in PPP (USA = 100), 2007

1	Zimbabwe[b]	0.4	10	Afghanistan[b]	1.5
2	Burundi	0.7		Sierra Leone	1.5
	Congo-Kinshasa	0.7	12	Timor-Leste	1.6
4	Liberia	0.8	13	Ethiopia	1.7
5	Central African Republic	0.9		Malawi	1.7
6	Guinea-Bissau	1.0		Togo	1.7
7	Somalia[b]	1.3	16	Mozambique	1.8
8	Eritrea	1.4	17	Myanmar[a]	1.9
	Niger	1.4		Rwanda	1.9

Note: for definition of purchasing power parity see page 249.
a 2005   b Estimate.   c 2004   d 2006   e 2003

The quality of life

Human development index[a]

Highest, 2006

1	Iceland	96.8		31	United Arab Emirates	90.3
	Norway	96.8		32	Bahrain	90.2
3	Canada	96.7		33	Portugal	90.0
4	Australia	96.5		34	Qatar	89.9
5	Ireland	96.0		35	Czech Republic	89.7
6	Netherlands	95.8		36	Malta	89.4
	Sweden	95.8		37	Barbados	88.9
8	Japan	95.6		38	Hungary	87.7
	Luxembourg	95.6		39	Poland	87.5
10	France	95.5		40	Chile	87.4
	Switzerland	95.5		41	Slovakia	87.2
12	Finland	95.4		42	Estonia	87.1
13	Denmark	95.2		43	Lithuania	86.9
14	Austria	95.1		44	Latvia	86.3
15	United States	95.0		45	Croatia	86.2
16	Spain	94.9		46	Argentina	86.0
17	Belgium	94.8		47	Uruguay	85.9
18	Greece	94.7		48	Cuba	85.5
19	Italy	94.5		49	Bahamas	85.4
20	New Zealand	94.4		50	Costa Rica	84.7
21	Hong Kong	94.2		51	Mexico	84.2
	United Kingdom	94.2		52	Libya	84.0
23	Germany	94.0		53	Oman	83.9
24	Israel	93.0		54	Saudi Arabia	83.5
25	South Korea	92.8		55	Bulgaria	83.4
26	Slovenia	92.3		56	Trinidad & Tobago	83.3
27	Brunei	91.9		57	Panama	83.2
28	Singapore	91.8		58	Venezuela	82.6
29	Cyprus	91.2		59	Romania	82.5
	Kuwait	91.2		60	Malaysia	82.3

Human development index[a]

Lowest, 2006

1	Sierra Leone	32.9		10	Chad	38.9
2	Central African Rep	35.2			Ethiopia	38.9
3	Congo-Kinshasa	36.1		12	Mali	39.1
4	Liberia	36.4		13	Guinea	42.3
5	Mozambique	36.6		14	Côte d'Ivoire	43.1
6	Niger	37.0		15	Rwanda	43.5
7	Burkina Faso	37.2		16	Eritrea	44.2
8	Burundi	38.2		17	Zambia	45.3
9	Guinea-Bissau	38.3		18	Malawi	45.7

a GDP or GDP per head is often taken as a measure of how developed a country is, but its usefulness is limited as it refers only to economic welfare. In 1990 the UN Development Programme published its first estimate of a Human Development Index, which combined statistics on two other indicators – adult literacy and life expectancy – with income levels to give a better, though still far from perfect, indicator of human development. In 1991 average years of schooling was combined with adult literacy to give a knowledge variable. The HDI is shown here scaled from 0 to 100; countries scoring over 80 are considered to have high human development, those scoring from 50 to 79 medium and those under 50 low.

Economic freedom index[a]

2009

1	Hong Kong	90.0	20	Belgium	72.1
2	Singapore	87.1	21	Macau	72.0
3	Australia	82.6	22	Barbados	71.5
4	Ireland	82.2	23	Austria	71.2
5	New Zealand	82.0	24	Cyprus	70.8
6	United States	80.7	25	Germany	70.5
7	Canada	80.5		Sweden	70.5
8	Denmark	79.6	27	Bahamas	70.3
9	Switzerland	79.4	28	Norway	70.2
10	United Kingdom	79.0	29	Spain	70.1
11	Chile	78.3	30	Lithuania	70.0
12	Netherlands	77.0	31	Armenia	69.9
13	Estonia	76.4	32	El Salvador	69.8
14	Iceland	75.9		Georgia	69.8
15	Luxembourg	75.2	34	Botswana	69.7
16	Bahrain	74.8	35	Taiwan	69.5
17	Finland	74.5	36	Czech Republic	69.4
18	Mauritius	74.3		Slovakia	69.4
19	Japan	72.8	38	Uruguay	69.1

Gender-related development index[b]

2006

1	Australia	96.3		New Zealand	93.7
	Iceland	96.3		United States	93.7
3	Canada	95.8	22	Hong Kong	93.5
	Norway	95.8	23	Austria	92.9
	Sweden	95.8	24	Slovenia	92.0
6	France	95.2	25	South Korea	91.7
7	Netherlands	95.1	26	Cyprus	91.0
8	Finland	94.9	27	Singapore	89.9
9	Denmark	94.6	28	Portugal	89.7
	Switzerland	94.6	29	Brunei	89.5
11	Spain	94.5	30	Czech Republic	89.4
12	Ireland	94.4	31	Kuwait	89.1
	Japan	94.4	32	Bahrain	88.9
14	United Kingdom	94.1		Malta	88.9
15	Greece	94.0	34	Barbados	88.2
16	Belgium	93.9	35	United Arab Emirates	87.6
	Italy	93.9	36	Hungary	87.5
18	Luxembourg	93.8	37	Poland	87.2
19	Germany	93.7			

a Ranks countries on the basis of indicators of how government intervention can restrict the economic relations between individuals, published by the Heritage Foundation. The ranking includes data on labour and business freedom as well as trade policy, taxation, monetary policy, the banking system, foreign-investment rules, property rights, the amount of economic output consumed by the government, regulation policy, the size of the black market and the extent of wage and price controls. Countries are scored from 80–100 (free) to 0–49.9 (repressed).
b Combines similar data to the HDI (and also published by the UNDP) to give an indicator of the disparities in human development between men and women in individual countries. The lower the index, the greater the disparity.

Economic growth

Highest economic growth
Average annual % increase in real GDP, 1997–2007

1	Equatorial Guinea[a]	66.2	28	Ireland	9.3
2	Turkmenistan	28.8	29	Sudan	9.0
3	Azerbaijan	25.3	30	Georgia	8.9
4	Myanmar	20.9		Lithuania	8.9
5	Armenia	17.0	32	United Arab Emirates	8.7
6	Qatar	15.4	33	Laos	8.6
7	China	15.1	34	Botswana	8.2
8	Angola[a]	14.8	35	Tanzania	8.1
9	Cambodia	14.4	36	Bahrain	7.8
10	Bhutan[a]	12.8	37	Mongolia	7.7
11	Mozambique	11.9	38	Belize	7.5
	Trinidad & Tobago	11.9	39	Ethiopia	7.4
13	Kazakhstan	11.8		Jordan	7.4
14	Tajikistan	11.3		Russia	7.4
15	Chad	11.2		Ukraine	7.4
	Latvia	11.2		Bangladesh	7.4
17	Bosnia[b]	11.1	44	Uzbekistan	7.3
18	Nigeria	10.7	45	Burkina Faso[a]	7.2
19	Sierra Leone	10.5		Dominican Republic	7.2
20	Belarus	10.3	47	Costa Rica	7.1
21	Cape Verde	10.2		Panama	7.1
22	Estonia	10.0	49	Kuwait	7.0
	Vietnam	10.0	50	Singapore	6.8
24	Albania	9.7	51	Gambia, The	6.7
	India	9.7		Luxembourg	6.7
	Uganda	9.7	53	Egypt	6.5
27	Rwanda	9.5		Iran	6.5

Lowest economic growth
Average annual % change in real GDP, 1997–2007

1	Zimbabwe[a]	-3.9	20	Brunei	2.3
2	Guinea-Bissau	-1.3		Papua New Guinea	2.3
3	Eritrea[a]	0.2		Switzerland	2.3
4	Côte d'Ivoire	0.4	23	Barbados	2.4
5	Gabon[a]	0.7	24	Belgium	2.5
6	Haiti	0.9		Burundi[a]	2.5
7	Japan	1.2	26	France	2.6
	Togo	1.2	27	Norway	2.7
9	Central African Rep[a]	1.3	28	Austria	2.8
	Guyana	1.3		Swaziland	2.8
11	Jamaica	1.4	30	Argentina	2.9
	Uruguay	1.4		Netherlands	2.9
13	Italy	1.6	32	Indonesia	3.0
14	Germany	1.7	33	Bahamas	3.1
15	Fiji	1.8	34	Brazil	3.2
16	Congo-Kinshasa[a]	2.1		United States	3.2
	Denmark	2.1	36	Macedonia	3.3
	Paraguay	2.1		United Kingdom	3.3
19	Portugal	2.2		Venezuela	3.3

a Estimate.   b Including Herzegovina.

Highest economic growth
Average annual % increase in real GDP, 1987–97

1	Equatorial Guinea	74.2	10	Belize	10.0
2	China	15.8	11	Taiwan	9.9
3	Malaysia	14.3	12	Indonesia	9.5
4	Singapore	13.9	13	Uganda	8.9
5	Thailand	12.3	14	Fiji	8.8
6	Botswana	11.8	15	United Arab Emirates	8.4
7	Chile	11.4	16	Laos	7.9
8	South Korea	11.0	17	Mauritius	7.8
9	Vietnam	10.9		Syria	7.8

Lowest economic growth
Average annual % change in real GDP, 1987–97

1	Sierra Leone	-4.8	11	Hungary	-0.7
2	Bulgaria	-4.5	12	Haiti	-0.3
3	Congo-Kinshasa	-4.0	13	Mongolia	-0.1
4	Lebanon	-3.1		Zambia	-0.1
5	Romania	-2.2	15	Central African Rep	0.0
6	Libya	-1.8	16	Czech Republic	0.3
	Rwanda	-1.8	17	Nicaragua	0.6
8	Albania	-1.7		Niger	0.6
9	Cameroon	-1.5		Peru	0.6
10	Burundi[a]	-1.0	20	Barbados	0.7

Highest services growth
Average annual % increase in real terms, 1997–2007

1	Azerbaijan	27.8	10	Kazakhstan	12.4
2	Armenia	18.0	11	Bosnia[b]	12.3
3	China	16.7	12	Ethiopia	11.9
4	Cambodia	15.8	13	United Arab Emirates[c]	11.8
5	Bhutan	14.8	14	Moldova	11.7
6	Uganda	13.5		Sudan	11.7
	Georgia	13.5	16	Albania	11.5
8	India	13.3	17	Syria	10.6
9	Latvia	12.6	18	Rwanda	10.5

Lowest services growth
Average annual % change in real terms, 1997–2007

1	Zimbabwe[d]	-4.0	9	Guinea	1.7
2	Guinea-Bissau	-1.6		Paraguay	1.7
3	Central African Rep	-0.9	11	Malawi	1.8
4	Papua New Guinea	-0.7	12	Germany	1.9
5	Côte d'Ivoire	0.0		Italy	1.9
	Jamaica	0.0	14	Switzerland[c]	2.1
7	Eritrea	0.1	15	Lebanon	2.2
8	Japan[c]	1.4	16	Austria	2.4

a Estimate.   b Including Herzegovina.   c 1996–2006   d 1995–2005
Note: Rankings of highest and lowest industrial growth 1997–2007 can be found on page 46 and highest and lowest agricultural growth 1997–2007 on page 49.

Trading places

Biggest exporters
% of total world exports (goods, services and income), 2007

1	Euro area (13)	16.36		22	Austria	1.19
2	United States	11.49		23	India	1.16
3	China	10.42		24	Luxembourg	1.15
4	Germany	8.81		25	Hong Kong	1.01
5	United Kingdom	6.10			Malaysia	1.01
6	Japan	4.69			Norway	1.01
7	France	4.40		28	Australia	1.00
8	Netherlands	3.35		29	Denmark	0.92
9	Italy	3.28		30	Brazil	0.91
10	Canada	2.62		31	Thailand	0.87
11	Belgium	2.34		32	United Arab Emirates	0.84
12	South Korea	2.15		33	Poland	0.73
13	Spain	2.14		34	Turkey	0.70
14	Russia	2.05		35	Czech Republic	0.69
15	Switzerland	1.83		36	Finland	0.64
16	Ireland	1.44		37	Indonesia	0.62
17	Taiwan	1.41		38	Hungary	0.57
18	Mexico	1.39		39	Iran	0.50
19	Sweden	1.38		40	South Africa	0.45
20	Singapore	1.25		41	Portugal	0.43
21	Saudi Arabia	1.20		42	Kuwait	0.42

Most trade dependent
Trade as % of GDP[a], 2007

1	Aruba	122.7
2	Singapore	85.5
3	Malaysia	84.5
4	Vietnam	78.3
5	Bahrain	78.1
6	Slovakia	77.7
7	New Caledonia	76.9
8	Guyana	76.8
9	Lesotho	75.3
10	United Arab Emirates	74.7
11	Belgium	71.3
12	Czech Republic	68.5
	Zimbabwe	68.5
14	Hungary	67.6
15	Equatorial Guinea	65.8
16	Swaziland	65.0
17	Tajikistan	62.9
18	Estonia	61.8
19	Qatar	60.7
20	Taiwan	60.5
21	Slovenia	59.9
22	Bulgaria	59.7

Least trade dependent
Trade as % of GDP[a], 2007

1	North Korea	6.4
2	Bermuda	9.5
3	Brazil	10.7
4	United States	11.3
5	Rwanda	12.3
6	Central African Rep	12.4
7	Japan	14.3
8	Colombia	14.9
9	Cuba	15.1
	Niger[b]	15.1
11	Madagascar[c]	15.3
12	Burundi	15.9
	Haiti	15.9
14	India	16.2
15	Benin[b]	16.4
	Pakistan	16.4
17	Ethiopia	16.6
	Euro area (13)	16.6
19	Burkina Faso	16.7
20	Greece	16.8
21	Albania	17.0
22	Myanmar[b]	17.6

Notes: The figures are drawn wherever possible from balance of payment statistics so have differing definitions from trade statistics taken from customs or similar sources. For Hong Kong and Singapore, domestic exports and retained imports only are used. Euro area data exclude intra-euro area trade.
a Average of imports plus exports of goods as % of GDP.   b 2006   c 2005

Biggest traders of goods
% of world, 2007

Exports			Imports		
1	Euro area (13)	15.49	1	Euro area (13)	14.99
2	Germany	10.12	2	United States	14.83
3	China	9.11	3	Germany	8.10
4	United States	8.61	4	China	6.82
5	Japan	5.07	5	United Kingdom	4.68
6	France	4.08	6	France	4.53
7	Italy	3.75	7	Japan	4.32
8	Netherlands	3.45	8	Italy	3.75
9	United Kingdom	3.30	9	Netherlands	3.07
10	Canada	3.23	10	Canada	2.92
11	South Korea	2.83	11	Spain	2.86
12	Russia	2.65	12	South Korea	2.63
13	Belgium	2.42	13	Belgium	2.43
14	Mexico	2.03	14	Mexico	2.12
15	Spain	1.92	15	India	1.74
16	Taiwan	1.84	16	Russia	1.68
17	Saudi Arabia	1.75	17	Taiwan	1.64
18	Switzerland	1.50	18	Switzerland	1.41
19	United Arab Emirates	1.35	19	Turkey	1.22
20	Malaysia	1.32	20	Australia	1.21
21	Sweden	1.27		Austria	1.21
22	Austria	1.21		Poland	1.21
23	Brazil	1.20	23	Sweden	1.15

Biggest earners from services and income
% of world exports of services and income, 2007

1	Euro area (13)	17.80	24	Norway	0.99
2	United States	16.27	25	Australia	0.91
3	China	12.60	26	Taiwan	0.69
4	United Kingdom	10.76	27	Greece	0.61
5	Germany	6.64	28	Finland	0.57
6	France	4.95	29	Portugal	0.50
7	Japan	4.08	30	Malaysia	0.49
8	Netherlands	3.18	31	Thailand	0.46
9	Luxembourg	2.82	32	Brazil	0.44
10	Spain	2.51		Turkey	0.44
11	Italy	2.48	34	Israel	0.39
12	Hong Kong	2.46	35	Hungary	0.36
13	Ireland	2.39	36	Mexico	0.32
	Switzerland	2.39	37	Kuwait	0.31
15	Belgium	2.21	38	Czech Republic	0.30
16	Canada	1.61	39	Egypt	0.29
17	Sweden	1.56	40	Saudi Arabia	0.28
18	Singapore	1.40	41	South Africa	0.25
19	India	1.23	42	Ukraine	0.22
20	Denmark	1.19	43	Argentina	0.21
21	Austria	1.16	44	Indonesia	0.20
22	Russia	1.07		Macau	0.20
23	South Korea	1.02	46	Lebanon	0.19

Balance of payments: current account

Largest surpluses
$m, 2007

1	China	371,833		26	Indonesia	10,347
2	Germany	252,930		27	Finland	10,121
3	Japan	210,490		28	Angola	9,402
4	Saudi Arabia	95,080		29	Azerbaijan	9,018
5	Switzerland	76,946		30	Belgium	7,216
6	Russia	76,241		31	Chile	7,200
7	Norway	60,459		32	Argentina	7,122
8	Netherlands	59,586		33	Philippines	6,301
9	Kuwait	47,471		34	South Korea	5,954
10	Singapore	39,106		35	Macau	5,863
11	Euro area (13)	38,560		36	Trinidad & Tobago	5,364
12	Sweden	38,416		37	Brunei[a]	5,232
13	United Arab Emirates	37,013		38	Luxembourg	4,928
14	Iran	34,081		39	Israel	4,523
15	Taiwan	31,701		40	Turkmenistan	4,037
16	Algeria	30,600		41	Bahrain	2,907
17	Malaysia	28,931		42	Botswana	2,434
18	Libya	28,454		43	Denmark	2,379
19	Hong Kong	25,746		44	Gabon[b]	1,983
20	Nigeria	21,972		45	Oman	1,918
21	Qatar	21,951		46	Bolivia	1,800
22	Venezuela	20,001		47	Uzbekistan	1,631
23	Thailand	15,755		48	Ecuador	1,598
24	Canada	12,639		49	Brazil	1,550
25	Austria	12,031		50	Peru	1,505

Largest deficits
$m, 2007

1	United States	-731,210		22	Latvia	-6,485
2	Spain	-145,355		23	Serbia	-6,346
3	United Kingdom	-78,760		24	Colombia	-5,866
4	Australia	-57,682		25	Lithuania	-5,692
5	Italy	-51,032		26	Ukraine	-5,272
6	Greece	-44,587		27	Croatia	-4,447
7	Turkey	-37,697		28	Slovakia	-4,103
8	France	-31,250		29	Estonia	-3,772
9	Romania	-23,032		30	Sudan	-3,447
10	Portugal	-21,418		31	Czech Republic	-3,232
11	South Africa	-20,780		32	Iceland	-3,179
12	Poland	-18,595		33	Belarus	-3,060
13	India	-13,799		34	Jordan	-2,776
14	Ireland	-12,695		35	Cyprus	-2,595
15	New Zealand	-10,635		36	Slovenia	-2,293
16	Bulgaria	-8,716		37	Congo-Brazzaville	-2,181
17	Hungary	-8,635		38	Ghana	-2,152
18	Pakistan	-8,295		39	Georgia	-2,119
19	Mexico	-8,115		40	Dominican Republic	-2,068
20	Kazakhstan	-7,333		41	Lebanon	-2,046
21	Vietnam	-6,992		42	Bosnia	-1,930

Note: Euro area data exclude intra-euro area trade.   a 2006   b 2005

Largest surpluses as % of GDP
%, 2007

1	Timor-Leste	298.0	26	Iran	11.9
2	Libya	48.8	27	China	11.6
3	Brunei[a]	45.6	28	Luxembourg	10.0
4	Kuwait	42.3	29	Namibia	9.9
5	Qatar	41.6	30	Aruba	9.5
6	Macau	41.3	31	Venezuela	8.8
7	Turkmenistan	31.2	32	Suriname	8.3
8	Azerbaijan	28.9		Sweden	8.3
9	Trinidad & Tobago	25.7		Taiwan	8.3
10	Saudi Arabia	24.8	35	Netherlands	7.8
11	Singapore	24.2	36	Germany	7.6
12	Algeria	22.6	37	Uzbekistan	7.3
13	Botswana	19.8	38	Papua New Guinea[b]	6.8
14	United Arab Emirates	18.6	39	Thailand	6.4
15	Bahrain	18.4	40	Russia	5.9
16	Switzerland	18.1	41	Equatorial Guinea	5.5
17	Gabon[b]	17.1	42	Oman	5.4
18	Norway	15.6	43	Japan	4.8
19	Malaysia	15.5	44	Chile	4.4
20	Angola	15.3		Philippines	4.4
21	Bolivia	13.7	46	Finland	4.1
22	Nigeria	13.3		Myanmar[a]	4.1
23	Lesotho	13.2	48	Ecuador	3.6
24	Hong Kong	12.4	49	Austria	3.2
25	Bhutan	12.0			

Largest deficits as % of GDP
%, 2007

1	Liberia	-52.1	21	Sierra Leone	-14.3
2	Montenegro	-32.4	22	Ghana	-14.2
3	Congo-Brazzaville	-28.5		Greece	-14.2
4	Burundi	-28.3	24	New Caledonia	-14.1
5	Latvia	-23.9	25	Romania	-13.9
6	Bulgaria	-22.0	26	Togo[a]	-13.6
7	Netherlands Antilles	-21.1	27	Tajikistan	-13.3
8	Fiji	-21.0	28	Bosnia	-12.7
9	Georgia	-20.8	29	Cyprus	-12.2
	West Bank and Gaza[b]	-20.8	30	Mauritania	-12.1
11	Bahamas	-20.0	31	Tanzania	-11.5
12	Nicaragua	-18.3	32	Guinea	-10.2
13	Estonia	-18.0		Mozambique	-10.2
14	Jordan	-17.5		Vietnam	-10.2
15	Moldova	-17.0	35	Spain	-10.1
16	Iceland	-15.9	36	Honduras	-10.0
17	Serbia	-15.8	37	Portugal	-9.6
18	Jamaica	-15.3	38	Cape Verde	-9.2
19	Zimbabwe[b]	-15.0	39	Gambia, The	-9.1
20	Lithuania	-14.8	40	Croatia	-8.7

a 2006 b 2005

Workers' remittances

Inflows, $m, 2007

1	India	35,262	16	Indonesia	6,174
2	China	32,833	17	Pakistan	5,998
3	Mexico	27,144	18	Lebanon	5,769
4	Philippines	16,291	19	Vietnam	5,500
5	France	13,746	20	Serbia and Mont.	4,910
6	Spain	10,687	21	Colombia	4,523
7	Poland	10,496	22	Ukraine	4,503
8	Nigeria	9,221	23	Brazil	4,382
9	Germany	8,570	24	Guatemala	4,254
10	Belgium	8,562	25	Russia	4,100
11	Romania	8,533	26	Portugal	3,945
12	United Kingdom	8,234	27	Australia	3,862
13	Egypt	7,656	28	El Salvador	3,711
14	Morocco	6,730	29	Jordan	3,434
15	Bangladesh	6,562	30	Dominican Republic	3,414

Official reserves[a]

$bn, end-2007

1	China	1,546.4	16	Malaysia	102.0
2	Japan	973.3	17	Italy	94.1
3	Euro area	510.4	18	Thailand	87.5
4	Russia	476.5	19	Mexico	87.2
5	United States	277.5	20	Libya	83.3
6	India	276.6	21	United Arab Emirates	77.2
7	Taiwan	271.1	22	Turkey	76.5
8	South Korea	262.5	23	Switzerland	75.2
9	Brazil	180.3	24	Poland	65.7
10	Singapore	163.0	25	Norway	60.8
11	Hong Kong	152.7	26	United Kingdom	57.3
12	Germany	135.9	27	Indonesia	56.9
13	France	115.5	28	Nigeria	51.9
14	Algeria	115.0	29	Argentina	46.1
15	Angola	110.3	30	Canada	41.1

Official gold reserves

Market prices, $bn, end-2007

1	Euro area	294.9	14	United Kingdom	8.3
2	United States	218.0	15	Lebanon	7.7
3	Germany	91.6	16	Austria	7.5
4	France	69.8		Spain	7.5
5	Italy	65.7	18	Belgium	6.1
6	Switzerland	30.7	19	Algeria	4.7
7	Japan	20.5	20	Sweden	4.0
8	Netherlands	16.7	21	Libya	3.9
9	China	16.1	22	Saudi Arabia	3.8
10	Russia	12.1	23	Philippines	3.5
11	Portugal	10.3	24	South Africa	3.3
12	India	9.6	25	Turkey	3.1
	Venezuela	9.6	26	Greece	3.0

a Foreign exchange, SDRs, IMF position and gold at market prices.

Exchange rates

The Economist's Big Mac index

		Big Mac prices		Implied	Actual $	Under (–)/
		in local currency	in $	PPP[a] of the $	exchange rate	over (+) valuation against $, %

Countries with the most under-valued currencies, January 2009

		in local currency	in $	Implied PPP[a] of the $	Actual $ exchange rate	Under (–)/ over (+) valuation against $, %
1	Malaysia	5.50	1.52	1.55	3.61	-57
2	South Africa	16.95	1.66	4.79	10.20	-53
3	Hong Kong	13.30	1.72	3.76	7.75	-52
4	Russia	62.00	1.73	17.50	35.70	-51
	Indonesia	19,800.00	1.74	5,593.00	11,380.00	-51
6	Thailand	62.00	1.77	17.50	35.00	-50
7	China	12.50	1.83	3.53	6.84	-48
8	Poland	7.00	2.01	1.98	3.48	-43
9	Philippines	98.00	2.07	27.70	47.40	-42
10	Australia	3.45	2.19	0.97	1.57	-38
11	Taiwan	75.00	2.23	21.20	33.60	-37
12	Mexico	33.00	2.30	9.32	14.40	-35
13	Egypt	13.00	2.34	3.67	5.57	-34
14	South Korea	3,300.00	2.39	932.00	1,380.00	-32
15	New Zealand	4.90	2.48	1.38	1.97	-30
16	Chile	1,550.00	2.51	438.00	617.00	-29
17	Peru	8.06	2.54	2.28	3.18	-28
18	Singapore	3.95	2.61	1.12	1.51	-26
19	Saudi Arabia	10.00	2.66	2.82	3.75	-25
20	Hungary	680.00	2.92	192.00	233.00	-18

Countries with the most over-valued or least under-valued currencies, Jan. 2009

		in local currency	in $	Implied PPP[a] of the $	Actual $ exchange rate	Under (–)/ over (+) valuation against $, %
1	Norway	40.00	5.79	11.30	6.91	63
2	Switzerland	6.50	5.60	1.84	1.16	58
3	Denmark	29.50	5.07	8.33	5.82	43
4	Sweden	38.00	4.58	10.70	8.30	29
5	Euro area[b]	3.42	4.38	1.04[c]	1.28[c]	24
6	Israel	15.00	3.69	4.24	4.07	4
7	Brazil	8.02	3.45	2.27	2.32	-2
8	Canada	4.16	3.36	1.18	1.24	-5
9	Argentina	11.50	3.30	3.25	3.49	-7
	United Kingdom	2.29	3.30	1.55[d]	1.44[d]	-7
11	Japan	290.00	3.23	81.90	89.80	-9
12	Turkey	5.15	3.13	1.45	1.64	-12
13	Czech Republic	65.94	3.02	18.60	21.86	-15

a Purchasing-power parity: local price in the 33 countries listed divided by United States price ($3.54, average of four cities).
b Weighted average of prices in euro area.
c Dollars per euro.
d Dollars per pound.

Inflation

Consumer price inflation

Highest, 2008, %

1	Zimbabwe[a]	24,411.0
2	Ethiopia	44.4
3	Myanmar[a]	35.0
4	Venezuela	30.6
5	Kenya	26.2
6	Iran	25.5
7	Mongolia	25.1
8	Kyrgyzstan	24.5
9	Vietnam	24.4
10	Burundi	24.2
11	Jamaica	22.0
12	Azerbaijan	20.8
13	Pakistan	20.3
14	Nicaragua	19.8
15	Cambodia	19.7
16	Egypt	18.3
17	Kazakhstan	17.1
18	Congo-Kinshasa[a]	16.9
19	Ghana	16.5
20	Sudan	16.0
21	Sri Lanka[a]	15.8
22	Haiti	15.5
23	Latvia	15.4

Lowest, 2008, %

1	Papua New Guinea[a]	0.9
2	Japan	1.4
3	Canada	2.4
	Switzerland	2.4
5	Netherlands	2.5
6	Germany	2.6
	Portugal	2.6
8	France	2.8
9	Austria	3.2
10	Bahrain[a]	3.3
	Italy	3.3
12	Albania	3.4
	Denmark	3.4
	Libya[b]	3.4
	Luxembourg	3.4
16	Sweden	3.5
	Taiwan	3.5
18	Central African Rep[a]	3.8
	Norway	3.8
	United States	3.8
21	Morocco	3.9
	Syria[a]	3.9

Highest average annual consumer price inflation, 2003–08, %

1	Zimbabwe[c]	1,357.3
2	Angola	20.4
3	Venezuela	20.0
4	Ethiopia	17.0
5	Myanmar[c]	16.7
6	Iran	16.5
7	Haiti	15.0
8	Dominican Republic	14.8
9	Kenya	14.3
10	Jamaica[c]	13.7
	Yemen	13.7
12	Congo-Kinshasa[c]	13.6
	Zambia	13.6
14	Ghana	13.1
15	Azerbaijan	12.7
16	Madagascar	12.5
17	Moldova[c]	12.4
18	Costa Rica	12.1
19	Sierra Leone[c]	11.9
20	Mongolia	11.8
21	Belarus	11.6
	Serbia	11.6

Lowest average annual consumer price inflation, 2003–08, %

1	Montenegro	0.0
2	Japan	0.3
3	Libya[d]	1.0
4	Switzerland	1.2
5	Netherlands	1.6
	Israel	1.6
	Sweden	1.6
8	Hong Kong	1.8
	Norway	1.8
	Papua New Guinea[c]	1.8
11	Finland	1.9
12	Chad	2.0
	Denmark	2.0
	France	2.0
	Germany	2.0
	Taiwan	2.0
17	Canada	2.1
	Central African Rep[c]	2.1
	Gabon	2.1
20	Austria	2.2

a 2007 b 2006 c 2003–07 d 2003-2006

Commodity prices

2008, % change on a year earlier		*2000–08, % change*	
1 Rice	101.5	1 Lead	359.4
2 Soyabeans	43.0	2 Copper	282.1
3 Soya oil	41.7	3 Tin	239.9
4 Corn	41.4	4 Oil[a]	226.3
5 Soya meal	40.0	5 Rice	222.6
Tea	40.0	6 Soya oil	220.4
7 Oil[a]	38.1	7 Gold	212.3
8 Coconut oil	33.3	8 Wheat	208.4
9 Cocoa	32.2	9 Palm oil	205.1
10 Tin	27.5	10 Cocoa	190.2
11 Sugar	26.7	11 Coconut oil	167.2
12 Wheat	25.6	12 Corn	152.0
13 Gold	25.4	13 Soybeans	146.1
14 Palm oil	20.1	14 Nickel	142.8
15 Beef (Aus)	19.7	15 Rubber	124.8
16 Coffee	15.2	16 Soya meal	96.0
17 Cotton	12.7	17 Coffee	70.3
18 Lamb	12.1	18 Beef (Aus)	69.1
19 Wool (NZ)	10.9	19 Zinc	65.8
20 Rubber	5.7	20 Aluminium	65.4
21 Beef (US)	0.7	21 Lamb	60.2
22 Copper	-2.8	22 Sugar	56.2
23 Aluminium	-2.9	23 Beef (US)	30.7
24 Wool (Aus)	-5.8	24 Wool (Aus)	27.5
25 Hides	-10.8	25 Cotton	21.0
26 Timber	-14.0	26 Tea	15.2

The Economist's house-price indicators

Q4 2008[b], % change on a year earlier		*1997–2008[b], % change*	
1 Switzerland	3.7	1 South Africa	389
2 Italy	1.1	2 Ireland	193
3 France	0.8	3 Spain	184
4 China	-0.9	4 Australia	163
5 South Africa	-1.3	5 France	152
6 Sweden	-1.6	6 Britain	150
7 Japan	-1.8	7 Sweden	145
8 Canada	-1.9	8 Denmark	119
9 Germany	-2.5	9 Italy	104
10 Spain	-3.2	10 New Zealand	102
11 Australia	-3.3	11 Netherlands	90
12 Singapore	-4.7	12 Canada	66
13 Denmark	-4.9	United States	66
14 Netherlands	-5.2	14 Swizerland	24
15 New Zealand	-8.9	15 Japan	-33
16 Ireland	-9.8	16 Hong Kong	-35
17 Hong Kong	-14.0		
18 Britain	-17.6		
19 United States	-18.2		

a West Texas Intermediate.   b Or latest.

Debt

Highest foreign debt[a]

$bn, 2007

1	China	373.6	26	Pakistan	40.7
2	Russia	370.2	27	Latvia	39.3
3	South Korea	268.8	28	Slovakia	36.8
4	Turkey	251.5	29	Bulgaria	33.0
5	Brazil	237.5	30	Peru	32.2
6	India	221.0	31	Egypt	30.4
7	Poland	195.4	32	Serbia	26.3
8	Mexico	178.1	33	Singapore	25.6
9	Indonesia	140.8	34	Lebanon	24.6
10	Argentina	127.8	35	Vietnam	24.2
11	United Arab Emirates	105.9	36	Bangladesh	22.0
12	Taiwan	98.4	37	Slovenia[b]	21.4
13	Kazakhstan	96.1	38	Morocco	20.3
14	Israel	89.1	39	Tunisia	20.2
15	Romania	85.4	40	Iran	20.1
16	Czech Republic	74.7	41	Sudan	19.2
17	Ukraine	73.6	42	Cuba	17.8
18	Philippines	65.8	43	Ecuador	17.5
19	Thailand	63.1	44	Sri Lanka	14.0
20	Chile	58.6	45	Côte d'Ivoire	13.9
21	Malaysia	53.7	46	Angola	12.7
22	Croatia	48.6	47	Congo-Kinshasa	12.3
23	Colombia	45.0		Uruguay	12.3
24	South Africa	43.4	49	Dominican Republic	10.3
25	Venezuela	43.1	50	Jamaica	10.1

Highest foreign debt[a]

As % of exports of goods and services, 2007

1	Liberia	976	20	Brazil	155
2	Burundi	882	21	Mauritania	150
3	Eritrea	660	22	Togo	148
4	Guinea-Bissau	529	23	Cuba	137
5	Sudan	382	24	Bulgaria	144
6	Latvia	373	25	Colombia	133
7	Congo-Kinshasa	326	26	Ukraine	131
	Zimbabwe	326	27	Peru	125
9	Central African Rep	325	28	Côte d'Ivoire	123
10	Laos	267		Pakistan	123
11	Argentina	219	30	Poland	121
12	Kazakhstan	218	31	Indonesia	120
13	Guinea	210	32	Myanmar	119
14	Turkey	200	33	Armenia	117
15	Serbia	198	34	Ecuador	115
16	Croatia	197		Lebanon	115
17	Uruguay	196	36	Burkina Faso	108
18	Jamaica	183	37	Tunisia	106
19	Romania	175			

a Foreign debt is debt owed to non-residents and repayable in foreign currency; the figures shown include liabilities of government, public and private sectors. Developed countries have been excluded.   b 2006

Highest foreign debt burden[a]
Foreign debt as % of GDP, 2007

1	Liberia	978		Romania	67
2	Guinea-Bissau	263	24	Ukraine	66
3	Latvia	192	25	Mauritius	65
4	Jamaica	131		Tunisia	65
	Kazakhstan	131	27	Guinea	64
6	Zimbabwe	121	28	Argentina	63
7	Congo-Kinshasa	111	29	Slovenia[c]	55
	Lebanon	111	30	Israel	54
9	Croatia	109		Jordan	54
10	Bulgaria	100		Macedonia	54
11	Burundi	97		United Arab Emirates	54
12	Congo-Brazzaville	93	34	Poland	53
13	Sudan	93	35	Philippines	51
14	Serbia	86	36	Ecuador	50
15	Mauritania	85		El Salvador	50
16	Laos	84	38	Slovakia	49
17	Togo	80	39	Central African Rep	48
18	Gabon	73	40	Turkey	47
19	Moldova	72	41	Cambodia	46
20	Panama	70		Myanmar	46
21	Uruguay	69	43	Chile	45
22	Côte d'Ivoire	67			

Highest debt service ratios[c]
%, average, 2007

1	Liberia	111.6	23	Argentina	13.0
2	Latvia	73.3	24	Israel	12.5
3	Kazakhstan	49.6		Mexico	12.5
4	Burundi	42.6	26	Gambia, The	12.4
5	Croatia	33.0	27	Bolivia	11.9
6	Turkey	32.1	28	Nicaragua	11.7
7	Brazil	27.8	29	Morocco	11.4
8	Poland	25.6	30	Tunisia	11.3
9	Peru	25.0	31	El Salvador	11.0
10	Colombia	22.0	32	Indonesia	10.5
11	Romania	19.1	33	Czech Republic	10.4
	Uruguay	19.1	34	Angola	10.2
13	Laos	18.9	35	Cameroon	9.9
	Slovenia[d]	18.9	36	Moldova	9.5
15	Ecuador	18.7	37	Cuba	9.4
	Lebanon	18.7	38	Russia	9.1
17	Jamaica	17.3	39	Pakistan	8.9
18	Ukraine	16.9	40	Dominican Republic	8.6
19	Bulgaria	15.5	41	Slovakia	8.4
20	Chile	14.2	42	Thailand	8.1
21	Philippines	13.7	43	Bosnia	8.0
22	Guinea	13.1	44	Venezuela	7.4

c Debt service is the sum of interest and principal repayments (amortisation) due on outstanding foreign debt. The debt service ratio is debt service expressed as a percentage of the country's exports of goods and services.   d 2006

Aid

Largest recipients of bilateral and multilateral aid[a]

$m, 2007

1	Iraq	9,115	24	Burkina Faso	930
2	Afghanistan	3,951	25	Madagascar	892
3	Tanzania	2,811	26	Senegal	843
4	Vietnam	2,497	27	Nicaragua	834
5	Ethiopia	2,422		Serbia	834
6	Pakistan	2,212	29	Turkey	797
7	Sudan	2,104	30	Indonesia	796
8	Nigeria	2,042	31	South Africa	794
9	Cameroon	1,933	32	Malawi	735
10	West Bank and Gaza	1,868	33	Colombia	731
11	Mozambique	1,777	34	Rwanda	713
12	Uganda	1,728	35	Haiti	701
13	Bangladesh	1,502	36	Liberia	696
14	China	1,439	37	Cambodia	672
15	India	1,298	38	Philippines	634
16	Kenya	1,275	39	Nepal	598
17	Congo-Kinshasa	1,217	40	Sri Lanka	589
18	Ghana	1,151	41	Niger	542
19	Morocco	1,090	42	Sierra Leone	535
20	Egypt	1,083	43	Jordan	504
21	Zambia	1,045	44	Bolivia	476
22	Mali	1,017	45	Benin	470
23	Lebanon	939	46	Burundi	466

Largest recipients of bilateral and multilateral aid[a]

$ per head, 2007

1	West Bank and Gaza	479.0	23	Serbia	84.2
2	Cape Verde	385.5	24	Jordan	84.1
3	Suriname	320.3	25	Haiti	79.7
4	Iraq	300.8	26	Belize	79.4
5	Lebanon	253.9	27	Rwanda	75.8
6	Timor-Leste	253.0	28	Guinea-Bissau	72.5
7	Liberia	198.9	29	Lesotho	72.0
8	Montenegro	154.5	30	Mali	71.1
9	Nicaragua	146.3	31	Tanzania	70.8
10	Afghanistan	122.3	32	Senegal	69.1
11	Armenia	117.2	33	Burkina Faso	66.5
12	Cameroon	114.4	34	Moldova	64.1
13	Mauritania	113.7	35	Laos	63.9
14	Bosnia	113.6	36	Swaziland	62.8
15	Macedonia	106.7	37	Fiji	62.5
16	Namibia	97.7	38	Honduras	61.9
17	Albania	95.4	39	Botswana	58.0
18	Sierra Leone	92.3	40	Burundi	57.6
19	Georgia	86.9	41	Mauritius	57.4
20	Mozambique	86.7	42	Uganda	55.9
21	Zambia	86.3	43	Sudan	55.7
22	Mongolia	84.4	44	Malawi	54.4

a Israel also receives aid, but does not disclose amounts.

Largest bilateral and multilateral donors[a]
$m, 2007

1	United States	21,787	15	Belgium	1,953
2	Germany	12,291	16	Austria	1,808
3	France	9,884	17	Switzerland	1,689
4	United Kingdom	9,849	18	Ireland	1,192
5	Japan	7,679	19	Finland	981
6	Netherlands	6,224	20	South Korea	699
7	Spain	5,140	21	Turkey	602
8	Sweden	4,339	22	Taiwan	514
9	Canada	4,080	23	Greece	501
10	Italy	3,971	24	Portugal	471
11	Norway	3,728	25	United Arab Emirates	429
12	Australia	2,669	26	Luxembourg	376
13	Denmark	2,562	27	Poland	363
14	Saudi Arabia	2,079	28	New Zealand	320

Largest bilateral and multilateral donors[a]
% of GDP, 2007

1	Norway	0.96		United Kingdom	0.36
2	Sweden	0.93	16	Australia	0.33
3	Denmark	0.82	17	Canada	0.31
4	Netherlands	0.81	18	Iceland	0.24
5	Luxembourg	0.76		New Zealand	0.24
6	Saudi Arabia	0.54	20	United Arab Emirates	0.22
7	Austria	0.48	21	Portugal	0.21
8	Ireland	0.46	22	Italy	0.19
9	Belgium	0.43	23	Japan	0.18
10	Finland	0.40	24	Greece	0.16
	Switzerland	0.40		United States	0.16
12	France	0.38	26	Taiwan	0.13
13	Germany	0.37	27	Czech Republic	0.10
14	Spain	0.36		Kuwait	0.10

Largest resource flow donors[b]
% of GNI, 2007

1	Austria	5.66	12	Canada	1.22
2	Switzerland	2.73	13	Germany	1.17
3	Ireland	2.70	14	Greece	1.10
4	Netherlands	2.35	15	Portugal	1.03
5	United Kingdom	2.10	16	Luxembourg	0.93
6	France	1.66		United States	0.93
7	Spain	1.55	18	Finland	0.86
8	Denmark	1.51	19	Belgium	0.83
9	Sweden	1.49	20	Japan	0.67
10	Norway	1.33	21	New Zealand	0.34
11	Australia	1.25	22	Iceland	0.27

a China also provides aid, but does not disclose amounts.
b Including other official flows eg, export credits, private grants and flows.

Industry and services

Largest industrial output
$bn, 2007

1	United States[a]	2,737	23	Sweden	114
2	China	1,555	24	Thailand	108
3	Japan[a]	1,313	25	Austria	105
4	Germany	895		Taiwan	105
5	United Kingdom	569	27	Switzerland[a]	101
6	Italy	508	28	Belgium	97
7	France	477	29	United Arab Emirates[a]	96
8	Russia	426	30	Malaysia	89
9	Spain	390	31	Argentina	81
10	Canada	378	32	Algeria	78
11	Mexico	354		South Africa	78
12	South Korea	339	34	Venezuela[b]	77
13	Brazil	323	35	Chile	73
14	India	318	36	Finland	69
15	Saudi Arabia	250	37	Colombia	68
16	Australia	219		Denmark	68
17	Indonesia	202	39	Ireland[a]	67
18	Netherlands	164	40	Nigeria	65
19	Turkey	161	41	Greece	64
20	Norway	148	42	Czech Republic	61
21	Iran	126	43	Romania	54
22	Poland	115			

Highest growth in industrial output
Average annual % increase in real terms, 1997–2007

1	Chad	39.3	11	Trinidad & Tobago	17.6
2	Azerbaijan	34.0	12	Belarus	15.8
3	Cambodia	31.5	13	Vietnam	15.5
4	Mozambique	29.3	14	Kazakhstan	15.4
5	Sudan	24.2	15	Uganda	14.9
6	Armenia	22.0	16	Burkina Faso[c]	14.7
7	Angola	21.0	17	Tajikistan	13.7
8	Bhutan	20.8	18	Albania	12.8
9	Laos	18.6	19	Georgia	12.7
10	China	17.8		Tanzania[c]	12.7

Lowest growth in industrial output
Average annual % change in real terms, 1997–2007

1	Zimbabwe[d]	-4.3		United Kingdom	0.5
2	Burundi[d]	-2.2	12	Japan[c]	0.7
3	Gabon	-1.3	13	Italy	0.8
	Guinea-Bissau	-1.3		Jamaica	0.8
5	Eritrea	-0.8	15	Denmark	0.9
6	Côte d'Ivoire	-0.5		Portugal	0.9
7	Moldova	-0.2	17	Brunei	1.0
8	Norway	0.4		Taiwan	1.0
	Paraguay	0.4		Venezuela	1.0
10	Kyrgyzstan	0.5	20	Fiji	1.2

a 2006   b 2005   c 1996–2006   d 1995–2005

Largest manufacturing output
$bn, 2007

1	United States[a]	1,700		21	Poland	65
2	Japan[a]	934		22	Belgium[a]	60
3	China[a]	893		23	Austria[a]	58
4	Germany[a]	595		24	Malaysia	52
5	Italy[a]	299		25	Argentina	51
6	France	283		26	South Africa	46
7	United Kingdom[b]	270		27	Ireland[a]	45
8	South Korea	240		28	Czech Republic	43
9	Russia	211			Finland[a]	43
10	Canada	202		30	Singapore	38
11	Brazil	200		31	Saudi Arabia	36
12	Mexico	183		32	Colombia	34
13	India	176			Norway	34
	Spain[a]	176		34	Romania	33
15	Indonesia	117		35	Philippines	32
16	Turkey	109		36	Denmark[b]	31
17	Taiwan	91			Greece[a]	31
18	Thailand	85		38	Iran	30
19	Australia	81		39	Ukraine	29
20	Netherlands[a]	79				

Largest services output
$bn, 2007

1	United States[a]	9,347		27	Hong Kong	183
2	Japan[a]	2,981		28	Indonesia	171
3	Germany	2,051		29	South Africa	164
4	United Kingdom	1,874		30	Portugal	139
5	France	1,792		31	Finland	138
6	Italy	1,332		32	Argentina	137
7	China	1,294		33	Iran	128
8	Canada	924		34	Ireland[a]	121
9	Spain	860			Saudi Arabia	121
10	Brazil	740		36	Thailand	110
11	Russia	629		37	Colombia	106
12	Mexico	594		38	Singapore	103
13	India	564		39	Czech Republic	93
14	Australia	518		40	Romania	82
15	Netherlands	501		41	Hungary	79
16	South Korea	496			Malaysia	79
17	Turkey	359		43	Philippines	78
18	Belgium	302		44	Chile	76
19	Sweden	278		45	Pakistan	71
20	Taiwan	272		46	Ukraine	69
21	Switzerland[a]	260		47	United Arab Emirates[a]	64
22	Poland	238		48	Egypt	62
23	Austria	225		49	Peru	55
24	Greece	203		50	Kazakhstan	52
25	Denmark	192		51	Venezuela[b]	51
26	Norway	191		52	Nigeria	46

a 2006 b 2005

Agriculture

Largest agricultural output
$bn, 2007

1	China	357	16	Pakistan		28
2	India	195		Thailand		28
3	United States[a]	131	18	Germany		27
4	Japan[a]	64	20	South Korea		26
5	Brazil	62	21	Argentina		23
6	Indonesia	60		United Kingdom		23
7	Nigeria	53	23	Philippines		20
	Russia	53	24	Malaysia		19
9	France	51	25	Australia		18
10	Turkey	49		Egypt		18
11	Italy	38	27	Colombia		17
12	Mexico	37	28	Poland		16
	Spain	37	29	Netherlands		14
14	Canada	29		Vietnam		14
	Iran	29				

Most economically dependent on agriculture
% of GDP from agriculture, 2007

1	Guinea-Bissau	63.6	14	Burundi[b]	34.8
2	Liberia	54.0	15	Malawi	34.3
3	Central African Rep	53.9	16	Ghana	33.6
4	Ethiopia	46.3	17	Kyrgyzstan	33.6
5	Tanzania[a]	45.3		Nepal	33.6
6	Sierra Leone	44.7	19	Burkina Faso[a]	33.3
7	Togo[b]	43.7	20	Nigeria	32.6
8	Congo-Kinshasa	42.5	21	Benin[b]	32.2
9	Laos	41.8	22	Cambodia	31.9
10	Rwanda	39.8	23	Guyana[b]	31.0
11	Mali	36.5	24	Gambia, The	28.7
12	Afghanistan[b]	36.1	25	Sudan	28.3
13	Papua New Guinea	35.5	26	Mozambique	27.6

Least economically dependent on agriculture
% of GDP from agriculture, 2007

1	Macau[a]	0.0		Taiwan	1.4
2	Hong Kong	0.1	15	Japan[a]	1.5
	Singapore	0.1		Sweden	1.5
4	Luxembourg	0.4	17	Ireland[a]	1.7
	Trinidad & Tobago	0.4	18	Botswana	1.8
6	Brunei	0.7	19	Austria	1.9
7	Belgium	0.9	20	Italy	2.0
	Germany	0.9		United Arab Emirates[a]	2.0
	United Kingdom	0.9	22	Netherlands	2.1
10	United States[a]	1.1	23	France	2.2
11	Switzerland[a]	1.2		Canada	2.2
12	Denmark	1.3	25	Australia	2.4
13	Norway	1.4		Slovenia	2.4

a 2006   b 2005

Highest growth in agriculture
Average annual % increase in real terms, 1997–2007

1	Angola	20.8		Mozambique	7.0
2	Tajikistan	12.5	11	Dominican Republic	6.8
3	United Arab Emirates[a]	10.9	12	Burkina Faso[a]	6.2
4	Azerbaijan	10.1		Chile	6.2
5	Armenia	9.2	14	Gambia, The	6.1
6	Uzbekistan	7.6	15	United States[a]	6.0
7	Rwanda	7.3	16	Panama	5.8
8	Benin[b]	7.2	17	Eritrea	5.6
9	Algeria	7.0	18	Guinea	5.4

Lowest growth in agriculture
Average annual % change in real terms, 1997–2007

1	Trinidad & Tobago	-4.2		Jamaica	-1.9
2	Bulgaria	-3.7	10	Botswana	-1.4
3	Moldova	-3.3	11	Taiwan	-1.1
4	Lesotho	-2.5	12	Zimbabwe[b]	-1.0
5	Ireland[a]	-2.2	13	Burundi[b]	-0.9
6	Luxembourg	-2.1		Slovakia	-0.9
7	Slovenia	-2.0	15	Switzerland[a]	-0.7
8	Greece	-1.9	16	Mauritius	-0.6

Biggest producers
'000 tonnes, 2007

Cereals

1	China	460,353	6	Brazil	68,832
2	United States	414,066	7	France	58,707
3	India	252,121	8	Canada	48,773
4	Russia	80,495	9	Bangladesh	44,669
5	Indonesia	69,430	10	Germany	42,295

Meat

1	China	90,577	6	Russia	5,602
2	United States	41,809	7	Mexico	5,572
3	Brazil	20,082	8	Spain	5,362
4	Germany	7,053	9	France	5,064
5	India	6,322	10	Argentina	4,439

Fruit

1	China	94,418	6	Spain	15,293
2	India	51,142	7	Mexico	15,041
3	Brazil	36,818	8	Turkey	12,390
4	United States	24,962	9	Iran	12,102
5	Italy	17,891	10	Indonesia	11,615

Vegetables

1	China	448,983	5	Russia	16,516
2	India	72,545	6	Egypt	16,041
3	United States	38,075	7	Iran	15,993
4	Turkey	24,454	8	Italy	13,587

a 1996–2006   b 1995–2005

Commodities

Wheat

Top 10 producers, 2007–08
'000 tonnes

1	EU27	119,690
2	China	109,300
3	India	75,810
4	United States	55,821
5	Russia	49,432
6	Pakistan	23,300
7	Canada	20,054
8	Kazakhstan	16,600
9	Argentina	16,300
10	Turkey	15,500

Top 10 consumers, 2007–08
'000s tonnes

1	EU27	117,590
2	China	102,350
3	India	75,770
4	Russia	36,800
5	United States	28,620
6	Pakistan	22,880
7	Turkey	16,960
8	Egypt	15,600
9	Iran	15,030
10	Ukraine	12,280

Rice[a]

Top 10 producers, 2007–08
'000 tonnes

1	China	130,224
2	India	96,690
3	Indonesia	35,800
4	Bangladesh	28,800
5	Vietnam	24,375
6	Thailand	19,300
7	Myanmar	10,730
8	Philippines	10,479
9	Brazil	8,199
10	Japan	7,930

Top 10 consumers, 2007–08
'000 tonnes

1	China	127,450
2	India	90,620
3	Indonesia	36,350
4	Bangladesh	30,747
5	Vietnam	19,400
6	Philippines	13,499
7	Myanmar	10,249
8	Thailand	9,600
9	Brazil	8,380
10	Japan	8,177

Sugar[b]

Top 10 producers, 2007
'000 tonnes

1	Brazil	33,199
2	India	29,090
3	EU27	18,445
4	China	13,895
5	United States	7,678
6	Thailand	7,147
7	Mexico	5,420
8	Australia	4,627
9	Pakistan	4,355
10	Russia	3,405

Top 10 consumers, 2007
'000 tonnes

1	India	20,878
2	EU27	19,315
3	China	13,825
4	Brazil	12,474
5	United States	9,107
6	Russia	6,500
7	Mexico	4,944
8	Indonesia	4,400
9	Pakistan	4,250
10	Egypt	2,700

Coarse grains[c]

Top 5 producers, 2007–08
'000 tonnes

1	United States	350,238
2	China	162,300
3	EU27	136,031
4	Brazil	61,224
5	India	40,630

Top 5 consumers, 2007–08
'000 tonnes

1	United States	274,747
2	China	160,457
3	EU27	154,751
4	Brazil	48,289
5	Mexico	42,777

Tea

Top 10 producers, 2007
'000 tonnes

1	China	1,166
2	India	945
3	Kenya	370
4	Sri Lanka	305
5	Turkey	178
6	Indonesia	150
7	Vietnam	148
8	Japan	100
9	Argentina	90
10	Bangladesh	58

Top 10 consumers, 2007
'000 tonnes

1	China	828
2	India	786
3	Russia	178
4	Japan	146
5	Turkey	145
6	United Kingdom	131
7	United States	109
8	Pakistan	106
9	Indonesia	75
10	Egypt	69

Coffee

Top 10 producers, 2007–08
'000 tonnes

1	Brazil	2,164
2	Vietnam	988
3	Colombia	751
4	Indonesia	465
5	Ethiopia	294
6	India	249
	Mexico	249
8	Guatemala	246
9	Honduras	231
10	Uganda	195

Top 10 consumers, 2007
'000 tonnes

1	United States	1,262
2	Brazil	1,016
3	Germany	496
4	Japan	437
5	Italy	348
6	France	338
7	Russia	243
8	Canada	212
9	Indonesia	192
	Spain	192

Cocoa

Top 10 producers, 2006–07
'000 tonnes

1	Côte d'Ivoire	1,229
2	Ghana	614
3	Indonesia	545
4	Nigeria	190
5	Cameroon	169
6	Brazil	126
7	Ecuador	115
8	Togo	78
9	Papua New Guinea	47
10	Dominican Republic	42

Top 10 consumers, 2006–07
'000 tonnes

1	United States	795
2	Germany	315
3	France	260
4	United Kingdom	223
5	Russia	195
6	Japan	167
7	Brazil	129
8	Spain	101
9	Italy	95
10	Canada	76

a Milled.
b Raw.
c Includes: maize (corn), barley, sorghum, rye, oats and millet.

Copper

| *Top 10 producers[a], 2007* | | *Top 10 consumers[b], 2007* | |
'000 tonnes		*'000 tonnes*	
1 Chile	5,557	1 China	4,863
2 Peru	1,190	2 United States	2,140
United States	1,190	3 Germany	1,392
4 China	928	4 Japan	1,252
5 Australia	871	5 South Korea	858
6 Indonesia	789	6 Italy	764
7 Russia	770	7 Russia	688
8 Canada	596	8 Taiwan	603
9 Zambia	550	9 India	516
10 Poland	452	10 Turkey	391

Lead

| *Top 10 producers[a], 2007* | | *Top 10 consumers[b], 2007* | |
'000 tonnes		*'000 tonnes*	
1 China	1,592	1 China	2,574
2 Australia	641	2 United States	1,570
3 United States	449	3 Germany	400
4 Peru	329	4 South Korea	344
5 Mexico	137	5 Italy	301
6 India	78	6 Japan	279
7 Canada	75	7 Spain	271
8 Sweden	63	8 United Kingdom	245
9 Ireland	57	9 Mexico	236
10 Russia	48	10 India	199

Zinc

| *Top 10 producers[a], 2007* | | *Top 10 consumers[c], 2007* | |
'000 tonnes		*'000 tonnes*	
1 China	3,048	1 China	3,631
2 Australia	1,518	2 United States	1,050
3 Peru	1,444	3 Japan	588
4 United States	803	4 Germany	534
5 Canada	630	5 South Korea	486
6 India	539	6 India	480
7 Mexico	452	7 Italy	396
8 Ireland	401	8 Belgium	364
9 Kazakhstan	386	9 Spain	271
10 Sweden	225	10 France	266

Tin

| *Top 5 producers[a], 2007* | | *Top 5 consumers[b], 2007* | |
'000 tonnes		*'000 tonnes*	
1 China	147.3	1 China	133.9
2 Indonesia	102.0	2 Japan	34.2
3 Peru	39.0	3 United States	33.7
4 Bolivia	16.0	4 Germany	22.7
5 Brazil	12.6	5 South Korea	16.1

Nickel

Top 10 producers[a], 2007
'000 tonnes

1	Russia	293.6
2	Canada	254.9
3	Indonesia	229.2
4	Australia	185.0
5	New Caledonia	125.4
6	Philippines	78.2
7	Cuba	75.2
8	China	66.4
9	Colombia	49.3
10	South Africa	37.9

Top 10 consumers[b], 2007
'000 tonnes

1	China	327.8
2	Japan	196.0
3	United States	118.5
4	Germany	110.2
5	Taiwan	75.6
6	South Korea	71.1
7	Italy	64.0
8	Belgium	55.4
9	South Africa	44.0
10	Spain	41.5

Aluminium

Top 10 producers[d], 2007
'000 tonnes

1	China	12,559
2	Russia	3,955
3	Canada	3,083
4	United States	2,560
5	Australia	1,959
6	Brazil	1,655
7	Norway	1,357
8	India	1,222
9	South Africa	898
10	United Arab Emirates	890

Top 10 consumers[e], 2007
'000 tonnes

1	China	12,347
2	United States	5,580
3	Japan	2,197
4	Germany	2,008
5	India	1,207
6	Italy	1,087
7	South Korea	1,081
8	Russia	1,020
9	Brazil	854
10	France	737

Precious metals

Gold [a]
Top 10 producers, 2007
tonnes

1	China	270.5
2	South Africa	254.7
3	Australia	245.0
4	United States	239.0
5	Peru	170.1
6	Russia	156.9
7	Indonesia	105.0
8	Canada	102.4
9	Ghana	76.5
10	Uzbekistan	72.9

Silver [a]
Top 10 producers, 2007
tonnes

1	Peru	3,494
2	Mexico	3,135
3	China	2,000
4	Chile	1,936
5	Australia	1,880
6	United States	1,260
7	Poland	1,240
8	Canada	860
9	Kazakhstan	722
10	Bolivia	525

Platinum
Top 3 producers, 2007
tonnes

1	South Africa	156.5
2	Russia	28.3
3	United States/Canada	10.1

Palladium
Top 3 producers, 2007
tonnes

1	Russia	141.2
2	South Africa	86.2
3	United States/Canada	30.8

a Mine production.   b Refined consumption.   c Slab consumption.
d Primary refined production.   e Primary refined consumption.

Rubber (natural and synthetic)

Top 10 producers, 2007 '000 tonnes		Top 10 consumers, 2007 '000 tonnes	
1 Thailand	3,212	1 China	5,985
2 China	2,815	2 United States	2,948
3 Indonesia	2,803	3 Japan	2,050
4 United States	2,697	4 India	1,141
5 Japan	1,655	5 Germany	993
6 Malaysia	1,267	6 Brazil	822
7 Russia	1,209	7 South Korea	724
8 South Korea	1,010	8 Russia	654
9 India	914	9 Thailand	591
10 Germany	901	10 Malaysia	569

Raw wool

Top 10 producers[a], 2007–08 '000 tonnes		Top 10 consumers[a], 2007–08 '000 tonnes	
1 Australia	277	1 China	425
2 China	183	2 India	84
3 New Zealand	173	Italy	84
4 Argentina	44	4 Turkey	50
5 India	36	5 Iran	40
6 Iran	33	6 Russia	24
7 Uruguay	32	7 Belgium	20
8 South Africa	28	8 New Zealand	19
9 United Kingdom	27	United Kingdom	19
10 Russia	23	10 South Korea	18

Cotton

Top 10 producers, 2007–08 '000 tonnes		Top 10 consumers, 2007–08 '000 tonnes	
1 China	8,071	1 China	10,900
2 India	5,355	2 India	3,986
3 United States	4,182	3 Pakistan	2,637
4 Pakistan	1,894	4 Turkey	1,325
5 Brazil	1,603	5 United States	1,003
6 Uzbekistan	1,206	6 Brazil	996
7 Turkey	625	7 Bangladesh	590
8 Greece	285	8 Indonesia	490
9 Turkmenistan	280	9 Mexico	430
10 Syria	250	10 Thailand	425

Major oil seeds[b]

Top 5 producers, 2007–08 '000 tonnes		Top 5 consumers, 2007–08 '000 tonnes	
1 United States	82,055	1 China	89,150
2 Brazil	62,865	2 United States	61,540
3 Argentina	51,900	3 EU25	42,290
4 China	48,465	4 Argentina	40,325
5 India	31,000	5 Brazil	38,004

Oil[c]

Top 10 producers, 2008
'000 barrels per day

1	Saudi Arabia[d]	10,846
2	Russia	9,886
3	United States	6,736
4	Iran[d]	4,325
5	China	3,795
6	Canada	3,238
7	Mexico	3,157
8	United Arab Emirates[d]	2,980
9	Kuwait[d]	2,784
10	Venezuela[d]	2,566

Top 10 consumers, 2008
'000 barrels per day

1	United States	19,419
2	China	7,999
3	Japan	4,845
4	India	2,882
5	Russia	2,797
6	Germany	2,505
7	Brazil	2,397
8	Canada	2,295
9	South Korea	2,291
10	Saudi Arabia[d]	2,224

Natural gas

Top 10 producers, 2008
Billion cubic metres

1	Russia	601.7
2	United States	582.2
3	Canada	175.2
4	Iran[d]	116.3
5	Norway	99.2
6	Algeria[d]	86.5
7	Saudi Arabia[d]	78.1
8	Qatar[d]	76.6
9	China	76.1
10	Indonesia[d]	69.7

Top 10 consumers, 2008
Billion cubic metres

1	United States	657.2
2	Russia	420.2
3	Iran[d]	117.6
4	Canada	100.0
5	United Kingdom	93.9
6	Japan	93.7
7	Germany	82.0
8	China	80.7
9	Saudi Arabia[d]	78.1
10	Italy	77.7

Coal

Top 10 producers, 2008
Million tonnes oil equivalent

1	China	1,414.5
2	United States	596.9
3	Australia	219.9
4	India	194.3
5	Russia	152.8
6	Indonesia[d]	141.1
	South Africa	141.1
8	Poland	60.5
9	Kazakhstan	58.8
10	Colombia	47.8

Top 10 consumers, 2008
Million tonnes oil equivalent

1	China	1,406.3
2	United States	565.0
3	India	231.4
4	Japan	128.7
5	South Africa	102.8
6	Russia	101.3
7	Germany	80.9
8	South Korea	66.1
9	Poland	59.4
10	Australia	51.3

Oil[c]

Top proved reserves, end 2008
% of world total

1	Saudi Arabia[d]	21.0		5	Venezuela[d]	7.9
2	Iran[d]	10.9		6	United Arab Emirates[d]	7.8
3	Iraq[d]	9.1		7	Russia	6.3
4	Kuwait[d]	8.1		8	Libya[d]	3.5

a Clean basis.   b Soybeans, sunflower seed, cottonseed, groundnuts and rapeseed.
c Includes crude oil, shale oil, oil sands and natural gas liquids.   d Opec members.

Energy

Largest producers
Million tonnes oil equivalent, 2006

1	China	1,749	16	United Kingdom	187
2	United States	1,654	17	United Arab Emirates	177
3	Russia	1,220	18	Algeria	173
4	Saudi Arabia	571	19	South Africa	159
5	Euro area	463	20	Kuwait	151
6	India	436	21	France	137
7	Canada	412		Germany	137
8	Iran	309	23	Kazakhstan	131
9	Indonesia	308	24	Libya	102
10	Australia	268	25	Iraq	101
11	Mexico	256		Japan	101
12	Nigeria	235	27	Malaysia	98
13	Norway	223	28	Qatar	95
14	Brazil	207	29	Colombia	85
15	Venezuela	196	30	Argentina	84

Largest consumers
Million tonnes oil equivalent, 2006

1	United States	2,321	16	Iran	171
2	China	1,879	17	Saudi Arabia	146
3	Euro area	1,269	18	Spain	145
4	Russia	676	19	Ukraine	137
5	India	566	20	South Africa	130
6	Japan	528	21	Australia	122
7	Germany	349	22	Nigeria	105
8	France	273	23	Thailand	103
9	Canada	270	24	Poland	98
10	United Kingdom	231	25	Turkey	94
11	Brazil	224	26	Netherlands	80
12	South Korea	217	27	Pakistan	79
13	Italy	184	28	Argentina	69
14	Indonesia	179	29	Malaysia	68
15	Mexico	177	30	Egypt	63

Energy efficiency[a]

Most efficient
GDP per unit of energy use, 2006

1	Hong Kong	14.8
2	Peru	14.4
3	Botswana	12.1
4	Panama	12.0
5	Colombia	11.3
	Ireland	11.3
7	Congo-Brazzaville	10.9
8	Uruguay	10.6
9	Gabon	10.2
	Switzerland	10.2
11	Malta	10.1

Least efficient
GDP per unit of energy use, 2006

1	Congo-Kinshasa	1.0
2	Uzbekistan	1.2
3	Mozambique	1.8
4	Trinidad & Tobago	2.0
	Zambia	2.0
6	Tanzania	2.1
	Togo	2.1
	Ukraine	2.1
9	Ethiopia	2.4
	Kazakhstan	2.4
11	Iceland	2.5

a 2005 PPP$, per kg of oil equivalent.

Net energy importers
% of commercial energy use, 2006

Highest			Lowest		
1	Hong Kong	100	1	Congo-Brazzaville	-1,180
	Malta	100	2	Norway	-754
	Netherlands Antilles	100	3	Brunei	-677
	Singapore	100	4	Angola	-671
5	Cyprus	98	5	Gabon	-566
	Luxembourg	98	6	Kuwait	-495
7	Moldova	97	7	Libya	-474
8	Jordan	96	8	Qatar	-424
	Lebanon	96	9	Algeria	-372
10	Morocco	95	10	Oman	-293
11	Ireland	90	11	Saudi Arabia	-291
12	Jamaica	89	12	United Arab Emirates	-278

Largest consumption per head
Kg of oil equivalent, 2006

1	Qatar	22,057	12	Finland	7,108
2	Iceland	14,237	13	Singapore	6,968
3	Bahrain	11,874	14	Saudi Arabia	6,170
4	United Arab Emirates	11,036	15	Oman	6,057
5	Trinidad & Tobago	10,768	16	Australia	5,917
6	Luxembourg	9,972	17	Belgium	5,782
7	Kuwait	9,729	18	Sweden	5,650
8	Netherlands Antilles	9,161	19	Norway	5,598
9	Canada	8,262	20	Netherlands	4,901
10	United States	7,768	21	Russia	4,745
11	Brunei	7,346	22	Czech Republic	4,485

Sources of electricity
% of total, 2006

Oil			Gas		
1	Cyprus	100.0	1	Qatar	100.0
	Malta	100.0		Turkmenistan	100.0
	Netherlands Antilles	100.0	3	Trinidad & Tobago	99.4
	Yemen	100.0	4	Brunei	99.0
5	Benin	100.0	5	United Arab Emirates	98.0

Hydropower			Nuclear power		
1	Paraguay	100.0	1	France	79.1
2	Mozambique	99.9	2	Lithuania	71.6
3	Congo-Kinshasa	99.7	3	Slovakia	57.6
	Ethiopia	99.7	4	Belgium	55.3
5	Nepal	99.6	5	Sweden	46.7
				Ukraine	46.7

Coal		
1	Botswana	99.4
2	Mongolia	96.9
3	Poland	93.6
4	South Africa	93.5
5	Estonia	90.2

Workers of the world

Highest % of population in labour force
2007 or latest

1	Cayman Islands	67.7		21	Cyprus	52.3
2	Laos	66.6		22	Japan	52.2
3	Bhutan	60.4			Latvia	52.2
4	Macau	60.3			Netherlands	52.2
5	China	59.5		25	Australia	52.0
6	Bermuda	59.4		26	Slovenia	51.8
	Switzerland	59.4		27	Austria	51.4
8	Canada	57.9			South Korea	51.4
9	Thailand	57.2		29	Estonia	51.2
10	Iceland	56.7		30	United Kingdom	51.1
11	Norway	55.7		31	Finland	51.0
12	Sweden	55.0			United States	51.0
13	Denmark	54.6		33	Germany	50.8
14	Peru	53.7		34	Ireland	50.7
15	Hong Kong	53.2		35	Czech Republic	50.4
16	Belgium	53.1		36	Indonesia	50.2
17	Portugal	53.0		37	Azerbaijan	49.8
18	Russia	52.9		38	Spain	49.7
19	New Zealand	52.8		39	Slovakia	49.1
20	Brazil	52.4			Uruguay	49.1

Most male workforce
Highest % men in workforce, 2007 or latest

1	Saudi Arabia	84.6
2	Algeria	83.0
3	Oman	81.6
4	West Bank and Gaza	81.5
5	Iran	80.6
	Syria	80.6
7	Pakistan	79.3
8	Bangladesh	77.7
9	Guatemala	77.4
10	Egypt	77.1
11	Bahrain	76.4
12	Turkey	73.8
13	Tunisia	73.4
14	Morocco	72.9
15	Fiji	69.3
16	Nicaragua	69.2
17	India	68.4
18	Malta	66.7
19	Honduras	65.3
20	Sri Lanka	64.9
21	Mauritius	64.4
22	Malaysia	63.9
23	Bosnia	63.5
24	Bhutan	63.4
25	Chile	63.2

Most female workforce
Highest % women in workforce, 2007 or latest

1	Benin	53.1
2	Belarus	52.9
3	Netherlands Antilles	51.9
4	Tanzania	51.0
5	Mongolia	50.7
6	Laos	50.2
7	Ghana	49.6
	Madagascar	49.6
9	Moldova	49.5
10	Lithuania	49.3
	Russia	49.3
12	Estonia	49.2
13	Guadeloupe	49.1
14	Azerbaijan	49.0
	Kazakhstan	49.0
16	Barbados	48.7
17	Bermuda	48.5
	Ethiopia	48.5
	Latvia	48.5
	Ukraine	48.5
21	Bahamas	48.4
22	Zimbabwe	48.2
23	Finland	48.1
24	Cayman Islands	48.0
25	Papua New Guinea	47.9

Lowest % of population in labour force
2007 or latest

1	West Bank and Gaza	22.2	21	Nicaragua	36.5
2	Algeria	27.6	22	Puerto Rico	36.6
3	Syria	29.3	23	Oman	37.3
4	Saudi Arabia	29.8	24	Sri Lanka	37.4
5	Sudan	30.5	25	Georgia	37.8
6	Armenia	30.7	26	Honduras	37.9
7	Egypt	31.0	27	India	39.1
8	Pakistan	31.8	28	Mongolia	39.5
9	Congo-Brazzaville	32.3	29	Guinea-Bissau	39.9
10	Turkey	32.4	30	Panama	40.8
11	Iran	33.6	31	Malta	40.9
12	Suriname	34.6	32	Fiji	41.1
	Tunisia	34.6	33	El Salvador	41.2
14	Bangladesh	34.7	34	Zimbabwe	41.5
15	Botswana	35.0	35	Italy	42.0
	Guatemala	35.0		Mexico	42.0
17	South Africa	35.8	37	Croatia	42.3
18	Bosnia	36.1	38	Albania	42.4
19	Moldova	36.4	39	Chile	42.5
	Morocco	36.4	40	Hungary	42.8

Highest rate of unemployment
% of labour force[a], 2007 or latest

1	Macedonia	34.9	27	Dominican Republic	10.0
2	Namibia	33.8	28	Turkey	9.9
3	Bosnia	29.0	29	Barbados	9.8
4	Guinea-Bissau	26.3	30	Croatia	9.6
5	Réunion	24.2		Poland	9.6
6	South Africa	23.0	32	Argentina	9.5
7	Guadeloupe	22.7		Morocco	9.5
8	West Bank and Gaza	21.3	34	Jamaica	9.4
9	Martinique	21.2	35	Greenland	9.3
10	Serbia	18.1	36	Uruguay	9.2
11	Botswana	17.6	37	Indonesia	9.1
12	Ethiopia	16.7	38	Brazil	8.9
13	Tunisia	14.2	39	Mali	8.8
14	Burundi	14.0	40	Bolivia	8.7
15	Albania	13.8	41	Germany	8.6
	Algeria	13.8	42	Afghanistan	8.5
17	Georgia	13.3		Mauritius	8.5
18	Jordan	13.2	44	Spain	8.3
19	Nicaragua	12.2	45	Greece	8.1
20	Netherlands Antilles	12.0		Kyrgyzstan	8.1
21	Egypt	11.2	47	France	8.0
22	Slovakia	11.0		Portugal	8.0
23	Colombia	10.9		Trinidad & Tobago	8.0
	Puerto Rico	10.9	50	Bahamas	7.9
25	Iran	10.5		Bhutan	7.9
26	Syria	10.3		Ecuador	7.9

a ILO definition.

The business world

Global competitiveness

2008

	Overall	Government	Infrastructure
1	United States	Singapore	United States
2	Hong Kong	Hong Kong	Sweden
3	Singapore	Switzerland	Finland
4	Switzerland	Denmark	Switzerland
5	Denmark	Qatar	Japan
6	Sweden	Finland	Denmark
7	Australia	New Zealand	Canada
8	Canada	Australia	Singapore
9	Finland	Canada	Germany
10	Netherlands	Sweden	Norway
11	Norway	Norway	Netherlands
12	Luxembourg	Ireland	Australia
13	Germany	Chile	Austria
14	Qatar	Netherlands	France
15	New Zealand	China	Belgium
16	Austria	Luxembourg	United Kingdom
17	Japan	Thailand	Luxembourg
18	Malaysia	Taiwan	Israel
19	Ireland	Malaysia	Hong Kong
20	China	United States	South Korea
21	United Kingdom	Kazakhstan	New Zealand
22	Belgium	Estonia	Ireland
23	Taiwan	Israel	Taiwan
24	Israel	Austria	Portugal
25	Chile	Lithuania	Czech Republic
26	Thailand	South Africa	Malaysia
27	South Korea	Germany	Slovenia
28	France	Bulgaria	Estonia
29	Czech Republic	Portugal	Lithuania
30	India	United Kingdom	Qatar
31	Lithuania	Czech Republic	Spain
32	Slovenia	Jordan	China
33	Slovakia	Indonesia	Hungary
34	Portugal	Slovakia	Italy
35	Estonia	India	Greece
36	Kazakhstan	South Korea	Chile
37	Peru	Belgium	Slovakia
38	Bulgaria	Slovenia	Russia
39	Spain	Russia	Poland
40	Brazil	Japan	Jordan
41	Jordan	Peru	Croatia
42	Indonesia	Philippines	Thailand
43	Philippines	Spain	Bulgaria
44	Poland	Poland	Kazakhstan

Notes: Overall competitiveness of 55 economies is calculated by combining four factors: economic performance, government efficiency, business efficiency and infrastructure. Column 1 is based on 331 criteria, using hard data and survey data. Column 2 measures government efficiency, looking at public finance, fiscal policy, institutional and societal frameworks and business legislation. Column 3 includes basic, technological and scientific infrastructure, health and environment, and education.

The business environment

		2009–13 score	2004–2008 score	2004–2008 ranking
1	Singapore	8.55	8.85	1
2	Finland	8.54	8.63	4
3	Denmark	8.51	8.65	2
4	Switzerland	8.48	8.64	3
5	Canada	8.46	8.61	6
6	Hong Kong	8.45	8.62	5
7	Australia	8.37	8.26	12
8	Sweden	8.35	8.36	10
9	Netherlands	8.33	8.57	7
10	Ireland	8.20	8.24	13
	New Zealand	8.20	8.51	9
12	Germany	8.15	8.14	14
13	United States	8.08	8.56	8
14	Norway	7.98	8.05	16
15	Austria	7.85	7.65	21
	Taiwan	7.85	8.01	17
17	Belgium	7.82	8.09	15
18	France	7.80	7.92	18
19	Chile	7.70	7.83	19
	United Kingdom	7.70	8.33	11
21	Qatar	7.61	6.97	32
22	Israel	7.56	7.32	23
23	Estonia	7.51	7.68	20
24	Japan	7.48	7.54	22
	Spain	7.48	7.22	27
26	Czech Republic	7.34	7.27	24
27	South Korea	7.28	7.25	25
	United Arab Emirates	7.28	7.11	29
29	Malaysia	7.15	7.25	26
30	Slovakia	7.14	6.94	33
31	Mexico	7.13	6.90	35
32	Slovenia	7.11	6.99	31
33	Cyprus	7.08	6.99	30
34	Poland	7.05	6.83	36
	Portugal	7.05	6.92	34
36	Bahrain	6.99	7.13	28
37	Hungary	6.90	6.82	37
38	Thailand	6.78	6.68	38
39	Lithuania	6.69	6.64	40
40	Latvia	6.61	6.66	39
41	Italy	6.59	6.54	41
42	South Africa	6.53	6.37	43
43	Brazil	6.52	6.54	42
44	Bulgaria	6.47	6.15	47
	Costa Rica	6.47	6.36	45
	Greece	6.47	6.36	44

Note: Scores reflect the opportunities for, and hindrances to, the conduct of business, measured by countries' rankings in ten categories including market potential, tax and labour-market policies, infrastructure, skills and the political environment. Scores reflect average and forecast average over given date range.

Business creativity and research

Innovation index[a]
2008

1	United States	5.84			Netherlands	4.82
2	Finland	5.57		14	Belgium	4.69
3	Switzerland	5.54		15	Austria	4.68
4	Japan	5.52		16	France	4.67
5	Sweden	5.42		17	United Kingdom	4.66
6	Israel	5.26		18	Iceland	4.62
7	Taiwan	5.23		19	Norway	4.60
8	Germany	5.22		20	Australia	4.46
9	South Korea	5.18		21	Ireland	4.39
10	Denmark	5.09		22	Malaysia	4.28
11	Singapore	5.08		23	Luxembourg	4.15
12	Canada	4.82		24	Hong Kong	4.11

Technological readiness index[b]
2008

1	Netherlands	6.01		13	South Korea	5.51
2	Sweden	5.99		14	Finland	5.46
3	Denmark	5.87		15	Austria	5.34
4	Norway	5.81			Taiwan	5.34
5	Switzerland	5.76		17	Estonia	5.30
6	Iceland	5.65		18	Germany	5.22
	Singapore	5.65		19	Australia	5.21
8	United Kingdom	5.62		20	France	5.16
9	Canada	5.61		21	Japan	5.11
10	Hong Kong	5.60		22	New Zealand	5.09
11	United States	5.57		23	Belgium	5.01
12	Luxembourg	5.52		24	Ireland	4.98

Brain drain[c]

Highest, 2008				*Lowest, 2008*		
1	Guyana	1.62		1	United States	6.08
2	Zimbabwe	1.74		2	United Arab Emirates	5.79
3	Nepal	1.84		3	Qatar	5.50
4	Serbia	1.92		4	Norway	5.42
5	Burundi	2.08		5	Switzerland	5.33
6	Egypt	2.10		6	Chile	5.27
7	Bulgaria	2.12		7	Finland	5.21
	Senegal	2.12		8	Iceland	5.07
9	Macedonia	2.17		9	Kuwait	5.06
10	Ghana	2.19		10	Ireland	5.05
11	Uganda	2.20		11	Netherlands	5.01
12	Algeria	2.26		12	Hong Kong	4.97

a The innovation index is a measure of the adoption of new technology, and the interaction between the business and science sectors. It includes measures of the investment into research institutions and protection of intellectual property rights.
b The technological readiness index measures the ability of the economy to adopt new technologies. It includes measures of Information and communication technology (ICT) usage, the regulatory framework with regard to ICT, and the availability of new technology to business.
c Scores: 1=talented people leave for other countries, 7=they always remain in home country.

Total expenditure on R&D
% of GDP, 2006

1	Israel	4.59
2	Sweden	3.73
3	Finland	3.45
4	Japan	3.39
5	South Korea	3.22
6	Switzerland[a]	2.90
7	United States	2.61
8	Taiwan	2.58
9	Germany	2.53
10	Austria	2.46
11	Denmark	2.45
12	Singapore	2.31
13	France	2.09
14	Canada	1.95
15	Australia[a]	1.84
16	Belgium	1.82
17	United Kingdom	1.76
18	Netherlands	1.65
19	Czech Republic	1.55
20	Norway	1.52
21	Slovenia	1.50
22	Luxembourg	1.47
23	China	1.36
24	Ireland	1.30
25	Spain	1.20

$bn, 2006

1	United States	343.7
2	Japan	148.4
3	Germany	73.8
4	France	47.5
5	United Kingdom	42.7
6	China	37.7
7	South Korea	28.6
8	Canada	25.0
9	Italy[b]	19.4
10	Spain	14.8
11	Sweden	14.7
12	Australia[a]	11.8
13	Netherlands	11.2
14	Russia	10.6
15	Switzerland[a]	10.5
16	Taiwan	9.4
17	Austria	7.9
18	Belgium	7.3
	Brazil[b]	7.3
20	Finland	7.2
21	Denmark	6.7
22	Israel	6.6
23	Norway	5.1
24	India	4.8
25	Mexico[b]	3.9

Patents
No. of patents granted to residents
Total, average 2004–06

1	Japan	116,806
2	United States	82,910
3	South Korea	59,335
4	Taiwan	36,538
5	Russia	19,236
6	China	16,807
7	Germany	13,822
8	Ukraine[c]	9,303
9	France	9,023
10	United Kingdom	3,503
11	Spain	1,959
12	Netherlands	1,833
13	Sweden	1,730
14	Canada	1,508
15	Australia	1,088
16	Finland	1,009
17	Poland	985
18	Austria	961
19	India	695
20	Romania	662

No. of patents in force
Per 100,000 people, 2006

1	Luxembourg	5,605
2	Taiwan	1,313
3	Sweden	1,149
4	South Korea	965
5	Singapore	960
6	Japan[b]	879
7	Belgium[c]	853
8	Ireland[c]	831
9	Finland	823
	New Zealand	823
11	United Kingdom[a]	792
12	United States	586
13	France[b]	566
14	Germany	559
15	Australia	463
16	Portugal	357
17	Canada	355
18	Slovenia	353
19	Spain	348
20	Greece[a]	283

a 2004   b 2005   c 2002

Business costs and FDI

Office occupation costs

Rent, taxes and operating expenses, $ per sq. metre, November 2008

1	London (West End), UK	2,677	13	New Delhi (CBD), India	1,315
2	Moscow, Russia	2,527	14	Dublin, Ireland	1,169
3	Hong Kong (CBD)	2,493	15	New York, (Midtown), US	1,055
4	Tokyo (Inner Central), Japan	1,983	16	Ho Chi Minh City, Vietnam	999
5	Mumbai (CBD), India	1,839	17	Madrid, Spain	952
6	Dubai, UAE	1,685	18	Zurich, Switzerland	947
7	Tokyo (Outer Central), Japan	1,633	19	Milan, Italy	923
8	London (City), UK	1,578	20	Birmingham, UK	911
9	Singapore	1,455	21	Oslo, Norway	900
10	Hong Kong (Prime Districts)	1,431	22	Luxembourg City, Luxembourg	885
11	Abu Dhabi, UAE	1,426	23	Edinburgh, UK	883
12	Paris, France	1,417	24	Manchester, UK	854

Employment costs

Pay, social security and other benefits, production worker, 2007, $ per hour

1	Norway	39.12	11	Canada	26.28
2	Denmark	36.90	12	Australia	26.04
3	Germany	33.49	13	France	25.63
4	Finland	33.01	14	United States	25.26
5	Netherlands	32.27	15	Ireland	23.98
6	Belgium	31.87	16	Italy	21.94
7	Switzerland	30.87	17	Japan	20.72
8	Austria	30.41	18	Spain	18.48
9	Sweden	29.97	19	New Zealand	14.44
10	United Kingdom	27.18	20	Singapore	8.55

Foreign direct investment[a]

Inflows, $m, 2007

1	United States	232,865
2	United Kingdom	223,966
3	France	157,970
4	Canada	108,655
5	Netherlands	99,438
6	China	83,521
7	Hong Kong	59,899
8	Spain	53,385
9	Russia	52,475
10	Germany	50,925
11	Belgium	40,628
12	Switzerland	40,391
13	Italy	40,199
14	Brazil	34,585
15	Austria	30,675
16	Ireland	30,591
17	Mexico	24,686
18	Saudi Arabia	24,318

Outflows, $m, 2007

1	United States	313,787
2	United Kingdom	265,791
3	France	224,650
4	Germany	167,431
5	Spain	119,605
6	Italy	90,781
7	Japan	73,549
8	Canada	53,818
9	Hong Kong	53,187
10	Luxembourg	51,649
11	Switzerland	50,968
12	Belgium	49,667
13	Russia	45,652
14	Sweden	37,707
15	Austria	31,437
16	Netherlands	31,162
17	Australia	24,209
18	China	22,469

a Investment in companies in a foreign country.

Business burdens and corruption

Number of days taken to register a new company

Lowest, 2009			Highest, 2009		
1	New Zealand	1	1	Suriname	694
2	Australia	2	2	Guinea-Bissau	233
3	Georgia	3	3	Haiti	195
4	Belgium	4	4	Congo-Kinshasa	155
	Singapore	4	5	Brazil	152
6	Canada	5	6	Venezuela	141
	Hungary	5	7	Equatorial Guinea	136
	Iceland	5	8	Brunei	116
9	Denmark	6	9	Laos	103
	Mauritius	6	10	Zimbabwe	96
	Portugal	6	11	Cambodia	85
	Qatar	6	12	Eritrea	84
	Turkey	6	13	Timor-Leste	83
	United States	6	14	Botswana	78
15	Egypt	7	15	Iraq	77

Corruption perceptions index[a]

2008, 10 = least corrupt

Lowest			Highest		
1	Denmark	9.3	1	Somalia	1.0
	New Zealand	9.3	2	Iraq	1.3
	Sweden	9.3		Myanmar	1.3
4	Singapore	9.2	4	Haiti	1.4
5	Finland	9.0	5	Afghanistan	1.5
	Switzerland	9.0	6	Chad	1.6
7	Iceland	8.9		Guinea	1.6
	Netherland	8.9		Sudan	1.6
9	Australia	8.7	9	Congo-Kinshasa	1.7
	Canada	8.7		Equatorial Guinea	1.7
11	Luxembourg	8.3	11	Cambodia	1.8
12	Austria	8.1		Kyrgyzstan	1.8
	Hong Kong	8.1	13	Togo	2.7
14	Germany	7.9	14	Egypt	2.8
	Norway	7.9		Malawi	2.8
16	Ireland	7.7		Mauritania	2.8
	United Kingdom	7.7		Niger	2.8
				Zambia	2.8

Business software piracy

% of software that is pirated, 2007

1	Armenia	93	9	Venezuela	87
2	Azerbaijan	92	10	Iraq	85
	Bangladesh	92		Vietnam	85
	Moldova	92	12	Algeria	84
5	Zimbabwe	91		Cameroon	84
6	Sri Lanka	90		Indonesia	84
7	Libya	89		Pakistan	84
	Yemen	89			

a This index ranks countries based on how much corruption is perceived by business people, academics and risk analysts to exist among politicians and public officials.

Businesses and banks

Largest non-bank businesses
By market capitalisation, $bn
End December 2007

1	PetroChina	China	724.6
2	Exxon Mobil	United States	504.2
3	General Electric	United States	370.2
4	China Mobile	China	354.2
5	Gazprom	Russia	329.7
6	Microsoft	United States	276.4
7	Royal Dutch Shell	United Kingdom/Netherlands	265.5
8	BP	United Kingdom	254.4
9	AT&T	United States	251.2
10	China Petroleum	China	249.9
11	Petrobras	Brazil	241.7
12	Berkshire Hathaway	United States	219.2
13	Google	United States	216.4
14	Toyota Motor	Japan	205.3
15	China Life	China	203.8
16	Wal-Mart Stores	United States	197.0
17	Chevron	United States	195.1
18	Procter & Gamble	United States	191.6
19	Johnson & Johnson	United States	191.4
20	Total	France	186.0
21	Cisco Systems	United States	176.7
22	Nestlé	Switzerland	172.2
23	BHP Billiton	Australia/United Kingdom	168.6
24	Pfizer	United States	153.7

End June 2009

1	PetroChina	China	366.7
2	Exxon Mobil	United States	341.1
3	Microsoft	United States	211.5
4	China Mobile	China	200.8
5	Wal-Mart Stores	United States	188.8
6	Petrobras	Brazil	164.8
7	Johnson & Johnson	United States	156.5
8	Royal Dutch Shell	United Kingdom/Netherlands	156.3
9	Procter & Gamble	United States	148.9
10	BP	United Kingdom	147.5
11	AT&T	United States	146.6
12	BHP Billiton	Australia/United Kingdom	144.6
13	Nestlé	Switzerland	144.4
14	Berkshire Hathaway	United States	138.1
15	IBM	United States	138.0
16	Google	United States	133.2
17	Chevron	United States	132.8
18	Toyota Motor	Japan	131.4
19	Total	France	128.2
20	Apple	United States	127.1
21	General Electric	United States	124.1
22	China Petroleum	China	121.9
23	Gazprom	Russia	118.6
24	Roche Holding	Switzerland	118.4

Largest banks
By market capitalisation, $bn
End December 2007

1	Industrial and Commercial Bank of China	China	339.2
2	China Construction Bank	China	198.0
3	Bank of China	China	197.9
4	HSBC Holdings	United Kingdom	197.5
5	Bank of America	United States	183.1
6	Citigroup	United States	147.0
	JPMorgan Chase	United States	147.0
8	Banco Santander	Spain	134.9
9	Mitsubishi UFJ Financial Group	Japan	115.5
10	UniCredit	Italy	110.0
11	Wells Fargo	United States	99.5
12	Intesa Sanpaolo	Italy	97.7
13	BNP Paribas	France	97.1
14	Banco Bradesco	Brazil	93.6
15	BBVA	Spain	91.2
16	Sberbank	Russia	90.4
17	UBS	Switzerland	88.4
18	Royal Bank of Scotland	United Kingdom	88.1
19	Bank of Communications	China	87.7
20	China Merchant Bank	China	76.3
21	Royal Bank of Canada	Canada	75.1
22	Mizuho Financial Group	Japan	74.9
23	Deutsche Bank	Germany	69.2
24	Sumitomo Mitsui	Japan	68.8

End June 2009

1	Industrial and Commercial Bank of China	China	257.0
2	China Construction Bank	China	182.2
3	Bank of China	China	153.1
4	HSBC Holdings	United Kingdom	143.2
5	JPMorgan Chase	United States	133.8
6	Wells Fargo	United States	115.4
7	Bank of America	United States	110.3
8	Banco Santander	Spain	98.1
9	Mitsubishi UFJ Financial Group	Japan	72.3
10	BNP Paribas	France	69.3
11	Bank of Communications	China	60.1
12	Itaú Unibanco Banco	Brazil	59.7
13	Royal Bank of Canada	Canada	57.7
14	Credit Suisse Group	Switzerland	54.2
15	Commonwealth Bank of Australia	Australia	47.8
16	Westpac Banking	Australia	47.6
17	China Merchant Bank	China	47.4
18	BBVA	Spain	47.1
19	Barclays	United Kingdom	45.3
20	Toronto-Dominion Bank	Canada	44.1
21	UniCredit	Italy	42.4
22	Banco Bradesco	Brazil	41.4
23	Sumitomo Mitsui	Japan	41.2
24	Intesa Sanpaolo	Italy	40.5

Stockmarkets

Largest market capitalisation

$bn, end 2008

1	United States	11,738	21	Saudi Arabia	246
2	Japan	3,220	22	Mexico	233
3	China	2,794	23	Malaysia	187
4	United Kingdom	1,852	24	Singapore	180
5	France	1,492	25	Belgium	167
6	Hong Kong	1,329	26	Finland	154
7	Russia	1,322	27	Israel	134
8	Germany	1,108	28	Chile	132
9	Canada	1,002		Denmark	132
10	Spain	946	30	Norway	126
11	Switzerland	863	31	Turkey	118
12	Australia	676	32	Kuwait	107
13	India	645	33	Thailand	103
14	Brazil	589	34	Indonesia	99
15	Italy	521	35	United Arab Emirates	98
16	South Korea	495	36	Greece	90
17	South Africa	491		Poland	90
18	Netherlands	388	38	Colombia	87
19	Taiwan	381	39	Egypt	86
20	Sweden	253	40	Qatar	76

Largest falls in global stockmarkets

$ terms, % decrease December 31 2007 to December 29 2008

1	Russia (RTS)	-71.9	24	Italy (S&P/MIB)	-51.6
2	Greece (Athex Comp)	-67.1	25	United Kingdom	
3	Pakistan (KSE)	-65.2		(FTSE 100)	-51.1
4	Norway (OSEAX)	-63.9	28	Denmark (OMXCB)	-51.0
5	Turkey (ISE)	-63.2	29	Thailand (SET)	-49.9
6	China (SSEA)	-62.5	30	Canada (S&P TSX)	-49.6
7	Austria (ATX)	-62.2	31	Taiwan (TWI)	-49.0
8	India (BSE)	-61.7	32	Singapore (STI)	-48.6
9	Venezuela (IBC)	-59.1	33	Hong Kong	
10	Egypt (Case 30)	-58.8		(Hang Seng)	-48.2
	Poland (WIG)	-58.8	34	South Africa (JSE AS)	-47.1
12	Indonesia (JSX)	-58.7	35	France (CAC 40)	-45.7
13	Saudi Arabia (Tadawul)	-57.4	36	Germany (DAX)[a]	-43.2
14	Hungary (BUX)	-57.2	37	Spain (Madrid SE)	-43.2
15	Brazil (BVSP)	-57.0	38	Malaysia (KLSE)	-43.0
16	Australia (All Ord.)	-56.6	39	United States	
17	South Korea (KOSPI)	-56.4		(S&P 500)	-40.8
18	Belgium (Bel 20)	-55.6	40	Mexico (IPC)	-38.8
19	Netherlands (AEX)	-54.5	41	Chile (IGPA)	-36.7
20	Argentina (MERV)	-54.2		Colombia (IGBC)	-36.7
21	Czech Republic (PX)	-53.5	43	Switzerland (SMI)	-30.0
22	Israel (TA-100)	-52.4	44	Japan (Topix)	-28.2
23	Sweden (Aff.Gen)	-52.2			

a Total return index.

Highest growth in value traded
$ terms, % increase, 2003–08

1	Vietnam	26,118.8		23	Austria	866.8
2	United Arab Emirates	14,331.3		24	Namibia	850.0
3	Mongolia	5,100.0		25	Tunisia	811.0
4	Morocco	3,059.8		26	Bulgaria	738.1
5	Colombia	2,982.5		27	Romania	731.4
6	Bangladesh	2,725.7		28	Georgia	700.0
7	Ukraine	2,292.5		29	Poland	699.7
8	Nigeria	2,225.1		30	Malawi	650.0
9	Egypt	2,024.4		31	Indonesia	649.1
10	West Bank and Gaza	1,891.7		32	Cyprus	641.5
11	El Salvador[a]	1,580.0		33	Russia	594.0
12	Croatia	1,351.5		34	Kenya	588.0
13	Macedonia	1,318.2		35	Oman	572.5
14	Kazakhstan	1,225.8		36	Zambia[b]	554.5
15	Côte d'Ivoire	1,212.5		37	Philippines	553.2
16	Nepal	1,162.1		38	Luxembourg	541.9
17	Papua New Guinea[a]	1,150.0		39	Peru	529.4
18	Brazil	1,104.3		40	Panama	468.9
19	China	1,047.3		41	Chile	458.7
20	Bahrain	983.9		42	Lebanon	438.2
21	Jordan	974.4		43	Norway	425.3
22	Kyrgyzstan	918.2		44	Belgium	395.2

Highest growth in number of listed companies
% increase, 2002–07

1	Vietnam	677.3		25	Oman	32.3
2	Croatia	469.7			Norway	32.3
3	Serbia[b]	417.8		27	Sweden	30.2
4	Montenegro	220.0		28	West Bank and Gaza[b]	29.6
	United Arab Emirates	220.0		29	Panama	29.2
6	Kuwait	108.2		30	Estonia	28.6
7	Nepal	104.1		31	Ecuador	26.7
8	Uganda	100.0		32	Zambia[b]	25.0
9	Taiwan	88.3		33	China	23.8
10	Kazakhstan	85.0		34	Indonesia	18.9
11	Saudi Arabia	81.4		35	Brazil	17.7
12	Malawi	75.0		36	Bangladesh	17.4
13	Poland	71.9		37	Tanzania	16.7
14	Ukraine	68.5		38	Bolivia	15.6
15	Papua New Guinea[b]	66.7		39	Denmark	15.5
16	Jordan	62.7		40	South Korea	15.0
17	El Salvador[b]	50.0		41	Thailand	13.1
18	Russia	46.7		42	Venezuela	11.1
19	Morocco	45.3		43	Spain	9.7
20	Qatar[c]	44.8		44	Israel	9.4
21	Ghana	40.0		45	Malaysia	8.9
	Swaziland	40.0		46	Italy	8.5
23	Malta	38.5		47	Bahrain	7.1
24	Australia	36.9		48	Fiji	6.7

a 2003–06   b 2003–07   c 2004–08

Transport: roads and cars

Longest road networks
Km, 2006 or latest

1	United States	6,544,257	21	Bangladesh	239,226
2	China	3,456,999	22	Argentina	231,374
3	India	3,316,452	23	Vietnam	222,179
4	Brazil	1,751,868	24	Saudi Arabia	221,372
5	Canada	1,408,900	25	Philippines	200,037
6	Japan	1,196,999	26	Romania	198,817
7	France	951,500	27	Nigeria	193,200
8	Russia	933,000	28	Iran	172,927
9	Australia	812,972	29	Ukraine	169,323
10	Sweden	697,794	30	Colombia	164,278
11	Spain	666,292	31	Hungary	159,700
12	Italy	487,700	32	Congo-Kinshasa	153,497
13	Turkey	426,951	33	Belgium	152,256
14	Poland	423,997	34	Czech Republic	128,512
15	United Kingdom	398,351	35	Netherlands	126,100
16	Indonesia	391,009	36	Greece	117,533
17	South Africa	364,131	37	Algeria	108,302
18	Mexico	356,945	38	Austria	107,262
19	Pakistan	260,420	39	South Korea	102,062
20	Germany	260,184	40	Malaysia	98,721

Densest road networks
Km of road per km² land area, 2006 or latest

1	Macau	21.3		Trinidad & Tobago	1.6
2	Malta	7.1		United Kingdom	1.6
3	Bahrain	5.1	24	Sri Lanka	1.5
	Singapore	5.1	25	Ireland	1.4
5	Belgium	5.0		Poland	1.4
6	Barbados	3.7	27	Austria	1.3
7	Japan	3.2		Cyprus	1.3
8	Netherlands	3.0		Estonia	1.3
9	Puerto Rico	2.8		Spain	1.3
10	Jamaica	2.0	31	Lithuania	1.2
	Luxembourg	2.0	32	Latvia	1.1
12	Slovenia	1.9		Netherlands Antilles	1.1
13	Hong Kong	1.8		Taiwan	1.1
14	Bangladesh	1.7	35	India	1.0
	Denmark	1.7		Mauritius	1.0
	France	1.7		South Korea	1.0
	Hungary	1.7	38	Greece	0.9
	Switzerland	1.7		Israel	0.9
19	Czech Republic	1.6		Portugal	0.9
	Italy	1.6		Slovakia	0.9
	Sweden	1.6			

Most crowded road networks

Number of vehicles per km of road network, 2006 or latest

1	Hong Kong	245.0	26	Switzerland	59.4
2	Qatar	218.0	27	Indonesia	58.8
3	Singapore	194.1	28	Croatia	56.6
4	Germany	189.3	29	Guatemala	52.7
5	Macau	185.5	30	Tunisia	49.1
6	Kuwait	180.7	31	Greece	46.9
7	Taiwan	174.2	32	Serbia	46.5
8	South Korea	155.7	33	Cyprus	45.8
9	Israel	114.4	34	Austria	42.7
10	Malta	113.2	35	France	38.5
11	Netherlands Antilles	95.3	36	Belgium	36.9
12	Jordan	90.8	37	Finland	36.4
13	Mauritius	88.6	38	Ukraine	35.6
14	Dominican Republic	81.4	39	Brunei	35.5
15	Italy	80.2	40	Slovakia	35.4
16	Bahrain	77.2	41	Russia	34.9
17	United Kingdom	76.6	42	Poland	34.7
18	Bulgaria	69.4		Spain	34.7
19	Malaysia	67.4	44	Denmark	32.7
20	Mexico	64.9	45	Chile	32.5
21	Portugal	63.8	46	New Zealand	32.4
22	Luxembourg	63.3	47	Czech Republic	31.3
23	Barbados	63.1	48	Honduras	30.7
24	Japan	62.6		Moldova	30.7
25	Netherlands	62.2	50	United States	30.6

Most used road networks

'000 vehicle-km per year per km of road network, 2006 or latest

1	Hong Kong	5,453	21	Denmark	629
2	Singapore	4,528	22	Ecuador	575
3	Germany	2,456		France	575
4	Israel	2,402	24	Bulgaria	571
5	Bahrain	1,528	25	New Zealand	434
6	South Korea	1,292	26	Norway	381
7	United Kingdom	1,257	27	Czech Republic	367
8	Tunisia	1,000	28	Ireland	351
9	Croatia	908	29	Romania	341
10	Netherlands	872	30	South Africa	339
11	Luxembourg	857	31	Spain	337
12	Switzerland	815	32	Poland	326
13	Cyprus	769	33	Guatemala	323
14	United States	733	34	Suriname	321
15	Greece	675	35	Egypt	311
16	Austria	667	36	Morocco	310
17	Finland	661	37	Mexico	309
18	Belgium	658	38	Slovenia	297
19	Japan	653	39	Senegal	296
20	Peru	634	40	Australia	272

Highest car ownership
Number of cars per 1,000 population, 2006 or latest

1	Luxembourg	647	26	Lebanon	403
2	Iceland	632	27	Greece	388
3	New Zealand	609	28	Ireland	382
4	Italy	595	29	Estonia	367
5	Germany	565	30	Netherlands Antilles	360
6	Canada	561	31	Czech Republic	358
7	Cyprus	550	32	Latvia	357
8	Australia	542	33	Denmark	354
9	Malta	523	34	Kuwait	349
10	Switzerland	520	35	Brunei	346
11	Austria	507	36	Barbados	343
12	France	496	37	Qatar	335
13	Slovenia	493	38	Bahrain	325
14	Belgium	474	39	Croatia	323
15	Portugal	471		Poland	323
16	Finland	470	41	Bulgaria	314
17	Lithuania	468	42	Bahamas	290
18	Sweden	462	43	Hungary	274
19	United States	461	44	Slovakia	247
20	United Kingdom	457		Taiwan	247
21	Spain	445	46	South Korea	240
22	Japan	441	47	Israel	239
23	Norway	439	48	Libya	232
24	Netherlands	424	49	United Arab Emirates	228
25	Saudi Arabia	415	50	Malaysia	225

Lowest car ownership
Number of cars per 1,000 population, 2006 or latest

1	Bangladesh	1		Congo-Kinshasa	8
	Burundi	1		Guinea	8
	Central African Rep	1		India	8
	Ethiopia	1	24	Kenya	9
	Rwanda	1		Philippines	9
	Tanzania	1	26	Pakistan	10
7	Sierra Leone	2		Senegal	10
	Uganda	2		Togo	10
9	Equatorial Guinea	3	29	Bhutan	12
	Mali	3	30	Benin	13
	Nepal	3	31	Bolivia	15
12	Myanmar	4	32	Nigeria	17
	Niger	4		Sri Lanka	17
14	Burkina Faso	5	34	China	18
	Gambia, The	5		Nicaragua	18
	Papua New Guinea	5	36	Syria	19
17	Liberia	6		Tajikistan	19
18	Côte d'Ivoire	7		Yemen	19
19	Angola	8	39	El Salvador	24
	Cameroon	8		Iran	24

Most injured in road accidents
Number of people injured per 100,000 population, 2006 or latest

1	Qatar	9,989	26	Germany	398
2	Kuwait	2,231	27	Croatia	380
3	Jordan	1,783	28	Colombia	366
4	Costa Rica	1,560	29	Cyprus	336
5	Mauritius	1,553		Portugal	336
6	Saudi Arabia	1,305	31	South Africa	322
7	Malaysia	1,222	32	United Kingdom	312
8	Panama	1,212	33	Malta	298
9	Botswana	1,025	34	Iceland	293
10	Suriname	913	35	Sri Lanka	290
11	Bosnia	867	36	Chile	287
12	Barbados	769		Switzerland	287
13	Japan	745	38	Peru	282
14	Brunei	710	39	Mongolia	275
15	Taiwan	702	40	Denmark	268
16	United States	626		New Zealand	268
17	Slovenia	561	42	Israel	246
18	Swaziland	501	43	Nicaragua	245
19	Austria	481	44	Bahrain	237
20	Canada	473	45	Bolivia	230
21	Belgium	468	46	Spain	220
22	South Korea	443	47	Hong Kong	217
23	Namibia	440	48	Czech Republic	215
24	Oman	406		Lesotho	215
25	Italy	405	50	Hungary	208

Most deaths in road accidents
Number of people killed per 100,000 population, 2006 or latest

1	Qatar	33		Namibia	17
	South Africa	33	19	Jordan	16
3	Botswana	30		Kuwait	16
4	Kazakhstan	28		Lesotho	16
5	Malaysia	26		Ukraine	16
6	Swaziland	24	23	Estonia	15
7	Gabon	23		Georgia	15
	Oman	23		Greece	15
	Russia	23		Suriname	15
	Thailand	23		Tunisia	15
11	Lithuania	22		United States	15
	United Arab Emirates	22	29	Bulgaria	14
13	Saudi Arabia	21		Croatia	14
14	Belarus	18		Ecuador	14
	Latvia	18		Poland	14
16	Kyrgyzstan	17		Taiwan	14
	Mongolia	17		Vietnam	14

Transport: planes and trains

Most air travel
Million passenger-km[a] per year, 2008

1	United States	1,332,096		16	Thailand	61,570
2	China	251,146		17	Ireland	60,560
3	United Kingdom	228,042		18	Brazil	56,834
4	Germany	152,081		19	India	55,964
5	Japan	144,490		20	Italy	52,410
6	France	129,655		21	Malaysia	40,019
7	Singapore	93,707		22	Indonesia	30,754
8	United Arab Emirates	89,195		23	Mexico	29,198
9	South Korea	83,707		24	New Zealand	28,289
10	Australia	82,881		25	South Africa	27,573
11	Spain	81,021		26	Belgium	25,936
12	Hong Kong	75,031		27	Switzerland	25,020
13	Netherlands	74,496		28	Turkey	24,995
14	Canada	74,468		29	Saudi Arabia	22,939
15	Russia	68,172		30	Portugal	20,782

Busiest airports

Total passengers, m, 2008

1	Atlanta, Hartsfield	89.4
2	Chicago, O'Hare	68.3
3	London, Heathrow	66.5
4	Tokyo, Haneda	65.9
5	Paris, Charles de Gaulle	60.2
6	Los Angeles, Intl.	58.6
7	Beijing, Capital	57.7
8	Dallas, Ft. Worth	56.3
9	Frankfurt, Main	52.5
10	Denver, Intl.	50.8
11	Madrid, Barajas	49.4
12	Hong Kong, Intl.	47.4
13	Amsterdam, Schiphol	46.2
14	New York, JFK	46.1
15	Las Vegas, Intl.	42.5

Total cargo, m tonnes, 2008

1	Memphis, Intl.	3.65
2	Hong Kong, Intl.	3.52
3	Shanghai, Pudong Intl.	2.50
4	Seoul, Incheon	2.33
5	Anchorage, Intl.	2.23
6	Frankfurt, Main	2.03
7	Paris, Charles de Gaulle	1.99
8	Tokyo, Narita	1.98
9	Louisville, Standiford Fd.	1.94
10	Dubai, Intl.	1.82
	Singapore, Changi	1.82
12	Miami, Intl.	1.73
13	Los Angeles, Intl.	1.53
14	Amsterdam, Schiphol	1.49
15	London, Heathrow	1.43

Average daily aircraft movements, take-offs and landings, 2008

1	Atlanta, Hartsfield	2,663		10	Beijing, Capital	1,339
2	Chicago, O'Hare	2,389		11	Phoenix, Skyharbor Intl.	1,335
3	Dallas, Ft. Worth	1,778		12	Philadelphia, Intl.	1,314
4	Denver, Intl.	1,676		13	London, Heathrow	1,301
5	Los Angeles, Intl.	1,649		14	Phoenix, Deer Valley	1,253
6	Houston, George Bush Intercont.	1,551		15	Frankfurt, Main	1,251
7	Charlotte/Douglas, Intl.	1,538		16	Detroit, Metro	1,227
8	Paris, Charles de Gaulle	1,516		17	Minneapolis, St Paul	1,221
9	Las Vegas, McCarran Intl.	1,463		18	Madrid, Barajas	1,205
				19	Toronto, Pearson Intl.	1,179
				20	Newark	1,167

a Air passenger–km data refer to the distance travelled by aircraft of national origin.

Longest railway networks
'000 km, 2007

1	United States	226.7	21	Australia	9.6
2	Russia	84.2	22	Czech Republic	9.5
3	China	63.6	23	Pakistan	7.8
4	India	63.3	24	Hungary	7.7
5	Canada	57.0	25	Iran	7.3
6	Argentina	35.8	26	Chile	5.9
7	Germany	33.9		Finland	5.9
8	Brazil	29.5	28	Austria	5.8
	France	29.5	29	Belarus	5.5
10	Mexico	26.7		Sudan	5.5
11	South Africa	24.5	31	Egypt	5.2
12	Ukraine	21.9	32	Norway	4.1
13	Japan	20.1	33	Bulgaria	4.0
14	Poland	19.4		Uzbekistan	4.0
15	Italy	16.7	35	Serbia	3.8
16	United Kingdom	16.2	36	Algeria	3.6
17	Spain	14.8		Congo-Brazzaville	3.6
18	Kazakhstan	14.2		Slovakia	3.6
19	Romania	10.6		Switzerland	3.6
20	Sweden	9.8	40	Nigeria	3.5

Most rail passengers
Km per person per year, 2007

1	Switzerland	2,103	11	Germany	908
2	Japan	1,978	12	Kazakhstan	878
3	France	1,350	13	United Kingdom	814
4	Russia	1,224	14	Italy	774
5	Ukraine	1,145	15	Finland	713
6	Austria	1,104	16	Sweden	711
7	Denmark	1,041	17	Czech Republic	666
8	Belarus	966	18	South Korea	651
9	Netherlands	948	19	Luxembourg	632
10	Belgium	937	20	Hungary	618

Most rail freight
Million tonnes-km per year, 2007

1	United States	2,820,061	11	Mexico	75,600
2	China	2,211,246	12	Belarus	47,933
3	Russia	2,090,337	13	Australia	46,036
4	India	480,993	14	Poland	43,548
5	Canada	353,227	15	France	42,635
6	Ukraine	240,810	16	Japan	23,145
7	Brazil	232,297	17	United Kingdom	21,200
8	Kazakhstan	191,189	18	Iran	20,542
9	South Africa	108,513	19	Uzbekistan	19,281
10	Germany	91,013	20	Austria	18,996

Transport: shipping

Merchant fleets

Number of vessels, by country of domicile, 2008

1	China	3,303	11	Singapore	869
2	Germany	3,208	12	Denmark	861
3	Greece	3,115	13	Indonesia	850
	Japan	3,115	14	Netherlands	792
5	Russia	2,111	15	Italy	773
6	Norway	1,827	16	Hong Kong	657
7	United States	1,769	17	Taiwan	590
8	South Korea	1,140	18	India	534
9	Turkey	1,026	19	United Arab Emirates	424
10	United Kingdom	876	20	Canada	419

By country of domicile, deadweight tonnage, m, January 2008

1	Greece	174.6	11	Taiwan	26.2
2	Japan	161.7	12	United Kingdom	26.0
3	Germany	94.2	13	Canada	18.7
4	China	84.9	14	Russia	18.0
5	Norway	46.9	15	Italy	17.7
6	United States	39.8	16	India	16.0
7	South Korea	37.7	17	Turkey	13.2
8	Hong Kong	33.4	18	Saudi Arabia	12.9
9	Singapore	28.6	19	Belgium	12.2
10	Denmark	27.4	20	Malaysia	11.2

Maritime trading

% of value of world trade generated, January 2008

1	United States	12.4		Spain	2.2
2	Germany	8.5	15	Mexico	2.0
3	China	7.8		Singapore	2.0
4	Japan	4.8	17	Taiwan	1.7
5	France	4.2	18	India	1.3
6	United Kingdom	3.8	19	Austria	1.2
7	Netherlands	3.7		Malaysia	1.2
8	Italy	3.6		Saudi Arabia	1.2
9	Belgium	3.0		Switzerland	1.2
10	Canada	2.9	23	Australia	1.1
11	Hong Kong	2.6		Poland	1.1
	South Korea	2.6		Sweden	1.1
13	Russia	2.2			

% of world fleet deadweight tonnage, by country of ownership, January 2008

1	Japan	15.6	10	Canada	1.8
2	Germany	9.1	11	Italy	1.7
3	China	8.2		Russia	1.7
4	United States	3.8	13	India	1.6
5	South Korea	3.6	14	Saudi Arabia	1.3
6	Hong Kong	3.2	15	Belgium	1.2
7	Singapore	2.8	16	Malaysia	1.1
8	Taiwan	2.5	17	Netherlands	0.8
	United Kingdom	2.5	18	Sweden	0.7

Note: Deadweight tonnage is the weight the ships can safely carry.

Tourism

Most tourist arrivals
Number of arrivals, '000, 2007

1	France	81,900	21	Netherlands	11,008
2	Spain	59,193	22	Egypt	10,610
3	United States	55,986	23	Croatia	9,307
4	China	54,720	24	South Africa	9,090
5	Italy	43,654	25	Hungary	8,638
6	United Kingdom	30,677	26	Switzerland	8,448
7	Germany	24,420	27	Japan	8,347
8	Ukraine	23,122	28	Singapore	7,957
9	Turkey	22,248	29	Morocco	7,408
10	Mexico	21,424	30	Belgium	7,045
11	Malaysia	20,973	31	Tunisia	6,762
12	Austria	20,766	32	Czech Republic	6,680
13	Canada	17,931	33	South Korea	6,448
14	Greece	17,518	34	Indonesia	5,506
15	Hong Kong	17,154	35	Bulgaria	5,151
16	Poland	14,975	36	Brazil	5,026
17	Thailand	14,464	37	India	4,977
18	Macau	12,945	38	Syria	4,566
19	Portugal	12,321	39	Argentina	4,562
20	Saudi Arabia	11,531	40	Vietnam	4,172

Biggest tourist spenders
$m, 2007

1	United States	78,612	11	Spain	17,876
2	Germany	74,068	12	Netherlands	17,645
3	United Kingdom	66,024	13	Belgium	15,996
4	France	31,936	14	Hong Kong	14,309
5	China	26,652	15	Norway	12,862
6	Japan	26,189	16	Sweden	12,186
7	Italy	23,804	17	Australia	12,054
8	Canada	22,535	18	Switzerland	10,640
9	South Korea	20,604	19	United Arab Emirates	9,843
10	Russia	18,903	20	Taiwan	8,799

Largest tourist receipts
$m, 2007

1	United States	96,712	13	Malaysia	14,047
2	Spain	57,795	14	Hong Kong	13,766
3	France	54,228	15	Netherlands	13,428
4	Italy	42,651	16	Mexico	12,901
5	China	41,919	17	Switzerland	11,818
6	United Kingdom	37,617	18	India	10,729
7	Germany	36,029	19	Belgium	10,662
8	Australia	22,244	20	Poland	10,627
9	Austria	18,887	21	Portugal	10,132
10	Turkey	18,487	22	Russia	9,607
11	Greece	15,513	23	Japan	9,334
12	Canada	15,486	24	Egypt	9,303

Education

Primary enrolment
Number enrolled as % of relevant age group

Highest		Lowest	
1 Rwanda	208	1 Eritrea	49
2 Sierra Leone	180	2 Congo-Brazzaville	66
3 Madagascar	169	3 Gambia, The	68
4 Nicaragua	168	Niger	68
5 Burundi	164	5 Côte d'Ivoire	70
6 Mozambique	148	6 Central African Rep	72
7 Uganda	146	7 Thailand	77
8 Malawi	142	8 Oman	78
9 Nepal	141	9 Sudan	80
10 Myanmar	138	10 Burkina Faso	81
11 Cambodia	137	11 Cape Verde	83
Ecuador	137	12 Mali	85
13 Ethiopia	136	13 Andorra	88
14 Honduras	134	China	88
15 India	130	Lebanon	88

Highest tertiary enrolment[a]
Number enrolled as % of relevant age group

1 Cuba	122	Sweden	75
2 South Korea	95	15 Iceland	73
3 Finland	94	16 Latvia	71
4 Greece	91	17 Belarus	69
5 Slovenia	86	Hungary	69
6 United States	82	Spain	69
7 Denmark	80	20 Italy	68
New Zealand	80	21 Argentina	67
9 Lithuania	76	Poland	67
Norway	76	23 Estonia	65
Ukraine	76	24 Uruguay	64
12 Australia	75	25 Belgium	62
Russia	75	Canada	62

Education spending
% of GDP

Highest		Lowest	
1 Cuba	13.3	1 Equatorial Guinea	0.6
Lesotho	13.3	2 Bermuda	1.2
3 Denmark	8.3	3 Central African Rep	1.4
Moldova	8.3	United Arab Emirates	1.4
5 Botswana	8.1	5 Zambia	1.5
6 Swaziland	8.0	6 Cambodia	1.6
7 Iceland	7.7	7 Guinea	1.7

Notes: Latest available year 2004–08. The gross enrolment ratios shown are the actual number enrolled as a percentage of the number of children in the official primary age group. They may exceed 100 when children outside the primary age group are receiving primary education.
a Tertiary education includes all levels of post-secondary education including courses leading to awards not equivalent to a university degree, courses leading to a first university degree and postgraduate courses.

Least literate
% adult literacy rate[a]

1	Mali	26.2		25	Angola	67.4
2	Burkina Faso	28.7		26	Cameroon	67.9
	Niger	28.7		27	Zambia	70.6
4	Guinea	29.5		28	Malawi	71.8
5	Chad	31.8		29	Nigeria	72.0
6	Ethiopia	35.9		30	Tanzania	72.3
7	Sierra Leone	38.1		31	Laos	72.7
8	Benin	40.5		32	Guatemala	73.2
9	Senegal	41.9		33	Uganda	73.6
10	Mozambique	44.4		34	Algeria	75.4
11	Eritrea	52.5		35	Cambodia	76.3
12	Bhutan	52.8		36	Tunisia	77.7
13	Bangladesh	53.5		37	Nicaragua	78.0
14	Pakistan	54.2		38	El Salvador	82.0
15	Liberia	55.5		39	Lesotho	82.2
16	Morocco	55.6		40	Iran	82.3
17	Mauritania	55.8		41	Botswana	82.9
18	Nepal	56.5		42	Syria	83.1
19	Papua New Guinea	57.8		43	Honduras	83.6
20	Yemen	58.9		44	Cape Verde	83.8
21	Ghana	65.0		45	Ecuador	84.2
22	India	66.0		46	Oman	84.4
23	Egypt	66.4		47	Saudi Arabia	85.0
24	Congo-Kinshasa	67.2		48	Jamaica	86.0

Top universities[b]
2008

1	Harvard, US		18	Michigan, US
2	Yale, US		19	Tokyo, Japan
3	Cambridge, UK		20	McGill, Canada
4	Oxford, UK		21	Carnegie Mellon, US
5	California Institute of Technology, US		22	King's College London, UK
6	Imperial College London, UK		23	Edinburgh, UK
7	University College London, UK		24	ETH Zurich, Switzerland
8	Chicago, US		25	Kyoto, Japan
9	Massachusetts Institute of Technology, US		26	Hong Kong
10	Columbia, US		27	Brown, US
11	Pennsylvania, US		28	École Normale Supérieure, France
12	Princeton, US		29	Manchester, UK
13	Duke, US		30	California, Los Angeles, US
	Johns Hopkins, US			National University of Singapore
15	Cornell, US		32	Bristol, UK
16	Australian National University		33	Northwestern, US
17	Stanford, US		34	British Columbia, Canada
				École Polytechnique, France

a Latest available year 2001–08.
b Based on academic peer review, employer review, faculty/student ratio, research strength and international factors.

Life expectancy

Highest life expectancy
Years, 2005–10

1	Japan	82.7		Malta	79.7
2	Andorra[a]	82.5	26	Finland	79.6
3	Hong Kong	82.2		Martinique	79.6
4	Italy	82.1	28	Luxembourg	79.5
5	Iceland	81.8	29	Faroe Islands[a]	79.4
	Switzerland	81.8		South Korea	79.4
7	Australia	81.5		United Kingdom	79.4
8	France	81.2	32	Greece	79.2
9	Spain	80.9		United States	79.2
	Sweden	80.9	34	Channel Islands	79.1
11	Canada	80.7		Guadeloupe	79.1
	Israel	80.7	36	Virgin Islands (US)	78.9
	Macau	80.7	37	Costa Rica	78.8
14	Norway	80.6	38	Portugal	78.7
15	Bermuda[a]	80.4		Puerto Rico	78.7
	Cayman Islands[a]	80.4	40	Cuba	78.6
17	Singapore	80.3	41	Chile	78.5
18	New Zealand	80.2	42	Slovenia	78.4
19	Austria	80.0	43	Denmark	78.3
	Netherlands	80.0	44	Taiwan[a]	78.0
21	Germany	79.9	45	Kuwait	77.6
	Ireland	79.9	46	United Arab Emirates	77.4
23	Belgium	79.7	47	Barbados	77.2
	Cyprus	79.7	48	Brunei	77.1

Highest male life expectancy
Years, 2005–10

1	Andorra[a]	80.3	10	Canada	78.3
2	Iceland	80.2		Norway	78.3
3	Hong Kong	79.4	12	New Zealand	78.2
4	Switzerland	79.3	13	Italy	78.1
5	Australia	79.1	14	Singapore	77.9
6	Japan	79.0	15	Cayman Islands[a]	77.8
7	Sweden	78.7		Malta	77.8
8	Israel	78.6		Netherlands	77.8
9	Macau	78.5			

Highest female life expectancy
Years, 2005–10

1	Japan	86.2	10	Iceland	83.3
2	Hong Kong	85.1	11	Cayman Islands[a]	83.1
3	Andorra[a]	84.8	12	Finland	83.0
4	France	84.7		Sweden	83.0
5	Italy	84.1	14	Canada	82.9
	Spain	84.1	15	Israel	82.8
	Switzerland	84.1		Macau	82.8
8	Australia	83.8		Norway	82.8
9	Bermuda[a]	83.7		Singapore	82.8

a 2009 estimate.

Lowest life expectancy
Years, 2005–10

1	Afghanistan	43.8	26	Kenya	54.2
2	Zimbabwe	44.1	27	Botswana	54.9
3	Zambia	45.2	28	Ethiopia	55.0
4	Lesotho	45.3	29	Senegal	55.4
5	Swaziland	45.8		Tanzania	55.4
6	Angola	46.8	31	Gambia, The	55.8
7	Central African Rep	46.9	32	Ghana	56.5
8	Sierra Leone	47.4	33	Mauritania	56.6
9	Congo-Kinshasa	47.5	34	Côte d'Ivoire	57.2
10	Guinea-Bissau	47.6	35	Guinea	57.6
11	Mozambique	47.8	36	Sudan	58.0
	Nigeria	47.8	37	Liberia	58.1
13	Mali	48.3	38	Eritrea	59.4
14	Chad	48.7	39	Madagascar	60.1
15	Somalia	49.6	40	Gabon	60.3
16	Rwanda	49.9	41	Papua New Guinea	60.8
17	Equatorial Guinea	50.1		Timor-Leste	60.8
18	Burundi	50.3	43	Cambodia	60.9
19	Cameroon	51.0	44	Haiti	61.2
20	Niger	51.1		Myanmar	61.2
21	South Africa	51.6	46	Benin	61.3
22	Uganda	52.4	47	Namibia	61.4
23	Burkina Faso	52.9	48	Togo	62.4
	Malawi	52.9	49	Yemen	62.7
25	Congo-Brazzaville	53.6	50	India	63.5

Lowest male life expectancy
Years, 2005–10

1	Zimbabwe	43.4	11	Mozambique	46.9
2	Afghanistan	43.9	12	Nigeria	47.3
3	Lesotho	44.5	13	Chad	47.4
4	Zambia	44.6	14	Mali	47.6
5	Angola	44.9	15	Rwanda	48.1
6	Central African Rep	45.4	16	Somalia	48.2
7	Congo-Kinshasa	45.9	17	Burundi	48.8
8	Guinea-Bissau	46.1	18	Equatorial Guinea	48.9
	Sierra Leone	46.1	19	South Africa	49.9
10	Swaziland	46.3	20	Niger	50.3

Lowest female life expectancy
Years, 2005–10

1	Afghanistan	43.8	10	Angola	48.8
2	Zimbabwe	44.3	11	Congo-Kinshasa	49.0
3	Swaziland	45.2		Mali	49.0
4	Zambia	45.6	13	Guinea-Bissau	49.2
5	Lesotho	45.8	14	Chad	50.0
6	Nigeria	48.3	15	Somalia	51.0
7	Central African Rep	48.4	16	Equatorial Guinea	51.3
8	Mozambique	48.7	17	Cameroon	51.5
	Sierra Leone	48.7	18	Rwanda	51.6

Death rates and infant mortality

Highest death rates
Number of deaths per 1,000 population, 2005–10

1	Afghanistan	19.7	49	Czech Republic	10.8
2	Zambia	17.5	50	Liberia	10.6
3	Guinea-Bissau	17.4	51	Mauritania	10.5
4	Congo-Kinshasa	17.2	52	Denmark	10.3
5	Angola	17.1		Germany	10.3
	Central African Rep	17.1		Sudan	10.3
7	Lesotho	16.9	55	Greece	10.2
8	Chad	16.8		Montenegro	10.2
9	Nigeria	16.5	57	Portugal	10.1
10	Zimbabwe	16.2		Sweden	10.1
11	Mozambique	16.1	59	Poland	10.0
12	Sierra Leone	16.0		Slovakia	10.0
	Ukraine	16.0	61	Italy	9.9
14	Mali	15.9		Myanmar	9.9
	Somalia	15.9		North Korea	9.9
16	Swaziland	15.7		United Kingdom	9.9
17	Niger	15.2	65	Bosnia	9.8
18	Equatorial Guinea	15.1		Gabon	9.8
	Russia	15.1	67	Belgium	9.7
	South Africa	15.1	68	Channel Islands	9.5
21	Belarus	14.7		Slovenia	9.5
	Rwanda	14.7	70	Finland	9.4
23	Bulgaria	14.6	71	Austria	9.3
24	Cameroon	14.3		Benin	9.3
25	Burundi	14.0		Madagascar	9.3
26	Latvia	13.8		Uruguay	9.3
27	Hungary	13.4	75	Haiti	9.1
28	Burkina Faso	13.1		Japan	9.1
	Lithuania	13.1		Macedonia	9.1
30	Congo-Brazzaville	12.9	78	Thailand	8.9
	Estonia	12.9	79	Timor-Leste	8.8
	Uganda	12.9	80	Armenia	8.7
33	Malawi	12.4		Faroe Islands[a]	8.7
34	Moldova	12.3		Norway	8.7
	Romania	12.3		Spain	8.7
36	Ethiopia	12.0	84	Eritrea	8.6
37	Georgia	11.9		France	8.6
38	Botswana	11.7	86	India	8.5
	Kenya	11.7		Namibia	8.5
40	Serbia	11.6	88	Cambodia	8.4
41	Croatia	11.5		Netherlands	8.4
	Tanzania	11.5	90	Switzerland	8.3
43	Gambia, The	11.4	91	Greenland[a]	8.2
44	Kazakhstan	11.3		Luxembourg	8.2
45	Ghana	11.2		Togo	8.2
	Guinea	11.2	94	Bermuda[a]	8.0
47	Senegal	11.0		Papua New Guinea	8.0
48	Côte d'Ivoire	10.9		Trinidad & Tobago	8.0

Note: Both death and, in particular, infant mortality rates can be underestimated in certain countries where not all deaths are officially recorded. a 2008 estimate.

Highest infant mortality
Number of deaths per 1,000 live births, 2005–10

1	Afghanistan	157.0	23	Congo-Brazzaville	79.3
2	Chad	129.9	24	Ethiopia	79.1
3	Angola	117.5	25	Gambia, The	76.5
4	Congo-Kinshasa	116.8	26	Myanmar	75.4
5	Guinea-Bissau	114.0	27	Uganda	74.0
6	Somalia	109.6	28	Ghana	73.4
7	Nigeria	109.4	29	Mauritania	72.8
8	Mali	106.4	30	Togo	71.4
9	Central African Rep	105.5	31	Lesotho	69.6
10	Sierra Leone	104.3	32	Sudan	69.1
11	Equatorial Guinea	99.6	33	Timor-Leste	66.7
	Rwanda	99.6	34	Swaziland	65.7
13	Guinea	98.4	35	Madagascar	65.2
14	Burundi	98.3	36	Tanzania	64.8
15	Liberia	91.5	37	Zambia	64.6
16	Mozambique	90.1	38	Kenya	63.9
17	Niger	88.2		Pakistan	63.9
18	Cameroon	86.9	40	Haiti	62.4
19	Côte d'Ivoire	86.8	41	Cambodia	62.3
20	Benin	84.9	42	Tajikistan	60.2
21	Malawi	83.7	43	Yemen	58.6
22	Burkina Faso	80.1	44	Senegal	58.4

Lowest death rates
No. deaths per 1,000 pop., 2005–10

1	United Arab Emirates	1.5
2	Kuwait	1.9
3	Qatar	2.0
4	Bahrain	2.6
5	Oman	2.7
6	Brunei	2.8
7	Syria	3.4
8	Saudi Arabia	3.6
9	Belize	3.7
	West Bank and Gaza	3.7
11	Costa Rica	4.1
	Libya	4.1
13	Jordan	4.2
14	Macau	4.4
15	Malaysia	4.5
16	Mexico	4.7
	Nicaragua	4.7
18	Cayman Islands[a]	4.8
	Philippines	4.8
20	Algeria	4.9
21	Cape Verde	5.0
	Panama	5.0

Lowest infant mortality
No. deaths per 1,000 live births, 2005–10

1	Bermuda[a]	2.5
2	Iceland	2.9
3	Singapore	3.0
4	Sweden	3.1
5	Finland	3.2
	Japan	3.2
7	Norway	3.5
8	Hong Kong	3.7
	Slovenia	3.7
10	Andorra[a]	3.8
	Czech Republic	3.8
	Greece	3.8
13	France	3.9
	Italy	3.9
	Spain	3.9
16	Belgium	4.1
	Germany	4.1
	Switzerland	4.1
19	Luxembourg	4.2
	Portugal	4.2
21	Austria	4.3
22	Denmark	4.4
	South Korea	4.4

a 2009 estimate.

Death and disease

Diabetes

% of population aged 20–79, 2008

1	United Arab Emirates	19.5
2	Saudi Arabia	16.7
3	Bahrain	15.2
	Qatar	15.2
5	Kuwait	14.4
6	French Polynesia	13.5
	Réunion	13.5
8	Oman	13.1
9	Brunei	12.2
10	Trinidad & Tobago	11.5
11	Netherlands Antilles	11.3
12	Mauritius	11.1
13	Egypt	11.0
14	Malaysia	10.7
	Puerto Rico	10.7
16	Mexico	10.6
	Syria	10.6
18	Jamaica	10.3

Cardiovascular disease

Deaths per 100,000 population, age standardised, 2002

1	Turkmenistan	844
2	Tajikistan	753
3	Kazakhstan	713
4	Afghanistan	706
5	Russia	688
6	Uzbekistan	663
7	Ukraine	637
8	Moldova	619
9	Azerbaijan	613
10	Kyrgyzstan	602
11	Belarus	592
12	Georgia	584
13	Somalia	580
14	Egypt	560
15	Bulgaria	554
16	Yemen	553
17	Turkey	542
18	Albania	537
19	Sierre Leone	515

Cancer

Deaths per 100,000 population, age standardised, 2002

1	Mongolia	306
2	Bolivia	256
3	Hungary	201
4	Sierra Leone	181
5	Poland	180
6	Angola	179
7	Czech Republic	177
8	Peru	175
9	Slovakia	170
	Uruguay	170
11	Liberia	169
	Niger	169
	South Korea	169
14	Croatia	167
	Denmark	167
	Kazakhstan	167
17	Mali	166
18	Burkina Faso	162
	Swaziland	162
20	Congo-Kinshasa	161
	Lithuania	161
22	Côte d'Ivoire	160
	Slovenia	160

Tuberculosis

Incidence per 100,000 population, 2007

1	Swaziland	1,198
2	South Africa	948
3	Zimbabwe	782
4	Namibia	767
5	Botswana	731
6	Lesotho	637
7	Sierra Leone	574
8	Zambia	506
9	Cambodia	495
10	Mozambique	431
11	Togo	429
12	Côte d'Ivoire	420
13	Gabon	406
14	Congo-Brazzaville	403
15	Rwanda	397
16	Congo-Kinshasa	392
17	Ethiopia	378
18	Burundi	367
19	Kenya	353
20	Malawi	346
21	Central African Rep	345
22	North Korea	344
23	Uganda	330

Note: Statistics are not available for all countries. The number of cases diagnosed and reported depends on the quality of medical practice and administration and can be under-reported in a number of countries.

Measles immunisation
Lowest % of children aged 12–23 months, 2007

1	Chad	23
2	Somalia	34
3	Laos	40
4	Niger	47
5	Equatorial Guinea	51
6	Lebanon	53
7	Gabon	55
	Venezuela	55
9	Haiti	58
	Papua New Guinea	58
11	Benin	61
12	Central African Rep	62
	Nigeria	62
14	Timor-Leste	63
15	Ethiopia	65
16	Zimbabwe	66
17	Congo-Brazzaville	67
	Côte d'Ivoire	67
	India	67
	Sierra Leone	67

DPT[a] immunisation
Lowest % of children aged 12–23 months, 2007

1	Chad	20
2	Equatorial Guinea	33
3	Gabon	38
4	Niger	39
	Somalia	39
6	Laos	50
7	Haiti	53
8	Central African Rep	54
	Nigeria	54
10	Papua New Guinea	60
11	India	62
	Zimbabwe	62
13	Guinea-Bissau	63
14	Sierra Leone	64
	Uganda	64
16	Paraguay	66
17	Benin	67
18	Mali	68
19	Timor-Leste	70
20	Venezuela	71

HIV/AIDS
Prevalence among population aged 15–49, %, 2007

1	Swaziland	26.1
2	Botswana	23.9
3	Lesotho	23.2
4	South Africa	18.1
5	Namibia	15.3
	Zimbabwe	15.3
7	Zambia	15.2
8	Mozambique	12.5
9	Malawi	11.9
10	Central African Rep	6.3
11	Tanzania	6.2
12	Gabon	5.9
13	Uganda	5.4
14	Cameroon	5.1
15	Côte d'Ivoire	3.9
16	Chad	3.5
	Congo-Brazzaville	3.5
18	Equatorial Guinea	3.4
19	Togo	3.3
20	Nigeria	3.1
21	Bahamas	3.0
22	Rwanda	2.8
23	Suriname	2.4
24	Haiti	2.2

AIDS
Estimated deaths per 100,000 pop., 2007

1	Zimbabwe	1,060
2	Lesotho	1,000
	Swaziland	1,000
4	South Africa	734
5	Botswana	611
6	Malawi	504
7	Zambia	463
8	Mozambique	395
9	Central African Rep	262
10	Uganda	249
11	Namibia	243
12	Tanzania	242
13	Cameroon	231
14	Côte d'Ivoire	202
15	Gabon	164
16	Congo-Brazzaville	152
17	Togo	140
18	Burundi	136
	Chad	136
20	Nigeria	124
21	Ghana	91
22	Ethiopia	83
	Rwanda	83
24	Haiti	82

a Diptheria, pertussis and tetanus

Health

Highest health spending
As % of GDP, 2006

1	Timor-Leste	17.7
2	United States	15.3
3	Malawi	12.9
4	France	11.0
5	Rwanda	10.9
6	Denmark	10.8
	Switzerland	10.8
8	Argentina	10.7
9	Germany	10.6
10	Austria	10.2
	Portugal	10.2
12	Canada	10.0
13	Belgium	9.9
14	Jordan	9.7
15	Nicaragua	9.6
16	Bosnia	9.5
	Greece	9.5
18	Moldova	9.4
	Netherlands	9.4
20	New Zealand	9.3
	Zimbabwe	9.3
22	Afghanistan	9.2
	Sweden	9.2
24	Iceland	9.1
25	Italy	9.0
26	Lebanon	8.8
27	Australia	8.7
	Burundi	8.7
	Namibia	8.7
	Norway	8.7

Lowest health spending
As % of GDP, 2006

1	Brunei	1.9
2	Pakistan	2.0
3	Congo-Brazzaville	2.1
	Equatorial Guinea	2.1
5	Kuwait	2.2
	Mauritania	2.2
	Myanmar	2.2
8	Oman	2.3
9	Libya	2.4
10	Indonesia	2.5
	United Arab Emirates	2.5
12	Angola	2.6
13	Bangladesh	3.2
	Madagascar	3.2
	Papua New Guinea	3.2
16	Saudi Arabia	3.3
	Singapore	3.3
18	Bhutan	3.5
	Iraq	3.5
	North Korea	3.5
	Thailand	3.5
22	Bahrain	3.6
	Eritrea	3.6
	India	3.6
	Kazakhstan	3.6
26	Fiji	3.7

Highest pop. per doctor
2007 or latest

1	Malawi	50,752
2	Niger	50,338
3	Tanzania	48,297
4	Bhutan	44,231
5	Ethiopia	41,942
6	Burundi	40,500
7	Mozambique	39,883
8	Sierra Leone	35,802
9	Liberia	33,981
10	Chad	29,855
11	Benin	28,939
12	Togo	28,889
13	Botswana	24,658
14	Eritrea	21,860
15	Rwanda	21,759
16	Senegal	20,539
17	Lesotho	20,225

Lowest pop. per doctor
2007 or latest

1	Turkmenistan	140
2	Cuba	170
3	Greece	189
4	Ukraine	193
5	Belarus	213
6	Georgia	222
7	Russia	224
8	Bulgaria	232
9	Malta	240
10	Belgium	244
11	Lithuania	249
	Norway	249
13	Netherlands	250
	Switzerland	250
15	Hungary	255
16	Kazakhstan	262
17	Germany	265

Most hospital beds
Beds per 1,000 pop., 2007 or latest

1	Japan	14.0	21	Luxembourg	6.3
2	Belarus	11.3	22	Mongolia	6.1
3	Russia	9.7	23	Israel	6.0
4	Ukraine	8.7	24	Estonia	5.7
5	South Korea	8.6	25	Ireland	5.6
6	Germany	8.3	26	Switzerland	5.5
7	Czech Republic	8.2	27	Tajikistan	5.4
8	Kazakhstan	8.1	28	Belgium	5.3
	Lithuania	8.1		Croatia	5.3
10	Azerbaijan	8.0		Iceland	5.3
11	Austria	7.6	31	Moldova	5.2
	Malta	7.6		Poland	5.2
13	Latvia	7.5	33	Palau	5.0
14	France	7.3	34	Cuba	4.9
15	Hungary	7.1		Kyrgyzstan	4.9
16	Finland	6.8	36	Greece	4.8
	Slovakia	6.8		Netherlands	4.8
18	Barbados	6.6		Slovenia	4.8
19	Romania	6.5	39	Uzbekistan	4.7
20	Bulgaria	6.4	40	Macedonia	4.6

Obesity[a]

Men, % of total population

1	Lebanon	36.3
2	Qatar	34.6
3	United States	31.1
4	Panama	27.9
5	Kuwait	27.5
6	Cyprus	26.6
7	Saudi Arabia	26.4
8	Greece	26.0
9	New Zealand	24.7
10	Mexico	24.4
11	England	23.6
12	Austria	23.3
	Bahrain	23.3
14	Canada	22.9
	Malta	22.9
16	Albania	22.8
17	Scotland	22.4
18	Croatia	21.6
19	Germany	21.0
20	Lithuania	20.6
21	Wales	20.0
22	Chile	19.6
23	Argentina	19.5
24	Australia	19.3
25	Luxembourg	18.8

Women, % of total population

1	Qatar	45.3
2	Saudi Arabia	44.0
3	Lebanon	38.3
4	Panama	36.1
5	Albania	35.6
6	Mexico	34.5
7	Bahrain	34.1
8	United States	33.2
9	Egypt	33.1
10	United Arab Emirates	31.4
11	Kuwait	29.9
12	Turkey	29.4
13	Chile	29.3
14	Jordan	26.3
15	New Zealand	26.0
	Scotland	26.0
17	England	24.4
18	Jamaica	23.9
19	Oman	23.8
20	Cyprus	23.7
21	Canada	23.2
22	Peru	23.0
23	Croatia	22.7
24	Australia	22.2
25	Morocco	21.7

a   Defined as body mass index of 30 or more – see page 248.

Marriage and divorce

Highest marriage rates
Number of marriages per 1,000 population, 2007 or latest available year

1	Mongolia	19.0		Indonesia	7.0
2	Cayman Islands	16.8		Turkmenistan	7.0
3	Bermuda	13.7	28	South Korea	6.8
4	Vietnam	12.1		Uzbekistan	6.8
5	Iran	11.0	30	Moldova	6.5
6	Jordan	10.1		Philippines	6.5
7	Azerbaijan	9.4		Turkey	6.5
8	Mauritius	9.2	33	Romania	6.4
9	Algeria	8.9	34	Cyprus	6.3
10	Jamaica	8.7		Egypt	6.3
11	Fiji	8.6		Lithuania	6.3
12	Kyrgyzstan	8.4	37	Belize	6.1
13	Tajikistan	8.2		Costa Rica	6.1
14	Belarus	8.1		Malta	6.1
15	Guam	8.0	40	Hong Kong	6.0
	Lebanon	8.0		Puerto Rico	6.0
17	Russia	7.7	42	Bahamas	5.8
	United States	7.7		China	5.8
19	Channel Islands[a]	7.6		Malaysia	5.8
20	Taiwan	7.4		Netherlands Antilles	5.8
21	Macedonia	7.3		Trinidad & Tobago	5.8
	West Bank and Gaza	7.3		Tunisia	5.8
23	Denmark	7.1		Ukraine	5.8
	Kazakhstan	7.1	49	Aruba	5.7
25	Albania	7.0		Finland	5.7

Lowest marriage rates
Number of marriages per 1,000 population, 2007 or latest available year

1	Colombia	1.7		Bulgaria	4.0
2	Venezuela	2.7		France	4.0
3	Peru	2.9		Suriname	4.0
4	Argentina	3.1	21	Belgium	4.2
5	Qatar	3.2		French Polynesia	4.2
	Slovenia	3.2		Macau	4.2
7	Chile	3.3		Netherlands	4.2
	Panama	3.3		Nicaragua	4.2
9	United Arab Emirates	3.5	26	Dominican Republic	4.3
10	Andorra	3.6	27	Guatemala	4.4
11	Martinique	3.7		Hungary	4.4
	New Caledonia	3.7		Italy	4.4
	Uruguay	3.7		Saudi Arabia	4.4
14	Guadeloupe	3.8	31	Canada	4.5
	Réunion	3.8		Luxembourg	4.5
	South Africa	3.8		Thailand	4.5
17	Brazil	4.0	34	Estonia	4.6

a Jersey only
Note: The data are based on latest available figures (no earlier than 2001) and hence will be affected by the population age structure at the time. Marriage rates refer to registered marriages only and, therefore, reflect the customs surrounding registry and efficiency of administration.

Highest divorce rates
Number of divorces per 1,000 population, 2007 or latest available year

1	Guam	5.3	26	Finland	2.5
2	Aruba	4.4		Hong Kong	2.5
3	Uruguay	4.3		Norway	2.5
4	South Korea	4.2	29	Australia	2.4
5	Moldova	4.0		Bulgaria	2.4
	Puerto Rico	4.0		Hungary	2.4
	Russia	4.0		Kazakhstan	2.4
8	Ukraine	3.5		Latvia	2.4
9	Lithuania	3.4		Luxembourg	2.4
	Taiwan	3.4		Portugal	2.4
	United States	3.4	36	Costa Rica	2.3
12	Czech Republic	3.3		Cyprus	2.3
13	Channel Islands[a]	3.2	38	Austria	2.2
	Cuba	3.2		Canada	2.2
15	Estonia	3.1		France	2.2
16	Belgium	3.0		Slovakia	2.2
	Cayman Islands	3.0		Sweden	2.2
	Denmark	3.0	43	Guadeloupe	2.1
19	United Kingdom	2.9		Jordan	2.1
20	Bermuda	2.8	45	Japan	2.0
	Germany	2.8	46	Iceland	1.9
22	Belarus	2.7	47	Dominican Republic	1.8
23	Netherlands Antilles	2.6		Kuwait	1.8
	New Zealand	2.6		Netherlands	1.8
	Switzerland	2.6		Romania	1.8

Lowest divorce rates
Number of divorces per 1,000 population, 2007 or latest available year

1	Guatemala	0.1		Montenegro	0.8
2	Belize	0.2		Turkey	0.8
	Colombia	0.2	22	Armenia	0.9
4	Libya	0.3		Azerbaijan	0.9
5	Bosnia	0.4		Ecuador	0.9
	Tajikistan	0.4		Panama	0.9
7	Chile	0.5		Qatar	0.9
	Georgia	0.5		Venezuela	0.9
	Vietnam	0.5	28	Saudi Arabia	1.0
10	Mexico	0.6		South Africa	1.0
	Mongolia	0.6		United Arab Emirates	1.0
	Uzbekistan	0.6		West Bank and Gaza	1.0
13	Egypt	0.7	32	Mauritius	1.1
	Jamaica	0.7		New Caledonia	1.1
	Macedonia	0.7		Réunion	1.1
16	Brazil	0.8		Serbia	1.1
	Indonesia	0.8		Spain	1.1
	Ireland	0.8		Thailand	1.1
	Italy	0.8		Tunisia	1.1

a Jersey only

Households and living costs

Number of households
Biggest, m, 2007

1	China	380.8	14	Mexico	25.5
2	India	213.5	15	Pakistan	23.2
3	United States	115.2	16	Italy	22.7
4	Indonesia	60.6	17	Ukraine	19.9
5	Russia	53.0	18	Congo-Kinshasa	17.9
6	Brazil	51.4	19	Philippines	17.8
7	Japan	49.0		South Korea	17.8
8	Germany	39.5		Thailand	17.8
9	Nigeria	28.1	22	Egypt	16.9
10	United Kingdom	26.4	23	Turkey	15.9
11	Vietnam	26.3	24	Spain	15.5
12	Bangladesh	26.2	25	Ethiopia	15.1
13	France	25.8	26	Myanmar	13.8

Households with single occupation
% of total, 2007

1	Sweden	44.7	16	United Kingdom	28.0
2	Estonia	44.4	17	Canada	27.4
3	Norway	41.5		Italy	27.4
4	Denmark	40.1	19	Australia	27.1
5	Finland	38.7	20	United States	26.8
6	Switzerland	38.6	21	Hungary	26.4
7	Germany	37.7	22	Czech Republic	25.2
8	Netherlands	35.2	23	Lithuania	24.5
9	Croatia	34.8	24	Poland	24.1
10	Latvia	34.2	25	Russia	24.0
11	France	34.1	26	Romania	23.5
12	Belgium	33.0	27	Spain	23.0
13	Austria	30.7	28	South Africa	22.7
14	Slovakia	30.1	29	Belarus	22.3
15	Japan	29.7		New Zealand	22.3

Highest cost of living[a]
February 2009, USA=100

1	Japan	152	12	Germany	104
2	France	132	13	New Caledonia	103
3	Denmark	124	14	Spain	102
4	Norway	123	15	Venezuela	101
5	Finland	118	16	Netherlands	99
6	Switzerland	115		United Kingdom	99
7	Singapore	112	18	Italy	98
8	Hong Kong	110	19	Israel	96
9	Austria	109	20	Luxembourg	94
10	Ireland	108	21	Australia	92
11	Belgium	107	22	China	91

a The cost of living index shown is compiled by the Economist Intelligence Unit for use by companies in determining expatriate compensation: it is a comparison of the cost of maintaining a typical international lifestyle in the country rather than a comparison of the purchasing power of a citizen of the country. The index is based on typical urban prices an international executive and family will face abroad. The prices

Number of households
Smallest, m, 2007

1	Cayman Islands	0.01	14	Guadeloupe	0.11
2	Bermuda	0.02	15	Cape Verde	0.12
3	Aruba	0.03		Malta	0.12
4	French Polynesia	0.04	17	Equatorial Guinea	0.13
	Guam	0.04		Iceland	0.13
	New Caledonia	0.04		Réunion	0.13
7	Netherlands Antilles	0.05	20	Macau	0.15
8	Barbados	0.06	21	Fiji	0.16
9	Bahamas	0.07		Luxembourg	0.16
10	Brunei	0.08	23	Qatar	0.17
11	Suriname	0.09	24	Bahrain	0.20
12	Belize	0.10	25	Swaziland	0.21
	Martinique	0.10	26	Gabon	0.23

Households with five or more occupants
% of total, 2007

1	Pakistan	68.4	16	Colombia	37.8
2	Tunisia	64.8	17	Mexico	35.0
3	Morocco	60.3	18	Turkey	31.1
4	Jordan	59.2	19	Taiwan	27.3
5	India	56.6	20	Argentina	26.0
6	Egypt	55.9	21	Israel	24.8
7	Nigeria	55.4	22	Brazil	23.2
8	Philippines	52.9	23	Thailand	22.9
9	Malaysia	51.3	24	Venezuela	22.3
10	Kuwait	50.9	25	Chile	20.3
11	Vietnam	46.9	26	Bulgaria	19.1
12	Bolivia	44.3	27	Turkmenistan	17.7
13	Ecuador	43.8	28	South Africa	16.6
14	Peru	41.7	29	Hong Kong	16.0
15	Indonesia	40.3	30	Kazakhstan	13.9

Lowest cost of living[a]
February 2009, USA=100

1	Pakistan	37	12	Bangladesh	56
2	Iran	43	13	Argentina	57
3	India	45	14	Kazakhstan	58
4	Nepal	46	15	Costa Rica	59
5	Libya	49		Uzbekistan	59
6	Philippines	50		Zambia	59
7	Paraguay	52	18	Peru	60
	Ukraine	52	19	Brunei	61
9	Romania	53		Ecuador	61
	South Africa	53		Panama	61
11	Algeria	54		Sri Lanka	61

are for products of international comparable quality found in a supermarket or department store. Prices found in local markets and bazaars are not used unless the available merchandise is of the specified quality and the shopping area itself is safe for executive and family members. New York City prices are used as the base, so United States = 100.

Telephones and computers

Telephone

Telephone lines per 100 people, 2007

1	Bermuda	89.5	18	Denmark	51.9
2	Switzerland	74.7	19	Barbados	50.0
3	United States	65.3	20	Andorra	49.8
4	Germany	64.7	21	Australia	47.1
5	Taiwan	62.8	22	South Korea	46.4
6	Sweden	62.5	23	Italy	46.3
7	Virgin Islands (US)	62.2	24	Faroe Islands	45.9
8	Iceland	62.0	25	Cyprus	44.9
9	Montenegro	58.9	26	Netherlands	44.7
10	United Kingdom	58.8	27	Belgium	44.6
11	Hong Kong	57.2	28	Israel	44.4
12	Malta	56.6	29	Norway	42.4
13	France	56.5		Spain	42.4
14	Canada	55.5	31	Singapore	41.9
15	Greece	53.9	32	New Zealand	41.8
16	Luxembourg	53.2	33	Slovenia	41.1
17	Ireland	52.0	34	Austria	40.8

Mobile telephone

Subscribers per 100 people, 2007

1	United Arab Emirates	176.5	26	Saudi Arabia	114.7
2	Macau	165.1	27	Russia	114.6
3	Italy	150.7	28	Denmark	114.5
4	Qatar	150.4	29	Sweden	113.7
5	Hong Kong	149.2	30	Trinidad & Tobago	113.2
6	Estonia	148.4	31	Bahamas	112.9
7	Bahrain	148.3	32	Slovakia	112.6
8	Lithuania	145.2	33	Netherlands Antilles	110.6
9	Aruba	140.4	34	Croatia	110.5
10	Singapore	133.5		Norway	110.5
11	Bulgaria	129.6	36	Greece	110.3
12	Luxembourg	129.5	37	Hungary	110.0
13	Israel	128.5	38	Switzerland	109.7
14	Portugal	126.6	39	Spain	109.4
15	Czech Republic	124.9	40	Iceland	108.9
16	Thailand	123.8	41	Poland	108.7
17	Ukraine	119.6	42	Montenegro	107.3
18	Austria	118.6	43	Faroe Islands	106.7
19	United Kingdom	118.5	44	Taiwan	106.1
20	Germany	117.6	45	Belgium	102.7
21	Netherlands	117.5	46	Australia	102.5
22	Greenland	115.9	47	Argentina	102.2
	Ireland	115.9	48	New Zealand	101.7
24	Cyprus	115.6	49	Latvia	97.4
25	Finland	115.2	50	Kuwait	97.3

Computer
Computers per 100 people, 2007

1	Canada	94.3	26	Latvia	32.7
2	Switzerland	91.8	27	Armenia	31.9
3	Netherlands	91.2	28	Czech Republic	27.4
4	Sweden	88.1	29	Hungary	25.6
5	United States	80.5	30	Serbia	24.4
6	United Kingdom	80.2	31	Namibia	24.0
7	Singapore	74.3	32	Kuwait	23.7
8	Hong Kong	68.6	33	Costa Rica	23.1
9	Germany	65.6		Malaysia	23.1
10	France	65.2	35	Romania	19.2
11	Norway	62.9	36	Lithuania	18.3
12	Austria	60.7	37	Mauritius	17.6
13	Ireland	58.2	38	Portugal	17.2
14	South Korea	57.6	39	Poland	16.9
15	Denmark	54.9	40	Brazil	16.1
16	New Zealand	52.6	41	Saudi Arabia	14.8
17	Estonia	52.2	42	Mexico	14.4
18	Slovakia	51.4	43	Chile	14.1
19	Finland	50.0	44	Mongolia	13.9
20	Slovenia	42.5	45	Uruguay	13.6
21	Belgium	41.7	46	Russia	13.3
22	Spain	39.3	47	Trinidad & Tobago	13.2
23	Macedonia	36.8	48	Ecuador	13.0
24	Italy	36.7	49	Sudan	11.2
25	United Arab Emirates	33.0	50	Moldova	11.1

Broadband
Subscribers per 100 people, 2007

1	Denmark	35.9	19	New Zealand	20.2
	Sweden	35.9	20	Austria	19.5
3	Netherlands	33.6		Singapore	19.5
4	Switzerland	31.5	22	Ireland	18.5
5	Finland	30.6	23	Italy	18.3
	Norway	30.6	24	Spain	18.0
7	South Korea	30.4	25	Slovenia	17.1
8	Canada	27.5	26	Lithuania	15.0
9	Hong Kong	27.4	27	Portugal	14.4
10	Belgium	25.6	28	Hungary	14.2
	United Kingdom	25.6	29	Czech Republic	12.7
12	France	25.2	30	Greece	9.1
13	United States	24.3		Romania	9.1
14	Germany	23.8	32	Poland	9.0
15	Australia	23.0	33	Slovakia	8.8
16	Japan	22.1	34	Croatia	8.7
17	Israel	21.3		United Arab Emirates	8.7
18	Estonia	20.7	36	Bulgaria	8.2

The internet and music

Internet hosts

By country, January 2009		Per 1,000 pop., January 2009	
1 United States[a]	332,229,937	1 United States[a]	1,093.2
2 Japan	43,461,277	2 Iceland	887.7
3 Germany	23,304,039	3 Finland	762.5
4 Italy	19,487,125	4 Netherlands	712.3
5 Brazil	14,678,982	5 Denmark	690.1
6 China	13,964,313	6 Norway	662.4
7 France	13,650,159	7 Australia	550.4
8 Mexico	12,515,249	8 Estonia	504.7
9 Netherlands	11,682,001	9 Switzerland	474.6
10 Australia	11,337,838	10 Luxembourg	436.2
11 United Kingdom	8,980,515	11 New Zealand	432.3
12 Poland	8,350,365	12 Sweden	425.1
13 Canada	6,511,157	13 Belgium	416.0
14 Russia	6,010,631	14 Austria	354.1
15 Taiwan	5,463,496	15 Japan	338.7
16 Argentina	4,391,681	16 Italy	334.8
17 Belgium	4,367,700	17 Czech Republic	306.5
18 Finland	4,041,241	18 Ireland	291.6
19 Sweden	3,868,362	19 Andorra	289.3
20 Denmark	3,795,480	20 Germany	281.8
21 Switzerland	3,464,568	21 Croatia	254.7
22 Spain	3,325,990	22 Lithuania	251.4
23 Czech Republic	3,126,690	23 Greenland	243.6
24 Norway	3,113,496	24 Taiwan	238.6
25 India	3,096,335	25 France	224.1
26 Austria	2,903,737	26 Israel	217.5
27 Turkey	2,596,496	27 Cyprus	217.1
28 Greece	2,263,303	28 Poland	216.9
29 Romania	2,183,544	29 Hungary	216.8
30 Hungary	2,168,182	30 Greece	202.1

Music sales

Total including downloads, $m, 2007		$ per head, 2007	
1 United States	10,394	1 Norway	50.4
2 Japan	4,897	2 United Kingdom	49.6
3 United Kingdom	2,976	3 Japan	38.2
4 Germany	2,277	4 Austria	35.7
5 France	1,609	5 Denmark	34.4
6 Canada	650	6 United States	34.2
7 Australia	619	7 Ireland	33.5
8 Italy	536	8 Switzerland	31.9
9 Russia	426	9 Australia	30.0
10 Spain	423	10 Germany	27.5
11 Netherlands	402	11 France	26.4
12 South Korea	334	12 New Zealand	25.1
13 Mexico	304	13 Netherlands	24.5
14 Austria	293	14 Sweden	24.4
15 Brazil	276	15 Finland	24.3
16 Belgium	249	16 Belgium	23.7

a Includes all hosts ending ".com", ".net" and ".org", which exaggerates the numbers.

How we spend the day

Sleeping
Minutes per day

1	France	530
2	United States	518
3	Spain	514
4	New Zealand	513
5	Australia	512
	Turkey	512
7	Canada	509
8	Poland	508
9	Finland	507
10	Belgium	505
11	United Kingdom	503
12	Mexico	501
13	Italy	498
14	Germany	492
15	Sweden	486

Eating and drinking
Minutes per day

1	Turkey	162
2	France	135
3	New Zealand	130
4	Japan	117
5	Italy	114
6	Belgium	109
7	Spain	106
8	Germany	105
9	South Korea	96
10	Poland	94
	Sweden	94
12	Australia	89
13	United Kingdom	85
14	Norway	82
15	Finland	81

Leisure time
% of the day

1	Belgium	27.7	10	New Zealand	24.3
2	Germany	27.4	11	Poland	24.1
3	Norway	26.6	12	United States	24.0
4	Finland	26.1	13	Canada	23.7
5	Spain	25.4		South Korea	23.7
6	Italy	25.1	15	Turkey	22.8
7	France	24.9	16	Australia	22.5
8	United Kingdom	24.7	17	Japan	21.3
9	Sweden	24.4	18	Mexico	15.8

Minutes of leisure time per day

Men			Women		
1	Norway	384	1	Norway	380
2	Belgium	382	2	Germany	349
3	Finland	376	3	Finland	348
4	Germany	371	4	Belgium	332
5	United Kingdom	355	5	Sweden	331
6	Sweden	352	6	United Kingdom	322

Leisure time spent watching TV
%

1	Mexico	48	10	South Korea	35
2	Japan	47	11	Canada	34
3	United States	44		France	34
4	Australia	41	13	Norway	31
	Poland	41		Spain	31
6	United Kingdom	41		Sweden	31
7	Turkey	40	16	Germany	28
8	Finland	37		Italy	28
9	Belgium	36	18	New Zealand	25

Note: OECD survey of 18 member countries, 2006 or nearest year.

Cinema and films

Cinema attendances

Total visits, m, 2007			Visits per head, 2007	
1	China	1,497.1	1	New Zealand	8.9
2	United States	1,446.7	2	Australia	7.0
3	India	1,341.4	3	United States	4.8
4	Indonesia	297.0	4	Iceland	4.6
5	France	194.9	5	Canada	4.2
6	Mexico	178.6		Ireland	4.2
7	Japan	165.1	7	Singapore	3.5
8	United Kingdom	153.2	8	France	3.2
9	Australia	143.6	9	Venezuela	2.8
10	Canada	139.6	10	Spain	2.7
11	Germany	133.9	11	United Kingdom	2.6
12	Spain	117.1	12	Luxembourg	2.5
13	Italy	106.5		Malta	2.5
14	Russia	98.5		Norway	2.5
15	Philippines	90.8	15	Denmark	2.3
16	Venezuela	76.5		Belgium	2.3
17	South Africa	70.9	17	Switzerland	2.2
18	Argentina	51.1	18	Austria	2.1
19	South Korea	46.9	19	Italy	1.8
20	Brazil	41.7	20	Germany	1.6
21	Turkey	39.5		Mexico	1.6
22	Poland	37.0		Sweden	1.6
23	New Zealand	36.5		Ecuador	1.6
24	Belgium	24.2	24	Portugal	1.5
25	Netherlands	21.8	25	South Africa	1.5
26	Ecuador	21.5	26	Argentina	1.3
27	Ireland	18.0		Estonia	1.3
	Taiwan	18.0		Indonesia	1.3
29	Austria	17.3		Israel	1.3
30	Malaysia	16.5		Japan	1.3
31	Switzerland	16.4		Netherlands	1.3
32	Portugal	15.7		Slovenia	1.3

Top Oscar winners

	Film	Awards	Nominations
1	Ben-Hur (1959)	11	12
	Titanic (1997)	11	14
	The Lord of the Rings: The Return of the King (2003)	11	11
4	West Side Story (1961)	10	11
5	Gigi (1958)	9	9
	The Last Emperor (1987)	9	9
	The English Patient (1996)	9	12
8	Gone with the Wind (1939)	8	13
	From Here to Eternity (1953)	8	13
	On the Waterfront (1954)	8	12
	My Fair Lady (1964)	8	12
	Cabaret[a] (1972)	8	10
	Gandhi (1982)	8	11
	Amadeus (1984)	8	11
	Slumdog Millionaire (2009)	8	10

a   Did not win best picture award.

The press

Daily newspapers

Copies per '000 population, latest year

1	Iceland	821	16	Malta	259
2	Denmark	686	17	Germany	253
3	Japan	535	18	Slovenia	245
4	Sweden	532	19	Luxembourg	238
5	Switzerland	490	20	Ireland	236
6	Norway	473	21	Spain	227
7	Finland	456	22	United Arab Emirates	204
8	Hong Kong	428	23	Italy	197
9	South Korea	417	24	Canada	196
10	Austria	392	25	Croatia	194
11	Singapore	342		United States	184
12	United Kingdom	315	27	Taiwan	183
13	Czech Republic	311	28	Latvia	177
14	Estonia	292	29	Hungary	175
15	Netherlands	288		New Zealand	175

Press freedom[a]

Scores, 2008

Most free			Least free		
1	Iceland	1,50	1	Eritrea	97,50
	Luxembourg	1,50	2	North Korea	96,50
	Norway	1,50	3	Turkmenistan	95,50
2	Estonia	2,00	4	Burma	94,38
	Finland	2,00	5	Cuba	88,33
	Ireland	2,00	6	Vietnam	86,17
7	Belgium	3,00	7	China	85,50
	Latvia	3,00	8	Iran	80,33
	New Zealand	3,00	9	Sri Lanka	78,00
	Slovakia	3,00	10	Laos	70,00
	Sweden	3,00	11	West Bank and Gaza	66,88
	Switzerland	3,00	12	Uzbekistan	62,70
13	Canada	3,33	13	Saudi Arabia	61,75
14	Austria	3,50	14	Libya	61,50
	Denmark	3,50	15	Syria	59,63
16	Czech Republic	4,00	16	Iraq	59,38
	Lithuania	4,00	17	Equatorial Guinea	59,25
	Netherlands	4,00	18	Afghanistan	59,25
	Portugal	4,00	19	Yemen	59,00
20	Germany	4,50	20	Belarus	58,33
21	Jamaica	4,88	21	Somalia	58,00
22	Costa Rica	5,10	22	Pakistan	54,88
23	Hungary	5,50	23	Zimbabwe	54,00
	Namibia	5,50	24	Azerbaijan	53,63
	United Kingdom	5,50	25	Congo-Brazzaville	51,25
26	Suriname	6,00	26	Swaziland	50,50
27	Trinidad and Tobago	6,13	27	Egypt	50,25
28	Australia	6,25	28	Rwanda	50,00
29	Japan	6,50	29	Singapore	49,00
30	Slovenia	7,33	30	Tunisia	48,10

a Based on 50 questions about press freedom.

Olympics

Summer winners

2008		Gold	Silver	Bronze
1	China	51	21	28
2	United States	36	38	36
3	Russia	23	21	28
4	United Kingdom	19	13	15
5	Germany	16	10	15
6	Australia	14	15	17
7	South Korea	13	10	8
8	Japan	9	6	10
9	Italy	8	10	10
10	France	7	16	17
11	Ukraine	7	5	15
12	Netherlands	7	5	4
13	Jamaica	6	3	2
14	Spain	5	10	3
15	Kenya	5	5	4
16	Belarus	4	5	10
17	Romania	4	1	3
18	Ethiopia	4	1	2
19	Canada	3	9	6
20	Poland	3	6	1
21	Hungary	3	5	2
	Norway	3	5	2
23	Brazil	3	4	8
24	Czech Republic	3	3	0
25	Slovakia	3	2	1

Summer winners

1896–2008		Gold	Silver	Bronze
1	United States	931	728	640
2	Soviet Union (1952–92)	440	357	325
3	United Kingdom	208	255	252
4	Germany[a]	192	217	238
5	France	191	212	233
6	Italy	190	157	174
7	China	163	117	106
8	Hungary	159	141	159
9	Germany (East)	153	129	127
10	Sweden	142	159	174
11	Australia	131	137	164
12	Japan	123	112	125
13	Russia[b]	109	101	113
14	Finland	101	83	115
15	Romania	86	92	115
16	Netherlands	71	79	97
17	South Korea	68	74	73
18	Cuba	67	64	63

Note: Figures exclude mixed teams in 1896, 1900 and 1904 and Australasia teams in 1908 and 1912.
a Germany 1896–1936, unified teams in 1956–64, then since 1992.
b Russia 1896–1912, then since 1996.

Nobel prize winners: 1901–2008

Peace (two or more)

1	United States	18
2	United Kingdom	11
3	France	9
4	Sweden	5
5	Belgium	4
	Germany	4
7	Austria	3
	Norway	3
	South Africa	3
	Switzerland	3
11	Argentina	2
	Egypt	2
	Israel	2
	Russia	2

Economics[a]

1	United States	32
2	United Kingdom	8
3	Norway	2
	Sweden	2
5	France	1
	Germany	1
	Israel	1
	Netherlands	1
	Russia	1

Literature (three or more)

1	France	15
2	United States	12
3	United Kingdom	11
4	Germany	7
5	Sweden	6
6	Italy	5
7	Spain	5
8	Norway	3
	Poland	3
	Russia	3

Medicine (three or more)

1	United States	51
2	United Kingdom	22
3	Germany	15
4	France	7
	Sweden	7
6	Switzerland	6
7	Austria	5
	Denmark	5
9	Australia	3
	Belgium	3
	Italy	3

Physics

1	United States	49
2	Germany	19
3	United Kingdom	19
4	France	9
5	Netherlands	6
	Russia	6
7	Japan	5
8	Sweden	4
	Switzerland	4
10	Austria	3
	Italy	3
12	Canada	2
	Denmark	2
14	Colombia	1
	India	1
	Ireland	1
	Pakistan	1
	Poland	1

Chemistry

1	United States	43
2	United Kingdom	22
3	Germany	15
4	France	7
5	Switzerland	6
6	Sweden	5
7	Canada	4
	Japan	4
9	Argentina	1
	Austria	1
	Belgium	1
	Czech Republic	1
	Denmark	1
	Finland	1
	Israel	1
	Italy	1
	Netherlands	1
	Norway	1
	Russia	1

a Since 1969.
Notes: Prizes by country of residence at time awarded. When prizes have been shared in the same field, one credit given to each country. Only top rankings in each field are included.

Drinking and smoking

Beer drinkers

Retail sales, litres per head of population, 2007

1	Venezuela	83.0
2	Czech Republic	82.1
3	Australia	68.8
	Germany	68.8
5	Finland	66.6
6	Austria	66.1
7	Romania	65.7
8	Russia	65.0
9	Slovakia	64.8
10	Poland	64.4
11	United States	60.0
12	Denmark	59.6
13	Canada	54.6
	Netherlands	54.6
15	New Zealand	52.9
16	Hungary	51.5
17	Ukraine	49.3
18	Bulgaria	49.0
19	Mexico	43.6
20	Ireland	43.2
21	Belgium	43.0
22	Norway	40.9

Champagne drinkers

Bottles per head of population, 2008

1	Guadeloupe	4.25
2	Martinique	3.25
3	France	2.33
4	New Caledonia	1.37
5	Luxembourg	1.27
6	Réunion	1.25
7	Belgium	0.95
8	Switzerland	0.74
9	United Kingdom	0.60
10	United Arab Emirates	0.30
11	Singapore	0.27
12	Sweden	0.23
13	Ireland	0.21
	Netherlands	0.21
15	Australia	0.18
16	Denmark	0.17
17	Italy	0.16
18	Austria	0.15
	Norway	0.15
20	Germany	0.14
	Hong Kong	0.14
22	Finland	0.11

Alcoholic drinks

Retail sales, litres per head of population, 2008

1	Germany	100.4
2	Czech Republic	98.0
3	Finland	97.1
4	Denmark	89.3
5	Russia	88.5
6	Austria	87.0
7	Venezuela	83.0
8	Poland	80.1
9	Slovakia	78.9
10	Netherlands	77.5
11	Romania	77.1
12	Hungary	74.6
13	Australia	68.8
14	Ireland	67.7
15	United Kingdom	66.4
16	Belgium	66.2
17	Ukraine	64.5
18	Sweden	62.9
19	Switzerland	60.0
	United States	60.0
21	Portugal	58.9
22	Bulgaria	58.8
23	Norway	57.6

Smokers

Av. ann. consumption of cigarettes per head per day, 2008

1	Greece	8.1
2	Russia	7.2
3	Bulgaria	7.1
4	Ukraine	6.9
5	Bosnia	6.6
6	Slovenia	6.5
7	Moldova	6.4
8	Czech Republic	6.1
9	Spain	6.0
10	Kazakhstan	5.9
11	Belarus	5.8
	Cyprus	5.8
	Estonia	5.8
	Serbia	5.8
15	South Korea	5.4
16	Japan	5.3
	Macedonia	5.3
18	Croatia	5.2
	Lebanon	5.2
20	Taiwan	5.0
21	Azerbaijan	4.9
22	Austria	4.7
23	Armenia	4.6

Crime and punishment

Police

Personnel per 100,000 pop., 2006

1	Brunei	1,074
2	Montenegro	921
3	Mauritius	783
4	Cyprus	609
5	Latvia	602
6	Lebanon	584
7	Italy	552
8	Macedonia	480
9	Czech Republic	451
10	Serbia	439
11	Malta	434
12	Hong Kong	432
13	Portugal	420
14	Croatia	413
15	Singapore	395
16	Slovenia	393
17	Belize	386
18	Slovakia	378
19	Greece	375
20	Ukraine	359

Murders

Per 100,000 pop., 2006

1	Belize	32.7
2	Ecuador	18.1
3	Dominican Republic	16.0
4	Paraguay	12.3
5	Mongolia	11.9
6	Kazakhstan	11.3
7	Mexico	11.0
	Panama	11.0
9	Kyrgyzstan	8.5
10	Nicaragua	8.4
11	Lithuania	8.1
12	Costa Rica	7.9
	Thailand	7.9
14	Belarus	7.5
15	Georgia	7.3
16	Estonia	6.8
17	Latvia	6.5
18	Ukraine	6.4
19	Kenya	5.7
20	United States	5.6

Prisoners

Total prison pop., latest available year

1	United States	2,310,984
2	China	1,565,771
3	Russia	887,723
4	Brazil	440,013
5	India	373,271
6	Mexico	222,671
7	Thailand	166,338
8	South Africa	164,518
9	Iran	158,351
10	Ukraine	145,946
11	Indonesia	136,017
12	Turkey	101,100
13	Vietnam	92,153
14	Philippines	91,530
15	Pakistan[a]	90,000
16	Poland	85,440
17	Bangladesh[a]	83,000
18	United Kingdom	82,985
19	Japan	81,255
20	Ethiopia[a]	80,000
21	Spain	75,093
22	Germany	72,259
23	Colombia	69,979
24	Myanmar	65,063

Per 100,000 pop., latest available year

1	United States	760
2	Rwanda	631
3	Russia	626
4	Cuba[a]	531
5	Virgin Islands (US)	505
6	Belarus	473
7	Belize	452
8	Bahamas	451
9	Cayman Islands	440
10	Georgia	413
11	Kazakhstan	400
12	Bermuda	390
13	Barbados	365
14	South Africa	345
15	Suriname[a]	340
16	Puerto Rico	330
17	Botswana	329
18	Israel	326
19	Greenland	324
20	Ukraine	321
21	Netherlands Antilles	318
22	Chile	311
23	Panama	308
24	Guam	302

a Estimate.

Stars...

Space missions
Firsts and selected events

1957 Man-made satellite Dog in space, Laika
1961 Human in space, Yuri Gagarin
Entire day in space, Gherman Titov
1963 Woman in space, Valentina Tereshkova
1964 Space crew, one pilot and two passengers
1965 Space walk, Alexei Leonov
Eight days in space achieved (needed to travel to moon and back)
1966 Docking between space craft and target vehicle
Autopilot re-entry and landing
1968 Live television broadcast from space
Moon orbit
1969 Astronaut transfer from one craft to another in space
Moon landing
1971 Space station, Salyut
Drive on the moon
1973 Space laboratory, Skylab
1978 Non-Amercian, non-Soviet, Vladimir Remek (Czechoslovakia)
1982 Space shuttle, Columbia (first craft to carry four crew members)
1983 Five crew mission
1984 Space walk, untethered
Capture, repair and redeployment of satellite in space
Seven crew mission
1985 Classified US Defence Department mission
1986 Space shuttle explosion, Challenger
Mir space station activated
1990 Hubble telescope deployed
2001 Dennis Tito, first paying space tourist
2003 Space shuttle explosion, Columbia. Shuttle programme suspended
China's first manned space flight, Yang Liwei
2004 SpaceShipOne, first successful private manned space flight
2005 Space shuttle, resumption of flights
2008 *Phoenix* lander, mission on Mars

Space vehicle launches[a]

2005

1	Russia	21
2	United States	15
3	France	5
4	China	3
5	Japan	2
6	India	1
	Sweden	1

2006

1	United States	20
2	Russia	19
3	Japan	7
4	France	5
5	China	4
6	Sweden	3

2007

1	Russia	22
2	United States	20
3	China	6
4	France	5
5	India	3
	Japan	3
7	Brazil	2
8	Iran	1

2008

1	Russia	25
2	United States	13
3	China	10
4	France	4
5	India	3
6	Iran	2
7	Japan	1

a By host country and including
suborbital launches.

...and Wars

Defence spending
As % of GDP, 2007

1	Myanmar	33.4		United States	4.0
2	Jordan	10.3	17	Syria	3.9
3	Saudi Arabia	9.4	18	Egypt	3.4
4	Oman	8.1	19	Algeria	3.3
5	Burundi	7.9		Bahrain	3.3
6	Israel	7.2		Kuwait	3.3
7	Georgia	5.6		Lebanon	3.3
8	United Arab Emirates	5.5	23	Chile	3.2
9	Vietnam	5.2		Morocco	3.2
10	Angola	4.8		Pakistan	3.2
	El Salvador	4.8	26	Armenia	3.1
12	Singapore	4.4	27	Azerbaijan	3.0
13	Guinea-Bissau	4.3		Sri Lanka	3.0
	Yemen	4.3	29	Iran	2.9
15	Colombia	4.0			

Defence spending
$bn, 2007

1	United States	552.6	16	Turkey	13.6
2	United Kingdom	63.3	17	Israel	11.6
3	France	60.7	18	Netherlands	11.1
4	China[a]	46.2	19	United Arab Emirates	10.1
5	Germany	42.1	20	Taiwan	9.6
6	Japan	41.0	21	Greece	8.7
7	Italy	37.8	22	Poland	8.0
8	Saudi Arabia	35.4	23	Iran	7.5
9	Russia	32.2	24	Myanmar	7.0
10	South Korea	26.6		Singapore	7.0
11	India	26.5	26	Colombia	6.8
12	Brazil	20.6		Sweden	6.8
13	Australia	20.2	28	Norway	5.5
14	Canada	18.5	29	Chile	5.2
15	Spain	17.5	30	Belgium	5.0

Armed forces
'000, 2007

		Regulars	Reserves			Regulars	Reserves
1	China	2,185	800	13	Brazil	326	1,340
2	United States	1,540	979	14	Thailand	307	200
3	India	1,281	1,155	15	Indonesia	302	400
4	Russia	1,027	20,000	16	Italy	293	42
5	South Korea	687	4,500		Syria	293	314
6	Pakistan	617	0	18	Taiwan	290	1,657
7	Iraq	577	0	19	Colombia	267	62
8	Iran	523	350	20	Germany	244	162
9	Turkey	511	379	21	Japan	230	42
10	Vietnam	455	5,000	22	Saudi Arabia	222	0
11	Myanmar	406	0		Spain	222	319
12	France	353	70				

a Official budget only at market exchange rates.

Environment

Environmental performance index[a], 2008

Highest			Lowest		
1	Switzerland	95.5	1	Niger	39.1
2	Norway	93.1	2	Angola	39.5
	Sweden	93.1	3	Sierra Leone	40.0
4	Finland	91.4	4	Mauritania	44.2
5	Costa Rica	90.5	5	Burkina Faso	44.3
6	Austria	89.4		Mali	44.3
7	New Zealand	88.9	7	Chad	45.9
8	Latvia	88.8	8	Congo-Kinshasa	47.3
9	Colombia	88.3	9	Guinea-Bissau	49.7
10	France	87.8		Yemen	49.7
11	Iceland	87.6	11	Guinea	51.3
12	Canada	86.6	12	Cambodia	53.8
13	Germany	86.3	13	Iraq	53.9
	Slovenia	86.3	14	Mozambique	53.9
15	United Kingdom	86.3	15	Madagascar	54.6
16	Lithuania	86.2	16	Burundi	54.7
17	Slovakia	86.0	17	Rwanda	54.9
18	Portugal	85.8	18	Zambia	55.1
19	Estonia	85.2	19	Sudan	55.5
20	Croatia	84.6	20	Central African Rep	56.0
21	Japan	84.5	21	Benin	56.1
22	Ecuador	84.4	22	Nigeria	56.2
23	Hungary	84.2	23	Bangladesh	58.0
	Italy	84.2	24	Pakistan	58.7
25	Albania	84.0	25	Ethiopia	58.8
	Denmark	84.0	26	Eritrea	59.4
	Malaysia	84.0	27	Malawi	59.9
28	Russia	83.9	28	India	60.3
29	Chile	83.4	29	Haiti	60.7
30	Luxembourg	83.1	30	Swaziland	61.3
	Panama	83.1	31	Uganda	61.6
	Spain	83.1	32	Togo	62.3
33	Dominican Republic	83.0	33	Senegal	62.8
34	Brazil	82.7	34	Cameroon	63.8
	Ireland	82.7	35	Tanzania	63.9
36	Uruguay	82.3	36	United Arab Emirates	64.0
37	Georgia	82.2	37	Kuwait	64.5
38	Argentina	81.8	38	Bolivia	64.7
39	United States	81.0	39	Papua New Guinea	64.8
40	Taiwan	80.8	40	Kazakhstan	65.0
41	Cuba	80.7		Uzbekistan	65.0
42	Belarus	80.5	42	China	65.1
	Poland	80.5		Myanmar	65.1
44	Greece	80.2	44	Côte d'Ivoire	65.2
45	Venezuela	80.0	45	Indonesia	66.2
46	Australia	79.8	46	Laos	66.3
	Mexico	79.8	47	Mongolia	68.1
48	Bosnia	79.7	48	Syria	68.2

a Based on a range of factors including environmental health, biodiversity, air pollution, water use, agricultural methods, tackling climate change.

Air pollution in cities
Particulate matter[a] concentration per cubic metre, 2006

1	Cairo, Egypt	149	25	Guiyang, China		71
2	Delhi, India	136		Kunming, China		71
3	Tianjin, China	126	27	Pingxiang, China		67
4	Chongqing, China	124	28	Guangzhou, China		64
5	Kolkata, India	116	29	Sofia, Bulgaria		63
6	Shenyang, China	102	30	Quingdao, China		62
7	Kanpur, India	99	31	Liupanshui, China		60
	Lucknow, India	99	32	Wulumqi, China		57
9	Zhengzhou, China	98		Mumbai, India		57
10	Jinan, China	95	34	Córdoba, Argentina		55
11	Lanzhou, China	92	35	Santiago, Chile		54
12	Beijing, China	90	36	Dalian, China		50
13	Taiyuan, China	89		Nagpur, India		50
14	Chengdu, China	87		Tehran, Iran		50
15	Jakarta, Indonesia	84	39	Mexico City, Mexico		48
16	Anshan, China	83	40	Istanbul, Turkey		46
17	Wuhan, China	80	41	Turin, Italy		43
18	Nanchang, China	79	42	Pune, India		42
19	Harbin, China	77		Warsaw, Poland		42
20	Ahmadabad, India	76	44	Bengaluru, India		41
	Bangkok, Thailand	76		Singapore		41
22	Changchun, China	75	46	Nairobi, Kenya		40
	Zibo, China	75		Taegu, South Korea		40
24	Shanghai, China	74				

Water pollutant emissions
'000 kgs per day, 2005

1	China	6,088.7	23	Malaysia	187.6
2	United States	1,960.3	24	South Africa	183.8
3	India	1,519.8	25	Turkey	177.7
4	Russia	1,425.9	26	Cuba[b]	173.0
5	Japan	1,133.1	27	Iran	163.2
6	Germany	960.3	28	Argentina	155.5
7	Brazil[b]	780.4	29	Czech Republic	152.4
8	Indonesia	731.0	30	Swaziland[b]	146.0
9	France	604.7	31	Hungary	123.2
10	United Kingdom	539.7	32	Netherlands	119.2
11	Ukraine	527.2	33	Australia	111.7
12	Italy	481.3	34	Portugal	107.2
13	Vietnam	470.2	35	Algeria[b]	107.0
14	Spain	372.5	36	Pakistan[b]	104.1
15	Mexico[b]	370.8	37	Bulgaria	100.6
16	Poland	364.2	38	Sweden	100.1
17	Thailand	333.8	39	Belgium	99.6
18	South Korea	317.0	40	Philippines	98.5
19	Canada	310.3	41	Chile	96.5
20	Bangladesh	303.0		Venezuela[b]	96.5
21	Romania	235.1	43	Madagascar	88.9
22	Egypt	206.5	44	Dominican Republic	88.6

a Less than 10 microns in diameter. b 1990

Biggest emitters of carbon dioxide
Millions of tonnes, 2005

1	United States	5,776.4		26	Egypt	173.5
2	China	5,547.8		27	Argentina	152.7
3	Russia	1,503.3		28	Venezuela	148.1
4	India	1,402.4		29	Algeria	137.5
5	Japan	1,230.0		30	Pakistan	134.3
6	Germany	784.0		31	Netherlands	125.8
7	United Kingdom	546.4		32	United Arab Emirates	123.7
8	Canada	537.5		33	Czech Republic	119.7
9	South Korea	452.2		34	Nigeria	114.3
10	Italy	452.1		35	Uzbekistan	112.4
11	Iran	451.6		36	Belgium	102.6
12	Mexico	421.5		37	Vietnam	101.8
13	Indonesia	419.6		38	Greece	95.4
14	South Africa	408.8		39	Kuwait	93.6
15	Saudi Arabia	381.1		40	Romania	89.1
16	France	377.7		41	Iraq	84.5
17	Australia	368.9		42	North Korea	82.6
18	Spain	343.7		43	Philippines	75.0
19	Ukraine	327.1		44	Austria	73.6
20	Brazil	325.5		45	Syria	68.4
21	Poland	302.4		46	Chile	66.1
22	Thailand	270.9		47	Israel	63.6
23	Turkey	247.9		48	Belarus	63.3
24	Malaysia	239.8		49	Portugal	62.4
25	Kazakhstan	180.9		50	Colombia	58.6

Largest amount of carbon dioxide emitted per person
Tonnes, 2005

1	Kuwait	36.9		23	Israel	9.2
2	United Arab Emirates	30.1		24	United Kingdom	9.1
3	Trinidad & Tobago	24.7		25	Austria	8.9
4	United States	19.5		26	South Africa	8.7
5	Australia	18.1		27	Greece	8.6
6	Canada	16.6			Turkmenistan	8.6
7	Saudi Arabia	16.5		29	Denmark	8.5
8	Estonia	13.5		30	Poland	7.9
9	Singapore	13.2			Spain	7.9
10	Oman	12.5		32	Italy	7.7
11	Kazakhstan	11.9			Netherlands	7.7
12	Czech Republic	11.7		34	Slovenia	7.4
13	Norway	11.4		35	New Zealand	7.2
14	Russia	10.5		36	Bosnia	6.9
15	Ireland	10.2			Ukraine	6.9
16	Finland	10.1		38	Slovakia	6.8
17	Belgium	9.8		39	Belarus	6.5
18	Japan	9.6			Iran	6.5
19	Germany	9.5			Serbia	6.5
	Libya	9.5		42	France	6.2
21	South Korea	9.4		43	Portugal	5.9
22	Malaysia	9.3				

Average annual % change in carbon emissions

Biggest increase, 1990–2005		Biggest decrease, 1990–2005	
1 Namibia	51.7	1 North Korea	-10.4
2 Somalia	44.7	2 Tajikistan	-10.0
3 Bosnia	16.0	3 Afghanistan	-9.3
4 Laos	15.5	4 Gabon	-8.9
5 Uzbekistan	13.1	Puerto Rico	-8.9
6 Vietnam	11.6	6 Georgia	-8.8
7 Eritrea	11.2	7 Moldova	-8.1
8 Swaziland	10.8	8 Mauritania	-6.1
9 Nepal	9.4	9 Latvia	-5.9
10 Madagascar	8.4	10 Kyrgyzstan	-5.5
11 Oman	8.3	11 Congo-Kinshasa	-5.3
12 Benin	8.0	12 Ukraine	-5.1
Ethiopia	8.0	13 Lithuania	-4.2
Sri Lanka	8.0	14 Kazakhstan	-3.6
15 Honduras	7.6	15 Romania	-3.5
16 Malaysia	7.4	16 Belarus	-3.3
Uganda	7.4	17 Azerbaijan	-3.2
18 Haiti	6.9	Zimbabwe	-3.2
United Arab Emirates	6.9	19 Bulgaria	-3.1
20 Bangladesh	6.8	20 Estonia	-2.8
21 Sudan	6.5	21 Russia	-2.6
22 Guatemala	6.2	22 Serbia	-2.4
Mauritius	6.2	23 Cuba	-1.8
Nigeria	6.2	24 Mongolia	-1.7
Thailand	6.2	25 Slovakia	-1.6
26 Myanmar	6.1	26 Czech Republic	-1.5
27 Egypt	5.9	27 Denmark	-1.3
28 Indonesia	5.7	28 Poland	-1.2
29 Dominican Republic	5.4	29 Zambia	-1.1
El Salvador	5.4	30 Albania	-0.9

Clean energy[a]

As % of total energy use, 2006

1 Paraguay	116.5	17 Canada	20.9
2 Kyrgyzstan	45.5	18 Belgium	20.0
3 France	44.9	19 Albania	19.0
4 Sweden	44.5	20 Finland	18.6
5 Norway	39.6	21 South Korea	18.1
6 Tajikistan	39.1	22 Ukraine	17.9
7 Switzerland	35.9	23 Japan	17.1
8 Costa Rica	35.8	24 Czech Republic	15.8
9 Armenia	32.7	25 Brazil	15.0
10 Slovakia	27.5	26 Mozambique	14.4
11 Lithuania	27.4	27 Georgia	14.0
12 Bulgaria	26.5	Peru	14.0
13 El Salvador	24.4	29 Germany	13.9
14 Slovenia	24.2	30 Spain	13.8
15 New Zealand	24.0	31 Hungary	13.2
16 Philippines	22.9	32 Colombia	12.2

a Energy that does not produce carbon dioxide when generated.

Urban population with access to improved water source

Lowest, %, 2006

1	Angola	62		Myanmar	80
2	Somalia	63	17	Tanzania	81
3	Nigeria	65	18	Congo-Kinshasa	82
4	Yemen	68		Guinea-Bissau	82
5	Haiti	70		Rwanda	82
	Mauritania	70	21	Sierra Leone	83
7	Chad	71	22	Burundi	84
	Mozambique	71	23	Bangladesh	85
9	Liberia	72		Kenya	85
	Libya	72		Oman	85
11	Eritrea	74	26	Laos	86
12	Madagascar	76		Mali	86
13	Benin	78		Togo	86
	Sudan	78	29	Algeria	87
15	Cambodia	80		Swaziland	87

Rural population with access to water source

Lowest, %, 2006

1	Somalia	10	16	Cameroon	47
2	Mozambique	26		Gabon	47
3	Congo-Kinshasa	29		Guinea-Bissau	47
4	Nigeria	30	19	Mali	48
5	Ethiopia	31		Mongolia	48
6	Niger	32	21	Kenya	49
	Papua New Guinea	32	22	Central African Rep	51
	Sierra Leone	32		Haiti	51
9	Congo-Brazzaville	35		Swaziland	51
10	Madagascar	36	25	Liberia	52
11	Angola	39		Paraguay	52
12	Chad	40	27	Laos	53
	Togo	40	28	Mauritania	54
14	Zambia	41	29	Benin	57
15	Tanzania	46		Eritrea	57

Rural population with access to improved sanitation

Lowest, %, 2006

1	Eritrea	3	15	Côte d'Ivoire	12
	Niger	3		Guinea	12
	Togo	3		Haiti	12
4	Chad	4	18	Angola	16
5	Sierra Leone	5	19	India	18
6	Burkina Faso	6		Namibia	18
	Ghana	6	21	Cambodia	19
8	Liberia	7		Mozambique	19
	Somalia	7	23	Rwanda	20
10	Ethiopia	8	24	Congo-Brazzaville	21
11	Senegal	9	25	Bolivia	22
12	Madagascar	10	26	Nepal	24
	Mauritania	10		Sudan	24
14	Benin	11			

Country
profiles

ALGERIA

Area	2,381,741 sq km	Capital	Algiers
Arable as % of total land	3	Currency	Algerian dinar (AD)

People

Population	33.9m	Life expectancy: men	70.9 yrs
Pop. per sq km	14.2	women	73.7 yrs
Av. ann. growth		Adult literacy	75.4%
in pop. 2010–15	1.45%	Fertility rate (per woman)	2.3
Pop. under 15	27.3%	Urban population	64.6%
Pop. over 60	6.8%		per 1,000 pop.
No. of men per 100 women	102	Crude birth rate	22
Human Development Index	74.8	Crude death rate	4.9

The economy

GDP	AD9,374bn	GDP per head	$4,000
GDP	$135bn	GDP per head in purchasing	
Av. ann. growth in real		power parity (USA=100)	17.0
GDP 2002–2007	4.8%	Economic freedom index	56.6

Origins of GDP		**Components of GDP**	
	% of total		% of total
Agriculture	8.2	Private consumption	31.7
Industry, of which:	61.1	Public consumption	11.4
manufacturing	5.6	Investment	34.6
Services	30.8	Exports	47.3
		Imports	-25.0

Structure of employment

	% of total		% of labour force
Agriculture	21	Unemployed 2007	13.8
Industry	27	Av. ann. rate 1995–2007	23.7
Services	52		

Energy

	m TOE		
Total output	173.2	Net energy imports as %	
Total consumption	36.7	of energy use	-372
Consumption per head,			
kg oil equivalent	1,100		

Inflation and finance

Consumer price		*av. ann. increase 2002–07*	
inflation 2008	4.4%	Narrow money (M1)	24.5%
Av. ann. inflation 2003–08	3.1%	Broad money	15.5%
Treasury bill rate, 2008	0.20%		

Exchange rates

	end 2008		December 2008
AD per $	71.18	Effective rates	2000 = 100
AD per SDR	109.64	– nominal	89.27
AD per €	99.08	– real	89.89

Trade

Principal exports

	$bn fob
Hydrocarbons	58.8
Semi-finished goods	1.0
Raw materials	0.2
Total incl. others	**60.2**

Principal imports

	$bn cif
Capital goods	10.2
Semi-finished goods	7.1
Food	5.0
Total incl. others	**29.8**

Main export destinations

	% of total
United States	27.9
Italy	13.1
Spain	9.1
Canada	7.8

Main origins of imports

	% of total
France	20.8
China	9.7
Italy	9.4
Spain	6.7

Balance of payments, reserves and debt, $bn

Visible exports fob	60.6	Change in reserves	33.5
Visible imports fob	-26.4	Level of reserves	
Trade balance	34.2	end Dec.	115.0
Invisibles inflows	6.7	No. months of import cover	35.5
Invisibles outflows	-12.5	Official gold holdings, m oz	5.6
Net transfers	2.2	Foreign debt	6
Current account balance	30.6	– as % of GDP	5.5
– as % of GDP	22.6	– as % of total exports	4
Capital balance	-1.1	Debt service ratio[a]	9
Overall balance	29.6		

Health and education

Health spending, % of GDP	4.2	Education spending, % of GDP	...
Doctors per 1,000 pop.	1.2	Enrolment, %: primary	101
Hospital beds per 1,000 pop.	1.7	secondary	83
Improved-water source access,		tertiary	24
% of pop.	85		

Society

No. of households	5.6m	Colour TVs per 100 households	89.5
Av. no. per household	5.9	Telephone lines per 100 pop.	9.1
Marriages per 1,000 pop.	8.9	Mobile telephone subscribers	
Divorces per 1,000 pop.	...	per 100 pop.	81.4
Cost of living, Feb. 2009		Computers per 100 pop.	1.1
New York = 100	54	Internet hosts per 1,000 pop.	...

a 2006

ARGENTINA

Area	2,766,889 sq km	Capital	Buenos Aires
Arable as % of total land	10	Currency	Peso (P)

People

Population	39.5m	Life expectancy: men	71.6 yrs
Pop. per sq km	14.3	women	79.1 yrs
Av. ann. growth		Adult literacy	97.6%
in pop. 2010–15	0.91%	Fertility rate (per woman)	2.2
Pop. under 15	25.1%	Urban population	91.8%
Pop. over 60	14.6%		per 1,000 pop.
No. of men per 100 women	96	Crude birth rate	19
Human Development Index	86.0	Crude death rate	7.8

The economy

GDP	P812bn	GDP per head	$6,640
GDP	$262bn	GDP per head in purchasing	
Av. ann. growth in real		power parity (USA=100)	29.0
GDP 2002–2007	10.5%	Economic freedom index	52.3

Origins of GDP		**Components of GDP**	
	% of total		% of total
Agriculture	9.5	Private consumption	58.6
Industry, of which:	34.0	Public consumption	12.9
manufacturing	21.5	Investment	24.2
Services	56.5	Exports	24.6
		Imports	-20.3

Structure of employment

	% of total		% of labour force
Agricultural	1	Unemployed 2006	9.5
Industry	23	Av. ann. rate 1995–2006	15.0
Services	76		

Energy

	m TOE		
Total output	83.9	Net energy imports as %	
Total consumption	69.1	of energy use	-21
Consumption per head			
kg oil equivalent	1,766		

Inflation and finance

Consumer price		av. ann. increase 2002–07	
inflation 2008	8.6%	Narrow money (M1)	30.4%
Av. ann. inflation 2003–08	8.4%	Broad money	23.5%
Money market rate, 2008	10.07%		

Exchange rates

	end 2008		December 2008
		Effective rates	2000 = 100
P per $	3.43	Effective rates	2000 = 100
P per SDR	5.29	– nominal	...
P per €	4.77	– real	...

Trade

Principal exports		Principal imports	
	$bn fob		*$bn cif*
Agricultural products	19.2	Intermediate goods	15.5
Manufactures	17.4	Capital goods	10.8
Primary products	12.5	Consumer goods	5.2
Fuels	6.8	Fuels	2.8
Total incl. others	**55.9**	Total incl. others	**44.7**

Main export destinations		Main origins of imports	
	% of total		*% of total*
Brazil	17.4	Brazil	31.7
China	9.6	United States	14.4
United States	7.8	China	8.7
Chile	7.1	Germany	5.8

Balance of payments, reserves and debt, $bn

Visible exports fob	55.8	Change in reserves	14.1
Visible imports fob	-42.5	Level of reserves	
Trade balance	13.3	end Dec.	46.1
Invisibles inflows	16.9	No. months of import cover	8.4
Invisibles outflows	-23.4	Official gold holdings, m oz	1.8
Net transfers	0.3	Foreign debt	127.8
Current account balance	7.1	– as % of GDP	63
– as % of GDP	2.7	– as % of total exports	219
Capital balance	3.9	Debt service ratio	13
Overall balance	11.6		

Health and education

Health spending, % of GDP	10.7	Education spending, % of GDP	4.5
Doctors per 1,000 pop.	3.0	Enrolment, %: primary	109
Hospital beds per 1,000 pop.	...	secondary	84
Improved-water source access,		tertiary	67
% of pop.	96		

Society

No. of households	10.6m	Colour TVs per 100 households	95.4
Av. no. per household	3.6	Telephone lines per 100 pop.	24.0
Marriages per 1,000 pop.	3.1	Mobile telephone subscribers	
Divorces per 1,000 pop.	...	per 100 pop.	102.2
Cost of living, Feb. 2009		Computers per 100 pop.	9.0
New York = 100	57	Internet hosts per 1,000 pop.	111.1

AUSTRALIA

Area	7,682,300 sq km	Capital	Canberra
Arable as % of total land	6	Currency	Australian dollar (A$)

People

Population	20.6m	Life expectancy: men	79.1 yrs
Pop. per sq km	2.7	women	83.8 yrs
Av. ann. growth		Adult literacy	...
in pop. 2010–15	0.99%	Fertility rate (per woman)	1.9
Pop. under 15	19.0%	Urban population	88.6%
Pop. over 60	19.1%		per 1,000 pop.
No. of men per 100 women	99	Crude birth rate	14
Human Development Index	96.5	Crude death rate	6.9

The economy

GDP	A$1,046bn	GDP per head	$39,070
GDP	$821bn	GDP per head in purchasing	
Av. ann. growth in real		power parity (USA=100)	76.6
GDP 2002–2007	3.5%	Economic freedom index	82.6

Origins of GDP		Components of GDP	
	% of total		% of total
Agriculture	3.2	Private consumption	55.9
Industry, of which:	26.8	Public consumption	17.7
manufacturing	...	Investment	28.3
Services	70.1	Exports	20.1
		Imports	-21.9

Structure of employment

	% of total		% of labour force
Agriculture	3	Unemployed 2007	4.4
Industry	19	Av. ann. rate 1995–2007	6.6
Services	78		

Energy

	m TOE		
Total output	267.8	Net energy imports as %	
Total consumption	122.5	of energy use	-119
Consumption per head,			
kg oil equivalent	5,917		

Inflation and finance

Consumer price		av. ann. increase 2002–07	
inflation 2008	4.4%	Narrow money (M1)	10.1%
Av. ann. inflation 2003–08	3.0%	Broad money	15.3%
Money market rate, 2008	6.67%	Household saving rate, 2008	1.4%

Exchange rates

	end 2008		December 2008
			2000 = 100
A$ per $	1.44	Effective rates	
A$ per SDR	2.22	– nominal	99.80
A$ per €	2.00	– real	110.10

Trade

Principal exports		Principal imports	
	$bn fob		*$bn cif*
Coal	17.4	Intermediate & other goods	73.6
Meat & meat products	5.9	Consumption goods	48.3
Wheat	3.8	Capital goods	36.0
Total incl. others	**141.4**	Total incl. others	**158.0**

Main export destinations		Main origins of imports	
	% of total		*% of total*
Japan	18.7	China	15.6
China	14.3	United States	14.0
South Korea	7.9	Japan	9.9
India	5.8	Singapore	6.6
United States	5.8	Germany	5.6

Balance of payments, reserves and aid, $bn

Visible exports fob	142.4	Overall balance	-35.1
Visible imports fob	-160.2	Change in reserves	-28.2
Trade balance	-17.8	Level of reserves	
Invisibles inflows	72.9	end Dec.	26.9
Invisibles outflows	-112.6	No. months of import cover	1.2
Net transfers	-0.3	Official gold holdings, m oz	2.6
Current account balance	-57.7	Aid given	2.67
– as % of GDP	-7.0	– as % of GDP	0.33
Capital balance	22.4		

Health and education

Health spending, % of GDP	8.7	Education spending, % of GDP	5.2
Doctors per 1,000 pop.	2.5	Enrolment, %: primary	106
Hospital beds per 1,000 pop.	4.0	secondary	149
Improved-water source access,		tertiary	75
% of pop.	100		

Society

No. of households	7.7m	Colour TVs per 100 households	99.0
Av. no. per household	2.7	Telephone lines per 100 pop.	47.1
Marriages per 1,000 pop.	5.3	Mobile telephone subscribers	
Divorces per 1,000 pop.	2.4	per 100 pop.	102.5
Cost of living, Feb. 2009		Computers per 100 pop.	68.1
New York = 100	92	Internet hosts per 1,000 pop.	550.4

AUSTRIA

Area	83,855 sq km	Capital	Vienna
Arable as % of total land	17	Currency	Euro (€)

People

Population	8.2m	Life expectancy: men	77.2 yrs
Pop. per sq km	97.8	women	82.6 yrs
Av. ann. growth		Adult literacy	...
in pop. 2010–15	0.19%	Fertility rate (per woman)	1.4
Pop. under 15	14.9%	Urban population	66.9%
Pop. over 60	22.9%		per 1,000 pop.
No. of men per 100 women	95	Crude birth rate	9
Human Development Index	95.1	Crude death rate	9.3

The economy

GDP	€273bn	GDP per head	$44,880
GDP	$373bn	GDP per head in purchasing	
Av. ann. growth in real		power parity (USA=100)	82.0
GDP 2002–2007	2.7%	Economic freedom index	71.2

Origins of GDP		**Components of GDP**	
	% of total		% of total
Agriculture	1.9	Private consumption	53.1
Industry, of which:	30.5	Public consumption	18.0
manufacturing	...	Investment	22.9
Services	67.5	Exports	59.4
		Imports	-53.4

Structure of employment

	% of total		% of labour force
Agriculture	6	Unemployed 2007	4.4
Industry	28	Av. ann. rate 1995–2007	4.2
Services	66		

Energy

	m TOE		
Total output	9.9	Net energy imports as %	
Total consumption	34.2	of energy use	71
Consumption per head,			
kg oil equivalent	4,133		

Inflation and finance

Consumer price		av. ann. increase 2002–07	
inflation 2008	3.2%	Euro area:	
Av. ann. inflation 2003–08	2.2%	Narrow money (M1)	9.3%
Deposit rate, h'holds, 2008	3.88%	Broad money	8.4%
		Household saving rate, 2008	11.8%

Exchange rates

	end 2008		December 2008
€ per $	0.72	Effective rates	2000 = 100
€ per SDR	1.11	– nominal	107.20
		– real	103.30

Trade

Principal exports

	$bn fob
Machinery & transport equip.	68.8
Chemicals & related products	17.2
Food, drink & tobacco	10.4
Raw materials	5.5
Mineral fuels & lubricants	4.5
Total incl. others	**157.4**

Principal imports

	$bn cif
Machinery & transport equip.	60.8
Chemicals & related products	18.2
Mineral fuels & lubricants	15.5
Food, drink & tobacco	10.2
Raw materials	7.1
Total incl. others	**156.8**

Main export destinations

	% of total
Germany	31.0
Italy	8.9
United States	5.1
Switzerland	4.0
EU27	72.6

Main origins of imports

	% of total
Germany	41.5
Italy	8.2
Switzerland	4.4
France	3.2
EU27	79.3

Balance of payments, reserves and aid, $bn

Visible exports fob	162.1	Overall balance	2.5
Visible imports fob	-160.3	Change in reserves	5.3
Trade balance	1.8	Level of reserves	
Invisibles inflows	93.6	end Dec.	18.2
Invisibles outflows	-82.1	No. months of import cover	0.9
Net transfers	-1.4	Official gold holdings, m oz	9.0
Current account balance	12.0	Aid given	1.81
– as % of GDP	3.2	– as % of GDP	0.48
Capital balance	-6.1		

Health and education

Health spending, % of GDP	10.2	Education spending, % of GDP	5.4
Doctors per 1,000 pop.	3.7	Enrolment, %: primary	101
Hospital beds per 1,000 pop.	7.6	secondary	102
Improved-water source access,		tertiary	51
% of pop.	100		

Society

No. of households	3.5m	Colour TVs per 100 households	98.8
Av. no. per household	2.4	Telephone lines per 100 pop.	40.8
Marriages per 1,000 pop.	4.9	Mobile telephone subscribers	
Divorces per 1,000 pop.	2.2	per 100 pop.	118.6
Cost of living, Feb. 2009		Computers per 100 pop.	60.7
New York = 100	109	Internet hosts per 1,000 pop.	354.1

BANGLADESH

Area	143,998 sq km	Capital	Dhaka
Arable as % of total land	61	Currency	Taka (Tk)

People

Population	147.1m	Life expectancy: men	65.0 yrs
Pop. per sq km	1,021.5	women	67.0 yrs
Av. ann. growth		Adult literacy	53.5%
in pop. 2010–15	1.27%	Fertility rate (per woman)	2.2
Pop. under 15	31.5%	Urban population	26.6%
Pop. over 60	6.0%		per 1,000 pop.
No. of men per 100 women	102	Crude birth rate	24
Human Development Index	52.4	Crude death rate	6.6

The economy

GDP	Tk4,725bn	GDP per head	$430
GDP	$68.4bn	GDP per head in purchasing	
Av. ann. growth in real		power parity (USA=100)	2.7
GDP 2002–07	7.0%	Economic freedom index	47.5

Origins of GDP[a]		**Components of GDP**[a]	
	% of total		% of total
Agriculture	18.6	Private consumption	77
Industry, of which:	28.2	Public consumption	6
manufacturing	17.7	Investment	24
Services	53.2	Exports	20
		Imports	-27

Structure of employment

	% of total		% of labour force
Agriculture	52	Unemployed 2003	4.3
Industry	14	Av. ann. rate 1995–2003	2.7
Services	35		

Energy

			m TOE
Total output	20.3	Net energy imports as %	
Total consumption	25.0	of energy use	19
Consumption per head,			
kg oil equivalent	161		

Inflation and finance

Consumer price		av. ann. increase 2002–07	
inflation 2008	8.9%	Narrow money (M1)	18.2%
Av. ann. inflation 2002–08	8.2%	Broad money	15.7%
Deposit rate, Sep. 2008	10.21%		

Exchange rates

	end 2008		December 2008
			2000 = 100
Tk per $	68.92	Effective rates	
Tk per SDR	106.16	– nominal	...
Tk per €	95.94	– real	...

Trade

Principal exports[a]

	$bn fob
Clothing	7.5
Fish & fish products	0.5
Jute goods	0.3
Leather	0.3
Total incl. others	**11.4**

Principal imports[a]

	$bn cif
Capital goods	3.6
Textiles & yarns	3.4
Fuels	2.2
Iron & steel	1.0
Total incl. others	**17.2**

Main export destinations

	% of total
United States	24.1
Germany	12.3
United Kingdom	9.7
France	5.0
Belgium	4.0

Main origins of imports

	% of total
India	18.1
China	13.0
Kuwait	7.8
Singapore	5.0
Hong Kong	3.8

Balance of payments, reserves and debt, $bn

Visible exports fob	12.5	Change in reserves	1.4
Visible imports fob	-16.7	Level of reserves	
Trade balance	-4.2	end Dec.	5.3
Invisibles inflows	1.9	No. months of import cover	3.0
Invisibles outflows	-4.1	Official gold holdings, m oz	0.1
Net transfers	7.3	Foreign debt	22.0
Current account balance	0.9	– as % of GDP	22
– as % of GDP	1.3	– as % of total exports	84
Capital balance	1.4	Debt service ratio	4
Overall balance	1.4		

Health and education

Health spending, % of GDP	3.2	Education spending, % of GDP	2.7
Doctors per 1,000 pop.	0.3	Enrolment, %: primary	123
Hospital beds per 1,000 pop.	3.0	secondary	43
Improved-water source access,		tertiary	...
% of pop.	74		

Society

No. of households	26.2m	Colour TVs per 100 households	2.7
Av. no. per household	6.1	Telephone lines per 100 pop.	0.8
Marriages per 1,000 pop.	...	Mobile telephone subscribers	
Divorces per 1,000 pop.	...	per 100 pop.	21.7
Cost of living, Feb. 2009		Computers per 100 pop.	2.2
New York = 100	56	Internet hosts per 1,000 pop.	...

a Fiscal year ending June 30 2007.

BELGIUM

Area	30,520 sq km	Capital	Brussels
Arable as % of total land	28	Currency	Euro (€)

People

Population	10.5m	Life expectancy: men	76.7 yrs
Pop. per sq km	344.0	women	82.6 yrs
Av. ann. growth		Adult literacy	...
in pop. 2010–15	0.33%	Fertility rate (per woman)	1.8
Pop. under 15	16.8%	Urban population	97.3%
Pop. over 60	23.0%		per 1,000 pop.
No. of men per 100 women	96	Crude birth rate	12
Human Development Index	94.8	Crude death rate	9.7

The economy

GDP	€331bn	GDP per head	$42,610
GDP	$453bn	GDP per head in purchasing	
Av. ann. growth in real		power parity (USA=100)	76.6
GDP 2002–2007	2.4%	Economic freedom index	72.1

Origins of GDP		Components of GDP	
	% of total		% of total
Agriculture	0.8	Private consumption	52.2
Industry, of which:	24.0	Public consumption	22.2
manufacturing	...	Investment	22.6
Services	75.2	Exports	88.9
		Imports	-85.9

Structure of employment

	% of total		% of labour force
Agriculture	2	Unemployed 2007	7.5
Industry	24	Av. ann. rate 1995–2007	8.2
Services	74		

Energy

	m TOE		
Total output	15.5	Net energy imports as %	
Total consumption	61.0	of energy use	75
Consumption per head,			
kg oil equivalent	5,782		

Inflation and finance

Consumer price		av. ann. increase 2002–07	
inflation 2008	4.5%	Euro area:	
Av. ann. inflation 2003–08	2.6%	Narrow money (M1)	9.3%
Treasury bill rate, 2008	3.63%	Broad money	8.4%
		Household saving rate, 2008	7.9%

Exchange rates

	end 2008		December 2008
€ per $	0.72	Effective rates	2000 = 100
€ per SDR	1.11	– nominal	113.70
		– real	125.40

Trade

Principal exports		**Principal imports**	
	$bn fob		*$bn cif*
Chemicals & related products	127.6	Machinery & transport equip.	106.5
Machinery & transport equip.	104.6	Chemicals & related products	102.6
Food, drink & tobacco	34.2	Minerals, fuels & lubricants	48.8
Minerals, fuels & lubricants	30.6	Food, drink & tobacco	29.4
Total incl. others	**432.4**	Total incl. others	**413.7**

Main export destinations		**Main origins of imports**	
	% of total		*% of total*
Germany	19.6	Germany	17.8
France	16.7	Netherlands	17.6
Netherlands	11.9	France	11.2
United Kingdom	7.6	United Kingdom	6.3
EU27	76.3	EU27	70.9

Balance of payments, reserves and aid, $bn

Visible exports fob	323.7	Overall balance	1.2
Visible imports fob	-322.0	Change in reserves	3.1
Trade balance	1.7	Level of reserves	
Invisibles inflows	177.7	end Dec.	16.5
Invisibles outflows	-165.4	No. months of import cover	0.4
Net transfers	-6.8	Official gold holdings, m oz	7.3
Current account balance	7.2	Aid given	1.95
– as % of GDP	1.6	– as % of GDP	0.43
Capital balance	-8.1		

Health and education

Health spending, % of GDP	9.9	Education spending, % of GDP	6.1
Doctors per 1,000 pop.	4.2	Enrolment, %: primary	99
Hospital beds per 1,000 pop.	5.3	secondary	110
Improved-water source access, % of pop.	...	tertiary	62

Society

No. of households	4.5m	Colour TVs per 100 households	98.9
Av. no. per household	2.4	Telephone lines per 100 pop.	44.6
Marriages per 1,000 pop.	4.2	Mobile telephone subscribers	
Divorces per 1,000 pop.	3.0	per 100 pop.	102.7
Cost of living, Feb. 2009		Computers per 100 pop.	41.7
New York = 100	107	Internet hosts per 1,000 pop.	416.0

BRAZIL

Area	8,511,965 sq km	Capital	Brasilia
Arable as % of total land	7	Currency	Real (R)

People

Population	191.3m	Life expectancy: men	68.7 yrs
Pop. per sq km	22.5	women	76.0 yrs
Av. ann. growth		Adult literacy	90.0%
in pop. 2010–15	0.75%	Fertility rate (per woman)	1.7
Pop. under 15	25.9%	Urban population	85.2%
Pop. over 60	9.9%		per 1,000 pop.
No. of men per 100 women	97	Crude birth rate	20
Human Development Index	80.7	Crude death rate	6.4

The economy

GDP	R2,559bn	GDP per head	$6,860
GDP	$1,313bn	GDP per head in purchasing	
Av. ann. growth in real		power parity (USA=100)	21.0
GDP 2002–2007	4.2%	Economic freedom index	56.7

Origins of GDP		**Components of GDP**	
	% of total		% of total
Agriculture	6.0	Private consumption	60.8
Industry, of which:	28.1	Public consumption	19.9
manufacturing	17.4	Investment	17.7
Services	66.0	Exports	13.7
		Imports	-12.1

Structure of employment

	% of total		% of labour force
Agriculture	21	Unemployed 2004	8.9
Industry	19	Av. ann. rate 1995–2004	8.5
Services	60		

Energy

			m TOE
Total output	206.7	Net energy imports as %	
Total consumption	224.1	of energy use	8
Consumption per head,			
kg oil equivalent	1,184		

Inflation and finance

Consumer price		av. ann. increase 2002–07	
inflation 2008	5.7%	Narrow money (M1)	16.6%
Av. ann. inflation 2002–08	5.4%	Broad money	19.2%
Money market rate, 2008	12.36%		

Exchange rates

	end 2008		December 2008
R per $	2.34	Effective rates	2000 = 100
R per sdr	3.60	– nominal	...
R per €	3.26	– real	...

Trade

Principal exports	$bn fob	Principal imports	$bn cif
Transport equipment & parts	20.0	Machines & electrical	
Metal goods	18.7	equipment	31.5
Soyabeans, meal & oils	13.2	Oil & derivatives	20.1
Chemical products	3.0	Chemical products	18.6
		Transport equipment & parts	14.4
Total incl. others	**160.6**	Total incl. others	**120.6**

Main export destinations	% of total	Main origins of imports	% of total
United States	15.8	United States	15.7
Argentina	9.0	China	10.5
China	6.7	Argentina	8.6
Germany	4.5	Netherlands	0.9

Balance of payments, reserves and debt, $bn

Visible exports fob	160.6	Change in reserves	94.5
Visible imports fob	-120.6	Level of reserves	
Trade balance	40.0	end Dec.	180.3
Invisibles inflows	35.4	No. months of import cover	10.9
Invisibles outflows	-78.0	Official gold holdings, m oz	1.1
Net transfers	4.0	Foreign debt	237.5
Current account balance	1.6	– as % of GDP	25
– as % of GDP	0.1	– as % of total exports	155
Capital balance	89.1	Debt service ratio	28
Overall balance	87.5		

Health and education

Health spending, % of GDP	7.5	Education spending, % of GDP	5.1
Doctors per 1,000 pop.	1.0	Enrolment, %: primary	125
Hospital beds per 1,000 pop.	2.4	secondary	100
Improved-water source access,		tertiary	...
% of pop.	90		

Society

No. of households	51.4m	Colour TVs per 100 households	93.4
Av. no. per household	3.7	Telephone lines per 100 pop.	20.5
Marriages per 1,000 pop.	4.0	Mobile telephone subscribers	
Divorces per 1,000 pop.	0.8	per 100 pop.	63.1
Cost of living, Feb. 2009		Computers per 100 pop.	14.1
New York = 100	70	Internet hosts per 1,000 pop.	76.7

BULGARIA

Area	110,994 sq km	Capital	Sofia
Arable as % of total land	29	Currency	Lev (BGL)

People

Population	7.6m	Life expectancy: men	69.7 yrs
Pop. per sq km	68.5	women	76.8 yrs
Av. ann. growth		Adult literacy	98.3%
in pop. 2010–15	-0.63%	Fertility rate (per woman)	1.5
Pop. under 15	13.4%	Urban population	70.8%
Pop. over 60	24.2%		per 1,000 pop.
No. of men per 100 women	94	Crude birth rate	10
Human Development Index	83.4	Crude death rate	14.6

The economy

GDP	BGL56.5bn	GDP per head	$5,160
GDP	$39.5bn	GDP per head in purchasing	
Av. ann. growth in real		power parity (USA=100)	24.6
GDP 2002–2007	6.9%	Economic freedom index	64.6

Origins of GDP		**Components of GDP**	
	% of total		% of total
Agriculture	6.2	Private consumption	76.3
Industry, of which:	32.3	Public consumption	8.9
manufacturing	...	Investment	36.8
Services	61.5	Exports	63.4
		Imports	-85.5

Structure of employment

	% of total		% of labour force
Agriculture	9	Unemployed 2007	6.9
Industry	34	Av. ann. rate 1995–2007	13.7
Services	57		

Energy

		m TOE	
Total output	11.1	Net energy imports as %	
Total consumption	20.7	of energy use	46
Consumption per head,			
kg oil equivalent	2,688		

Inflation and finance

Consumer price			av. ann change 2002–07
inflation 2008	12.3%	Narrow money (M1)	25.4%
Av. ann. inflation 2002–08	7.8%	Broad money	25.5%
Money market rate, 2008	5.16%		

Exchange rates

	end 2008		December 2008
BGL per $	1.39	Effective rates	2000 = 100
BGL per SDR	2.14	– nominal	109.27
BGL per €	1.93	– real	141.45

Trade

Principal exports		Principal imports	
	$bn fob		*$bn cif*
Other metals	2.2	Crude oil & natural gas	4.9
Clothing	2.1	Machinery & equipment	3.1
Iron & steel	1.4	Textiles	2.1
Chemicals, plastics & rubber	1.0	Chemicals, plastics & rubber	2.0
Total incl. others	**18.6**	Total incl. others	**29.9**

Main export destinations		Main origins of imports	
	% of total		*% of total*
Turkey	11.5	Germany	14.8
Germany	10.2	Russia	10.6
Italy	10.1	Italy	7.5
Greece	9.0	Ukraine	5.1
EU27	60.8	EU27	58.5

Balance of payments, reserves and debt, $bn

Visible exports fob	18.6	Change in reserves	5.8
Visible imports fob	-28.6	Level of reserves	
Trade balance	-10.1	end Dec.	17.5
Invisibles inflows	8.4	No. months of import cover	5.8
Invisibles outflows	-7.5	Official gold holdings, m oz	1.3
Net transfers	0.5	Foreign debt	33.0
Current account balance	-8.7	– as % of GDP	100
– as % of GDP	-22.0	– as % of total exports	144
Capital balance	15.5	Debt service ratio	16
Overall balance	4.7		

Health and education

Health spending, % of GDP	7.2	Education spending, % of GDP	4.2
Doctors per 1,000 pop.	3.7	Enrolment, %: primary	100
Hospital beds per 1,000 pop.	6.4	secondary	106
Improved-water source access,		tertiary	50
% of pop.	99		

Society

No. of households	2.9m	Colour TVs per 100 households	91.5
Av. no. per household	2.5	Telephone lines per 100 pop.	30.1
Marriages per 1,000 pop.	4.0	Mobile telephone subscribers	
Divorces per 1,000 pop.	2.4	per 100 pop.	129.6
Cost of living, Feb. 2009		Computers per 100 pop.	8.9
New York = 100	62	Internet hosts per 1,000 pop.	83.7

CAMEROON

Area	475,442 sq km	Capital	Yaoundé
Arable as % of total land	13	Currency	CFA franc (CFAfr)

People

Population	16.9m	Life expectancy: men	50.4 yrs
Pop. per sq km	35.5	women	51.5 yrs
Av. ann. growth		Adult literacy	67.9%
in pop. 2010–15	2.10%	Fertility rate (per woman)	4.2
Pop. under 15	40.9%	Urban population	56.0%
Pop. over 60	5.4%		per 1,000 pop.
No. of men per 100 women	100	Crude birth rate	36
Human Development Index	51.4	Crude death rate	14.3

The economy

GDP	CFAfr9,913bn	GDP per head	$1,120
GDP	$20.7bn	GDP per head in purchasing	
Av. ann. growth in real		power parity (USA=100)	4.7
GDP 2002–07	3.6%	Economic freedom index	53.0

Origins of GDP		Components of GDP	
	% of total		% of total
Agriculture	19	Private consumption	73
Industry, of which:	31	Public consumption	9
manufacturing	17	Investment	17
Services	50	Exports	22
		Imports	-21

Structure of employment

	% of total		% of labour force
Agriculture	70	Unemployed 2007	...
Industry	13	Av. ann. rate 1995–2007	...
Services	17		

Energy

	m TOE		
Total output	10.3	Net energy imports as %	
Total consumption	7.1	of energy use	-46
Consumption per head,			
kg oil equivalent	390		

Inflation and finance

Consumer price		av. ann. change 2002–07	
inflation 2008	5.3%	Narrow money (M1)	7.8%
Av. ann. inflation 2003–08	2.7%	Broad money	7.5%
Deposit rate, Aug. 2008	3.25%		

Exchange rates

	end 2008		December 2008
CFAfr per $	471.34	Effective rates	2000 = 100
CFAfr per SDR	725.98	– nominal	113.70
CFAfr per €	656.11	– real	118.50

Trade

Principal exports[a]	$bn fob	Principal imports[b]	$bn cif
Crude oil	1.9	Capital goods	0.4
Timber	0.5	Intermediate goods	0.4
Cocoa	0.2	Minerals & raw materials	0.4
Cotton	0.1	Food, drink & tobacco	0.3
Total incl. others	**3.7**	Total incl. others	**2.5**

Main export destinations	% of total	Main origins of imports	% of total
Spain	20.2	France	23.7
Italy	16.0	Nigeria	12.3
France	11.9	Belgium	5.9
South Korea	8.3	United States	4.1

Balance of payments, reserves and debt, $bn

Visible exports fob	4.3	Change in reserves	1.2
Visible imports fob	-4.0	Level of reserves	
Trade balance	0.3	end Dec.	2.9
Invisible inflows	0.7	No. months of import cover	5.9
Invisible outflows	-1.9	Official gold holdings, m oz	0
Net transfers	0.4	Foreign debt	3.1
Current account balance	-0.5	– as % of GDP	5
– as % of GDP	-2.6	– as % of total exports	19
Capital balance	1.3	Debt service ratio[a]	10
Overall balance	0.8		

Health and education

Health spending, % of GDP	4.6	Education spending, % of GDP	3.9
Doctors per 1,000 pop.	0.2	Enrolment, %: primary	111
Hospital beds per 1,000 pop.	...	secondary	25
Improved-water source access,		tertiary	...
% of pop.	66		

Society

No. of households	4.5m	Colour TVs per 100 households	...
Av. no. per household	4.0	Telephone lines per 100 pop.	1.0
Marriages per 1,000 pop.	...	Mobile telephone subscribers	
Divorces per 1,000 pop.	...	per 100 pop.	24.5
Cost of living, Feb. 2009		Computers per 100 pop.	1.1
New York = 100	...	Internet hosts per 1,000 pop.	...

a 2006
b 2005

CANADA

Area[a]	9,970,610 sq km	Capital	Ottawa
Arable as % of total land	5	Currency	Canadian dollar (C$)

People

Population	32.9m	Life expectancy: men	78.3 yrs
Pop. per sq km	3.3	women	82.9 yrs
Av. ann. growth		Adult literacy	...
in pop. 2010–15	0.92%	Fertility rate (per woman)	1.6
Pop. under 15	16.5%	Urban population	80.3%
Pop. over 60	19.5%		per 1,000 pop.
No. of men per 100 women	98	Crude birth rate	11
Human Development Index	96.7	Crude death rate	7.4

The economy

GDP	C$1,428bn	GDP per head	$40,330
GDP	$1,330bn	GDP per head in purchasing	
Av. ann. growth in real		power parity (USA=100)	78.5
GDP 2002–2007	2.9%	Economic freedom index	80.5

Origins of GDP[b]		**Components of GDP**	
	% of total		% of total
Agriculture	2.6	Private consumption	55.5
Industry, of which:	31.5	Public consumption	19.3
manufacturing & mining	...	Investment	23.3
Services	69.0	Exports	34.7
		Imports	-32.7

Structure of employment

	% of total		% of labour force
Agriculture	3	Unemployed 2007	6.0
Industry	21	Av. ann. rate 1995–2007	7.7
Services	76		

Energy

	m TOE		
Total output	411.7	Net energy imports as %	
Total consumption	269.7	of energy use	-53
Consumption per head,			
kg oil equivalent	8,262		

Inflation and finance

		av. ann. increase 2002–07	
Consumer price			
inflation 2008	2.4%	Narrow money (M1)	2.2%
Av. ann. inflation 2003–08	2.1%	Broad money	-0.4%
Money market rate, 2008	2.96%	Household saving rate, 2008	2.8%

Exchange rates

	end 2008		December 2008
C$ per $	1.22	Effective rates	2000 = 100
C$ per SDR	1.89	– nominal	117.30
C$ per €	1.70	– real	125.30

Trade

Principal exports	$bn fob	Principal imports	$bn fob
Other industrial goods	97.1	Machinery & equipment	108.7
Machinery & equipment	88.9	Other industrial goods	79.3
Energy products	85.5	Motor vehicles & parts	74.5
Motor vehicles and parts	72.1	Consumer goods	51.0
Total incl. others	**415.6**	Total incl. others	**378.3**

Main export destinations	% of total	Main origins of imports	% of total
United States	79.9	United States	59.8
United Kingdom	2.9	China	10.4
China	2.1	Mexico	4.7
Japan	2.1	Japan	4.2

Balance of payments, reserves and aid, $bn

Visible exports fob	432.0	Overall balance	3.9
Visible imports fob	-387.7	Change in reserves	6.0
Trade balance	44.4	Level of reserves	
Invisibles inflows	130.0	end Dec.	41.1
Invisibles outflows	-160.8	No. months of import cover	0.9
Net transfers	-0.9	Official gold holdings, m oz	0.1
Current account balance	12.6	Aid given	4.08
– as % of GDP	1.0	– as % of GDP	0.31
Capital balance	-12.0		

Health and education

Health spending, % of GDP	10.0	Education spending, % of GDP	4.9
Doctors per 1,000 pop.	2.1	Enrolment, %: primary	96
Hospital beds per 1,000 pop.	3.6	secondary	102
Improved-water source access,		tertiary	62
% of pop.	100		

Society

No. of households	12.5m	Colour TVs per 100 households	99.1
Av. no. per household	2.6	Telephone lines per 100 pop.	55.5
Marriages per 1,000 pop.	4.5	Mobile telephone subscribers	
Divorces per 1,000 pop.	2.2	per 100 pop.	61.7
Cost of living, Feb. 2009		Computers per 100 pop.	94.3
New York = 100	85	Internet hosts per 1,000 pop.	197.9

a   Including freshwater.
b   2005

CHILE

Area	756,945 sq km	Capital	Santiago
Arable as % of total land	3	Currency	Chilean peso (Ps)

People

Population	16.6m	Life expectancy: men	75.5 yrs
Pop. per sq km	21.9	women	81.6 yrs
Av. ann. growth		Adult literacy	96.5%
in pop. 2010–15	0.90%	Fertility rate (per woman)	1.9
Pop. under 15	22.7%	Urban population	88.2%
Pop. over 60	12.8%		per 1,000 pop.
No. of men per 100 women	98	Crude birth rate	14
Human Development Index	87.4	Crude death rate	5.4

The economy

GDP	85,640bn pesos	GDP per head	$9,880
GDP	$164bn	GDP per head in purchasing	
Av. ann. growth in real		power parity (USA=100)	30.4
GDP 2002–07	5.5%	Economic freedom index	78.3

Origins of GDP		**Components of GDP**	
	% of total		% of total
Agriculture	5.5	Private consumption	54.5
Industry, of which:	36.1	Public consumption	11.0
manufacturing	18.1	Investment	20.6
Services	50.4	Exports	47.2
		Imports	-33.3

Structure of employment

	% of total		% of labour force
Agriculture	13	Unemployed 2007	7.2
Industry	23	Av. ann. rate 1995–2007	7.0
Services	64		

Energy

	m TOE		
Total output	10.0	Net energy imports as %	
Total consumption	29.8	of energy use	67
Consumption per head,			
kg oil equivalent	1,812		

Inflation and finance

			av. ann. increase 2002–07
Consumer price			
inflation 2008	8.7%	Narrow money (M1)	13.1%
Av. ann. inflation 2003–08	4.1%	Broad money	14.2%
Money market rate, 2008	7.11%		

Exchange rates

	end 2008		December 2008
Ps per $	629.11	Effective rates	2000 = 100
Ps per SDR	969.00	– nominal	83.60
Ps per €	875.72	– real	89.00

Trade

Principal exports		Principal imports	
	$bn fob		*$bn cif*
Copper	37.6	Intermediate goods	26.4
Paper products	2.9	Consumer goods	9.7
Fruit	2.7	Capital goods	7.0
Total incl. others	**67.7**	Total incl. others	**47.2**

Main export destinations		Main origins of imports	
	% of total		*% of total*
China	14.7	United States	15.5
United States	12.4	China	10.4
Japan	10.5	Brazil	9.5
Netherlands	5.8	Argentina	9.2
South Korea	5.7	Peru	3.6

Balance of payments, reserves and debt, $bn

Visible exports fob	67.6	Change in reserves	-2.6
Visible imports fob	-44.0	Level of reserves	
Trade balance	23.7	end Dec.	16.8
Invisibles inflows	14.4	No. months of import cover	2.6
Invisibles outflows	-33.8	Official gold holdings, m oz	0.0
Net transfers	3.0	Foreign debt	58.6
Current account balance	7.2	– as % of GDP	45
– as % of GDP	4.4	– as % of total exports	85
Capital balance	-9.4	Debt service ratio	14
Overall balance	-3.2		

Health and education

Health spending, % of GDP	5.3	Education spending, % of GDP	3.4
Doctors per 1,000 pop.	1.3	Enrolment, %: primary	99
Hospital beds per 1,000 pop.	2.4	secondary	91
Improved-water source access,		tertiary	52
% of pop.	95		

Society

No. of households	4.6m	Colour TVs per 100 households	93.9
Av. no. per household	3.6	Telephone lines per 100 pop.	17.2
Marriages per 1,000 pop.	3.3	Mobile telephone subscribers	
Divorces per 1,000 pop.	0.5	per 100 pop.	83.7
Cost of living, Feb. 2009		Computers per 100 pop.	14.1
New York = 100	64	Internet hosts per 1,000 pop.	52.1

CHINA

Area	9,560,900 sq km	Capital	Beijing
Arable as % of total land	15	Currency	Yuan

People

Population	1,331.4m	Life expectancy: men	71.3 yrs
Pop. per sq km	139.3	women	74.8 yrs
Av. ann. growth		Adult literacy	93.3%
in pop. 2010–15	0.61%	Fertility rate (per woman)	1.8
Pop. under 15	20.2%	Urban population	42.2%
Pop. over 60	11.9%		per 1,000 pop.
No. of men per 100 women	108	Crude birth rate	12
Human Development Index	76.2	Crude death rate	7.0

The economy

GDP	Yuan25,731bn	GDP per head	$2,430
GDP	$3,206bn	GDP per head in purchasing	
Av. ann. growth in real		power parity (USA=100)	11.8
GDP 2002–07	13.7%	Economic freedom index	53.2

Origins of GDP		**Components of GDP**	
	% of total		% of total
Agriculture	11.1	Private consumption	35.4
Industry, of which:	48.5	Public consumption	13.3
manufacturing	...	Investment	42.3
Services	40.4	Exports	38.8
		Imports	-29.9

Structure of employment

	% of total		% of labour force
Agriculture	41	Unemployed 2007	4.0
Industry	25	Av. ann. rate 1995–2007	3.5
Services	34		

Energy

	m TOE		
Total output	1,749.3	Net energy imports as %	
Total consumption	1,878.7	of energy use	7
Consumption per head,			
kg oil equivalent	1,433		

Inflation and finance

			av. ann. increase 2002–07
Consumer price			
inflation 2008	5.9%	Narrow money (M1)	16.6%
Av. ann. inflation 2003–08	3.6%	Broad money	17.9%
Deposit rate, 2008	2.25%		

Exchange rates

	end 2008		December 2008
Yuan per $	6.81	Effective rates	2000 = 100
Yuan per SDR	10.53	– nominal	111.11
Yuan per €	9.51	– real	113.43

Trade

Principal exports	$bn fob	Principal imports	$bn cif
Electrical machinery & equip.	128.2	Electrical machinery	209.0
Clothing & garments	115.3	Petroleum & products	99.0
Yarn & textiles	56.0	Industrial machinery	30.5
Petroleum & products	12.2	Textiles	16.6
Total incl. others	**1,218.1**	Total incl. others	**956.0**

Main export destinations	% of total	Main origins of imports	% of total
United States	19.1	Japan	14.0
Hong Kong	15.1	South Korea	10.9
Japan	8.4	Taiwan	10.6
South Korea	4.6	United States	7.3
EU27	20.1	EU27	11.6

Balance of payments, reserves and debt, $bn

Visible exports fob	1,220.0	Change in reserves	465.6
Visible imports fob	-904.6	Level of reserves	
Trade balance	315.4	end Dec.	1,546.4
Invisibles inflows	205.2	No. months of import cover	17.0
Invisibles outflows	-187.4	Official gold holdings, m oz	19.3
Net transfers	38.6	Foreign debt	373.6
Current account balance	371.8	– as % of GDP	13
– as % of GDP	11.6	– as % of total exports	32
Capital balance	73.5	Debt service ratio	2
Overall balance	461.7		

Health and education

Health spending, % of GDP	4.6	Education spending, % of GDP	...
Doctors per 1,000 pop.	1.5	Enrolment, %: primary	88
Hospital beds per 1,000 pop.	2.4	secondary	77
Improved-water source access,		tertiary	...
% of pop.	77		

Society

No. of households	380.8m	Colour TVs per 100 households	95.3
Av. no. per household	3.5	Telephone lines per 100 pop.	27.5
Marriages per 1,000 pop.	5.8	Mobile telephone subscribers	
Divorces per 1,000 pop.	1.5	per 100 pop.	41.2
Cost of living, Feb. 2009		Computers per 100 pop.	5.7
New York = 100	91	Internet hosts per 1,000 pop.	10.5

Note: Data excludes Special Administrative Regions ie, Hong Kong and Macau.

COLOMBIA

Area	1,141,748 sq km	Capital	Bogota
Arable as % of total land	2	Currency	Colombian peso (peso)

People

Population	47.0m	Life expectancy: men	69.2 yrs
Pop. per sq km	41.2	women	76.7 yrs
Av. ann. growth		Adult literacy	92.7%
in pop. 2010–15	1.29%	Fertility rate (per woman)	2.3
Pop. under 15	29.2%	Urban population	74.2%
Pop. over 60	8.3%		per 1,000 pop.
No. of men per 100 women	97	Crude birth rate	20
Human Development Index	78.7	Crude death rate	5.5

The economy

GDP	432trn pesos	GDP per head	$4,720
GDP	$208bn	GDP per head in purchasing	
Av. ann. growth in real		power parity (USA=100)	18.8
GDP 2002–07	6.6%	Economic freedom index	62.3

Origins of GDP		Components of GDP	
	% of total		% of total
Agriculture	9.3	Private consumption	63.3
Industry, of which:	36.9	Public consumption	16.6
manufacturing	18.4	Investment	24.9
Services	53.8	Exports	16.9
		Imports	-21.0

Structure of employment

	% of total		% of labour force
Agriculture	21	Unemployed 2007	10.7
Industry	20	Av. ann. rate 1995–2007	14.0
Services	59		

Energy

	m TOE		
Total output	84.6	Net energy imports as %	
Total consumption	30.2	of energy use	-180
Consumption per head,			
kg oil equivalent	696		

Inflation and finance

Consumer price		av. ann. increase 2002–07	
inflation 2008	7.0%	Narrow money (M1)	16.2%
Av. ann. inflation 2003–08	5.5%	Broad money	17.3%
Money market rate, 2008	9.72%		

Exchange rates

	end 2008		December 2008
		Effective rates	2000 = 100
Peso per $	2,198	– nominal	97.10
Peso per SDR	3,386	– real	107.90
Peso per €	3,060		

Trade

Principal exports		Principal imports	
	$bn fob		*$bn cif*
Petroleum & products	7.3	Intermediate goods &	
Coal	3.5	raw materials	14.2
Coffee	1.7	Capital goods	11.9
Nickel	1.7	Consumer goods	6.8
Total incl. others	**30.0**	Total	**32.9**

Main export destinations		Main origins of imports	
	% of total		*% of total*
United States	30.4	United States	28.6
Venezuela	12.3	Brazil	8.6
Ecuador	5.4	Mexico	8.5
Peru	3.7	China	7.3

Balance of payments, reserves and debt, $bn

Visible exports fob	30.6	Change in reserves	5.5
Visible imports fob	-31.2	Level of reserves	
Trade balance	-0.6	end Dec.	21.0
Invisibles inflows	5.5	No. months of import cover	5.3
Invisibles outflows	-16.0	Official gold holdings, m oz	0.2
Net transfers	5.2	Foreign debt	45.0
Current account balance	-5.9	– as % of GDP	28
– as % of GDP	-2.8	– as % of total exports	133
Capital balance	10.3	Debt service ratio	22
Overall balance	4.7		

Health and education

Health spending, % of GDP	7.3	Education spending, % of GDP	4.9
Doctors per 1,000 pop.	1.6	Enrolment, %: primary	122
Hospital beds per 1,000 pop.	1.0	secondary	85
Improved-water source access,		tertiary	...
% of pop.	93		

Society

No. of households	12.7m	Colour TVs per 100 households	79.9
Av. no. per household	3.7	Telephone lines per 100 pop.	17.2
Marriages per 1,000 pop.	1.7	Mobile telephone subscribers	
Divorces per 1,000 pop.	0.2	per 100 pop.	73.5
Cost of living, Feb. 2009		Computers per 100 pop.	8.0
New York = 100	69	Internet hosts per 1,000 pop.	40.6

CÔTE D'IVOIRE

Area	322,463 sq km	Capital	Abidjan/Yamoussoukro
Arable as % of total land	11	Currency	CFA franc (CFAfr)

People

Population	18.8m	Life expectancy: men	56.0 yrs
Pop. per sq km	58.3	women	58.6 yrs
Av. ann. growth		Adult literacy	48.7%
in pop. 2010–15	2.31%	Fertility rate (per woman)	4.2
Pop. under 15	40.6%	Urban population	48.2%
Pop. over 60	6.0%		per 1,000 pop.
No. of men per 100 women	104	Crude birth rate	38
Human Development Index	43.1	Crude death rate	10.9

The economy

GDP	CFAfr9,487bn	GDP per head	$1,030
GDP	$19.8bn	GDP per head in purchasing	
Av. ann. growth in real		power parity (USA=100)	3.7
GDP 2002–2007	0.8%	Economic freedom index	55.0

Origins of GDP

Components of GDP

	% of total		% of total
Agriculture	24	Private consumption	77
Industry, of which:	25	Public consumption	8
manufacturing	18	Investment	9
Services	51	Exports	47
		Imports	-41

Structure of employment

	% of total		% of labour force
Agriculture	...	Unemployed 2007	...
Industry	...	Av. ann. rate 1995–2007	...
Services	...		

Energy

	m TOE		
Total output	9.3	Net energy imports as %	
Total consumption	7.3	of energy use	-28
Consumption per head,			
kg oil equivalent	385		

Inflation and finance

		av. ann. change 2002–07	
Consumer price			
inflation 2008	6.3%	Narrow money (M1)	2.5%
Av. ann. inflation 2003–08	3.2%	Broad money	3.5%
Money market rate, 2008	3.94%		

Exchange rates

	end 2008		December 2008
CFAfr per $	471.34	Effective rates	2000 = 100
CFAfr per SDR	725.98	– nominal	118.00
CFAfr per €	656.11	– real	128.70

Trade

Principal exports[a]

	$bn fob
Cocoa beans & products	3.0
Petroleum products	3.0
Timber	0.3
Coffee & products	0.2
Total incl. others	**8.5**

Principal imports[a]

	$bn cif
Capital equipment & raw materials	2.1
Fuel & lubricants	1.8
Foodstuffs	1.0
Total incl. others	**5.8**

Main export destinations

	% of total
Germany	9.8
Nigeria	9.3
Netherlands	8.5
France	7.4
United States	7.1

Main origins of imports

	% of total
Nigeria	29.5
France	16.8
China	6.9
Belgium	3.5
Venezuela	3.0

Balance of payments, reserves and debt, $bn

Visible exports fob	8.5	Change in reserves	0.7
Visible imports fob	-5.9	Level of reserves	
Trade balance	2.5	end Dec.	2.5
Invisibles inflows	1.2	No. months of import cover	3.2
Invisibles outflows	-3.5	Official gold holdings, m oz	0.0
Net transfers	-0.4	Foreign debt	13.9
Current account balance	-0.1	– as % of GDP	67
– as % of GDP	-0.7	– as % of total exports	123
Capital balance	0.4	Debt service ratio	5
Overall balance	0.3		

Health and education

Health spending, % of GDP	3.8	Education spending, % of GDP	...
Doctors per 1,000 pop.	0.1	Enrolment, %: primary	70
Hospital beds per 1,000 pop.	...	secondary	25
Improved-water source access,		tertiary	...
% of pop.	84		

Society

No. of households	3.6m	Colour TVs per 100 households	28.0
Av. no. per household	5.1	Telephone lines per 100 pop.	1.4
Marriages per 1,000 pop.	...	Mobile telephone subscribers	
Divorces per 1,000 pop.	...	per 100 pop.	36.6
Cost of living, Feb. 2009		Computers per 100 pop.	1.7
New York = 100	80	Internet hosts per 1,000 pop.	0.5

a 2006

CZECH REPUBLIC

Area	78,864 sq km	Capital	Prague
Arable as % of total land	39	Currency	Koruna (Kc)

People

Population	10.2m	Life expectancy: men	73.4 yrs
Pop. per sq km	129.3	women	79.5 yrs
Av. ann. growth		Adult literacy	...
in pop. 2010–15	-0.19%	Fertility rate (per woman)	1.5
Pop. under 15	14.1%	Urban population	73.5%
Pop. over 60	21.8%		per 1,000 pop.
No. of men per 100 women	96	Crude birth rate	11
Human Development Index	89.7	Crude death rate	10.8

The economy

GDP	Kc3,551bn	GDP per head	$16,930
GDP	$175bn	GDP per head in purchasing	
Av. ann. growth in real		power parity (USA=100)	53.0
GDP 2002–2007	6.0%	Economic freedom index	69.4

Origins of GDP		**Components of GDP**	
	% of total		% of total
Agriculture	2.4	Private consumption	46.9
Industry, of which:	38.9	Public consumption	20.3
manufacturing	33.1	Investment	26.9
Services	58.7	Exports	80.1
		Imports	-75.1

Structure of employment

	% of total		% of labour force
Agriculture	4	Unemployed 2007	5.3
Industry	38	Av. ann. rate 1995–2007	6.8
Services	58		

Energy

	m TOE		
Total output	33.4	Net energy imports as %	
Total consumption	46.1	of energy use	27
Consumption per head,			
kg oil equivalent	4,485		

Inflation and finance

Consumer price		av. ann. increase 2002-07	
inflation 2008	6.4%	Narrow money (M1)	14.1%
Av. ann. inflation 2003–08	3.3%	Broad money	9.4%
Money market rate, 2008	3.63%	Household saving rate, 2008	3.3%

Exchange rates

	end 2008		December 2008
Kc per $	19.35	Effective rates	2000 = 100
Kc per SDR	29.80	– nominal	140.60
Kc per €	26.94	– real	148.52

Trade

Principal exports		Principal imports	
	$bn fob		*$bn cif*
Machinery & transport equipment	66.5	Machinery & transport equipment	58.3
Semi-manufactures	24.8	Semi-manufactures	28.0
Chemicals	7.1	Raw materials & fuels	18.4
Raw materials & fuels	6.5	Chemicals	14.6
Total incl. others	**122.8**	Total incl. others	**141.6**

Main export destinations		Main origins of imports	
	% of total		*% of total*
Germany	30.9	Germany	31.9
Poland	8.8	Netherlands	6.7
Slovakia	6.0	Poland	6.3
United Kingdom	5.0	Slovakia	6.3
EU27	85.3	EU27	80.1

Balance of payments, reserves and debt, $bn

Visible exports fob	122.8	Change in reserves	3.5
Visible imports fob	-116.9	Level of reserves	
Trade balance	5.9	end Dec.	34.9
Invisibles inflows	24.2	No. months of import cover	2.8
Invisibles outflows	-32.4	Official gold holdings, m oz	0.4
Net transfers	-0.9	Foreign debt	74.7
Current account balance	-3.2	– as % of GDP	43
– as % of GDP	-1.9	– as % of total exports	51
Capital balance	5.9	Debt service ratio	10
Overall balance	0.9		

Health and education

Health spending, % of GDP	6.9	Education spending, % of GDP	4.6
Doctors per 1,000 pop.	3.6	Enrolment, %: primary	109
Hospital beds per 1,000 pop.	8.2	secondary	96
Improved-water source access, % of pop.	100	tertiary	55

Society

No. of households	3.8m	Colour TVs per 100 households	97.9
Av. no. per household	2.7	Telephone lines per 100 pop.	23.6
Marriages per 1,000 pop.	5.1	Mobile telephone subscribers	
Divorces per 1,000 pop.	3.3	per 100 pop.	124.9
Cost of living, Feb. 2009		Computers per 100 pop.	27.4
New York = 100	81	Internet hosts per 1,000 pop.	306.5

DENMARK

Area	43,075 sq km	Capital	Copenhagen
Arable as % of total land	53	Currency	Danish krone (DKr)

People

Population	5.5m	Life expectancy: men	76.0 yrs
Pop. per sq km	127.7	women	80.6 yrs
Av. ann. growth		Adult literacy	...
in pop. 2010–15	0.15%	Fertility rate (per woman)	1.9
Pop. under 15	18.2%	Urban population	86.4%
Pop. over 60	23.0%		per 1,000 pop.
No. of men per 100 women	98	Crude birth rate	12
Human Development Index	95.2	Crude death rate	10.3

The economy

GDP	DKr1,696bn	GDP per head	$57,050
GDP	$312bn	GDP per head in purchasing	
Av. ann. growth in real		power parity (USA=100)	79.2
GDP 2002–2007	2.1%	Economic freedom index	79.6

Origins of GDP		Components of GDP	
	% of total		% of total
Agriculture	1.2	Private consumption	49.0
Industry, of which:	26.5	Public consumption	26.0
manufacturing	...	Investment	22.9
Services	72.4	Exports	52.3
		Imports	-50.2

Structure of employment

	% of total		% of labour force
Agriculture	3	Unemployed 2007	4.0
Industry	24	Av. ann. rate 1995–2007	5.3
Services	73		

Energy

	m TOE		
Total output	29.6	Net energy imports as %	
Total consumption	20.9	of energy use	-41
Consumption per head,			
kg oil equivalent	3,850		

Inflation and finance

Consumer price		av. ann. increase 2002–07	
inflation 2008	3.4%	Narrow money (M1)	11.9%
Av. ann. inflation 2003–08	2.0%	Broad money	10.9%
Money market rate, 2008	4.88%	Household saving rate, 2008	-1.9%

Exchange rates

	end 2008		December 2008
DKr per $	5.29	Effective rates	2000 = 100
DKr per SDR	8.14	– nominal	107.50
DKr per €	7.36	– real	118.40

Trade

Principal exports	$bn fob	Principal imports	$bn cif
Machinery & transport equip.	27.9	Machinery & transport equip.	35.1
Food, drinks & tobacco	18.1	Food, drinks & tobacco	11.3
Chemicals & related products	13.6	Chemicals & related products	11.1
Minerals, fuels & lubricants	10.6	Minerals, fuels & lubricants	5.1
Total incl. others	**101.5**	Total incl. others	**97.9**

Main export destinations	% of total	Main origins of imports	% of total
Germany	17.7	Germany	22.2
Sweden	14.8	Sweden	14.7
United Kingdom	8.1	Netherlands	6.8
United States	6.2	Norway	6.1
Norway	5.8	China	5.4
EU27	70.3	EU27	73.0

Balance of payments, reserves and aid, $bn

Visible exports fob	100.4	Overall balance	-0.2
Visible imports fob	-100.8	Change in reserves	3.2
Trade balance	-0.4	Level of reserves	
Invisibles inflows	96.3	end Dec.	34.3
Invisibles outflows	-88.4	No. months of import cover	2.2
Net transfers	-5.1	Official gold holdings, m oz	2.1
Current account balance	2.4	Aid given	2.56
– as % of GDP	0.8	– as % of GDP	0.82
Capital balance	-4.8		

Health and education

Health spending, % of GDP	10.8	Education spending, % of GDP	8.3
Doctors per 1,000 pop.	3.5	Enrolment, %: primary	98
Hospital beds per 1,000 pop.	3.8	secondary	119
Improved-water source access,		tertiary	80
% of pop.	100		

Society

No. of households	2.5m	Colour TVs per 100 households	98.1
Av. no. per household	2.2	Telephone lines per 100 pop.	51.9
Marriages per 1,000 pop.	7.1	Mobile telephone subscribers	
Divorces per 1,000 pop.	3.0	per 100 pop.	114.5
Cost of living, Feb. 2009		Computers per 100 pop.	54.9
New York = 100	124	Internet hosts per 1,000 pop.	690.1

EGYPT

Area	1,000,250 sq km	Capital	Cairo
Arable as % of total land	3	Currency	Egyptian pound (£E)

People

Population	76.9m	Life expectancy:	men	68.3 yrs
Pop. per sq km	76.9		women	71.8 yrs
Av. ann. growth		Adult literacy		66.4%
in pop. 2010–15	1.66%	Fertility rate (per woman)		2.7
Pop. under 15	32.3%	Urban population		42.7%
Pop. over 60	7.3%			per 1,000 pop.
No. of men per 100 women	101	Crude birth rate		27
Human Development Index	71.6	Crude death rate		5.9

The economy

GDP	£E745bn	GDP per head	$1,730
GDP	$130bn	GDP per head in purchasing	
Av. ann. growth in real		power parity (USA=100)	11.7
GDP 2002–2007	5.7%	Economic freedom index	58.0

Origins of GDP		**Components of GDP**[a]	
	% of total		% of total
Agriculture	14.1	Private consumption	70.4
Industry, of which:	36.7	Public consumption	11.5
manufacturing	18.0	Investment	21.2
Services	49.2	Exports	31.5
		Imports	-34.8

Structure of employment

	% of total		% of labour force
Agriculture	30	Unemployed 2005	11.2
Industry	21	Av. ann. rate 1995–2005	9.9
Services	49		

Energy

	m TOE		
Total output	77.8	Net energy imports as %	
Total consumption	62.5	of energy use	-25
Consumption per head,			
kg oil equivalent	843		

Inflation and finance

		av. ann. increase 2002–07	
Consumer price			
inflation 2008	18.3%	Narrow money (M1)	14.9%
Av. ann. inflation 2003–08	10.2%	Broad money	16.6%
Treasury bill rate, 2008	9.47%		

Exchange rates

	end 2008		December 2008
			2000 = 100
£E per $	5.60	Effective rates	
£E per SDR	8.62	– nominal	...
£E per €	7.80	– real	...

Trade

Principal exports[a]		Principal imports[a]	
	$bn fob		*$bn fob*
Petroleum & products	11.3	Intermediate goods	12.5
Finished goods incl. textiles	9.2	Capital goods	11.1
Semi-finished products	2.0	Consumer goods	6.9
Iron & steel	0.5	Fuels	4.0
Total incl. others	**24.5**	**Total incl. others**	**45.2**

Main export destinations		Main origins of imports	
	% of total		*% of total*
United States	9.7	United States	11.6
Italy	9.5	China	9.7
Spain	7.6	Italy	6.4
Syria	5.5	Germany	6.3

Balance of payments, reserves and debt, $bn

Visible exports fob	24.5	Change in reserves	6.2
Visible imports fob	-39.4	Level of reserves	
Trade balance	-14.9	end Dec.	32.2
Invisibles inflows	23.2	No. months of import cover	7.0
Invisibles outflows	-16.3	Official gold holdings, m oz	2.4
Net transfers	8.3	Foreign debt	30.4
Current account balance	0.4	– as % of GDP	25
– as % of GDP	0.3	– as % of total exports	60
Capital balance	3.0	Debt service ratio	4
Overall balance	3.7		

Health and education

Health spending, % of GDP	6.3	Education spending, % of GDP	3.8
Doctors per 1,000 pop.	0.6	Enrolment, %: primary	103
Hospital beds per 1,000 pop.	2.2	secondary	88
Improved-water source access,		tertiary	35
% of pop.	98		

Society

No. of households	16.9m	Colour TVs per 100 households	83.4
Av. no. per household	4.4	Telephone lines per 100 pop.	14.9
Marriages per 1,000 pop.	6.3	Mobile telephone subscribers	
Divorces per 1,000 pop.	0.7	per 100 pop.	39.8
Cost of living, Feb. 2009		Computers per 100 pop.	4.9
New York = 100	67	Internet hosts per 1,000 pop.	2.3

a   Year ending June 30, 2007.

ESTONIA

Area	45,200 sq km	Capital	Tallinn
Arable as % of total land	14	Currency	Kroon (EEK)

People

Population	1.3m	Life expectancy: men		67.6 yrs
Pop. per sq km	28.8	women		78.5 yrs
Av. ann. growth		Adult literacy		99.8%
in pop. 2010–15	-0.03%	Fertility rate (per woman)		1.8
Pop. under 15	15.1%	Urban population		69.4%
Pop. over 60	22.4%			per 1,000 pop.
No. of men per 100 women	86	Crude birth rate		12
Human Development Index	87.1	Crude death rate		12.9

The economy

GDP	EEK239bn	GDP per head	$15,580
GDP	$20.9bn	GDP per head in purchasing	
Av. ann. growth in real		power parity (USA=100)	44.7
GDP 2002–2007	9.5%	Economic freedom index	76.4

Origins of GDP		**Components of GDP**	
	% of total		% of total
Agriculture	2.8	Private consumption	55.2
Industry, of which:	30.4	Public consumption	17.2
manufacturing	17.2	Investment	37.9
Services	66.8	Exports	74.4
		Imports	-85.3

Structure of employment

	% of total		% of labour force
Agriculture	5	Unemployed 2007	4.7
Industry	32	Av. ann. rate 1995–2007	9.6
Services	63		

Energy

	m TOE		
Total output	3.6	Net energy imports as %	
Total consumption	4.9	of energy use	27
Consumption per head,			
kg oil equivalent	3,638		

Inflation and finance

Consumer price		av. ann. increase 2002–07	
inflation 2008	10.4%	Narrow money (M1)	22.8%
Av. ann. inflation 2003–08	5.7%	Broad money	21.8%
Money market rate, 2008	6.66%		

Exchange rates

	end 2008		December 2008
		Effective rates	2000 = 100
EEK per $	11.11	– nominal	...
EEK per SDR	17.11	– real	...
EEK per €	15.47		

Trade

Principal exports		Principal imports	
	$bn fob		*$bn cif*
Machinery & equipment	2.3	Machinery & equipment	3.3
Mineral products	1.4	Mineral products	2.2
Wood & paper	1.4	Transport equipment	2.1
Non-precious metals & products	1.1	Chemicals	1.8
Foodstuffs	1.0	Non-precious metals & products	1.6
Total incl. others	**11.0**	Total incl. others	**15.6**

Main export destinations		Main origins of imports	
	% of total		*% of total*
Finland	17.9	Finland	15.8
Sweden	13.2	Germany	12.7
Latvia	11.4	Russia	10.1
Russia	8.8	Sweden	10.0
Lithuania	5.8	Latvia	7.5
EU27	70.2	EU27	78.6

Balance of payments, reserves and debt, $bn

Visible exports fob	11.1	Change in reserves	0.5
Visible imports fob	-14.8	Level of reserves	
Trade balance	-3.7	end Dec.	3.3
Invisibles inflows	5.9	No. months of import cover	1.9
Invisibles outflows	-6.2	Official gold holdings, m oz	0.0
Net transfers	0.2	Foreign debt[a]	11.3
Current account balance	-3.8	– as % of GDP[a]	102
– as % of GDP	-18.1	– as % of total exports[a]	115
Capital balance	0.1	Debt service ratio[a]	14
Overall balance	0.1		

Health and education

Health spending, % of GDP	5.2	Education spending, % of GDP	4.9
Doctors per 1,000 pop.	3.4	Enrolment, %: primary	96
Hospital beds per 1,000 pop.	5.7	secondary	100
Improved-water source access,		tertiary	65
% of pop.	100		

Society

No. of households	0.6m	Colour TVs per 100 households	96.4
Av. no. per household	2.4	Telephone lines per 100 pop.	37.1
Marriages per 1,000 pop.	4.6	Mobile telephone subscribers	
Divorces per 1,000 pop.	3.1	per 100 pop.	148.4
Cost of living, Feb. 2009		Computers per 100 pop.	52.2
New York = 100	...	Internet hosts per 1,000 pop.	504.7

a 2005

FINLAND

Area	338,145 sq km	Capital	Helsinki
Arable as % of total land	7	Currency	Euro (€)

People

Population	5.3m	Life expectancy: men	76.2 yrs
Pop. per sq km	15.7	women	83.0 yrs
Av. ann. growth		Adult literacy	...
in pop. 2010–15	0.32%	Fertility rate (per woman)	1.9
Pop. under 15	16.7%	Urban population	63.0%
Pop. over 60	24.0%		*per 1,000 pop.*
No. of men per 100 women	96	Crude birth rate	11
Human Development Index	95.4	Crude death rate	9.4

The economy

GDP	€179bn	GDP per head	$46,260
GDP	$245bn	GDP per head in purchasing	
Av. ann. growth in real		power parity (USA=100)	75.7
GDP 2002–2007	3.7%	Economic freedom index	74.5

Origins of GDP		**Components of GDP**	
	% of total		*% of total*
Agriculture	3.1	Private consumption	50.5
Industry, of which:	32.6	Public consumption	21.4
manuf., mining & utilities	...	Investment	23.0
Services	64.3	Exports	45.7
		Imports	-40.7

Structure of employment

	% of total		*% of labour force*
Agriculture	5	Unemployed 2007	6.8
Industry	25	Av. ann. rate 1995–2007	10.2
Services	70		

Energy

	m TOE		
Total output	18.0	Net energy imports as %	
Total consumption	37.4	of energy use	52
Consumption per head,			
kg oil equivalent	7,108		

Inflation and finance

		av. ann. increase 2002–07	
Consumer price			
inflation 2008	4.1%	Euro area:	
Av. ann. inflation 2003–08	1.9%	Narrow money (M1)	9.3%
Money market rate, 2008	4.63%	Broad money	8.4%
		Household saving rate, 2008	-2.7%

Exchange rates

	end 2008		*December 2008*
€ per $	0.72	Effective rates	*2000 = 100*
€ per SDR	1.11	– nominal	116.60
		– real	112.60

Trade

Principal exports	$bn fob	Principal imports	$bn cif
Machinery & transport equipment	39.1	Machinery & transport equipment	31.7
Raw materials	5.3	Minerals & fuels	11.5
Chemicals & related products	5.2	Raw materials	8.7
Mineral fuels & lubricants	5.0	Chemical & related products	8.1
Total incl. others	**90.1**	Total incl. others	**81.8**

Main export destinations	% of total	Main origins of imports	% of total
Germany	10.9	Germany	16.0
Sweden	10.7	Sweden	13.8
Russia	10.2	Russia	13.7
United States	6.4	Netherlands	6.8
United Kingdom	5.8	China	5.3
Netherlands	5.6	United Kingdom	5.0
EU27	56.8	EU27	64.1

Balance of payments, reserves and aid, $bn

Visible exports fob	90.2	Overall balance	0.3
Visible imports fob	-78.2	Change in reserves	0.9
Trade balance	12.0	Level of reserves	
Invisibles inflows	46.3	end Dec.	8.4
Invisibles outflows	-46.2	No. months of import cover	0.8
Net transfers	-1.9	Official gold holdings, m oz	1.6
Current account balance	10.1	Aid given	0.98
– as % of GDP	4.1	– as % of GDP	0.40
Capital balance	-16.9		

Health and education

Health spending, % of GDP	8.2	Education spending, % of GDP	6.1
Doctors per 1,000 pop.	3.3	Enrolment, %: primary	96
Hospital beds per 1,000 pop.	6.8	secondary	111
Improved-water source access,		tertiary	94
% of pop.	100		

Society

No. of households	2.4m	Colour TVs per 100 households	97.1
Av. no. per household	2.2	Telephone lines per 100 pop.	33.0
Marriages per 1,000 pop.	5.7	Mobile telephone subscribers	
Divorces per 1,000 pop.	2.5	per 100 pop.	115.2
Cost of living, Feb. 2009		Computers per 100 pop.	50.0
New York = 100	118	Internet hosts per 1,000 pop.	762.5

FRANCE

Area	543,965 sq km	Capital	Paris
Arable as % of total land	34	Currency	Euro (€)

People

Population	60.9m	Life expectancy: men	77.6 yrs
Pop. per sq km	112.0	women	84.7 yrs
Av. ann. growth		Adult literacy	...
in pop. 2010–15	0.40%	Fertility rate (per woman)	1.9
Pop. under 15	18.4%	Urban population	77.1%
Pop. over 60	22.7%		*per 1,000 pop.*
No. of men per 100 women	95	Crude birth rate	13
Human Development Index	95.5	Crude death rate	8.6

The economy

GDP	€1,892bn	GDP per head	$41,970
GDP	$2,590bn	GDP per head in purchasing	
Av. ann. growth in real		power parity (USA=100)	73.9
GDP 2002–2007	2.0%	Economic freedom index	63.3

Origins of GDP		**Components of GDP**	
	% of total		*% of total*
Agriculture	2.2	Private consumption	56.7
Industry, of which:	20.6	Public consumption	23.2
manufacturing	...	Investment	22.1
Services	77.2	Exports	26.6
		Imports	-28.5

Structure of employment

	% of total		*% of labour force*
Agriculture	4	Unemployed 2007	8.0
Industry	26	Av. ann. rate 1995–2007	10.3
Services	70		

Energy

	m TOE		
Total output	137.0	Net energy imports as %	
Total consumption	272.7	of energy use	50
Consumption per head,			
kg oil equivalent	4,444		

Inflation and finance

Consumer price		*av. ann. increase 2002–07*	
inflation 2008	2.8%	Euro area:	
Av. ann. inflation 2003–08	2.0%	Narrow money (M1)	9.3%
Treasury bill rate, 2008	3.62%	Broad money	8.4%
		Household saving rate, 2008	12.7%

Exchange rates

	end 2008		*December 2008*
€ per $	0.72	Effective rates	*2000 = 100*
€ per SDR	1.11	– nominal	113.60
		– real	107.90

Trade

Principal exports		Principal imports	
	$bn fob		*$bn cif*
Machinery & transport equip.	218.7	Machinery & transport equip.	217.3
Chemicals & related products	97.1	Mineral fuels & lubricants	84.2
Food, drink & tobacco	59.0	Chemicals & related products	83.0
Mineral fuels & lubricants	21.1	Food, drink & tobacco	45.6
Raw materials	14.6	Raw materials	17.2
Total incl. others	**542.5**	Total incl. others	**618.6**

Main export destinations		Main origins of imports	
	% of total		*% of total*
Germany	15.2	Germany	18.8
Spain	9.5	Belgium	11.3
Italy	9.1	Italy	8.4
United Kingdom	8.3	Spain	7.1
Belgium	7.5	Netherlands	6.9
United States	6.3	United Kingdom	5.6
EU27	64.8	EU27	68.8

Balance of payments, reserves and aid, $bn

Visible exports fob	546.0	Overall balance	-0.3
Visible imports fob	-600.9	Change in reserves	17.2
Trade balance	-54.9	Level of reserves	
Invisibles inflows	398.5	end Dec.	115.5
Invisibles outflows	-344.2	No. months of import cover	1.5
Net transfers	-30.7	Official gold holdings, m oz	83.7
Current account balance	-31.3	Aid given	9.88
– as % of GDP	-1.2	– as % of GDP	0.38
Capital balance	27.9		

Health and education

Health spending, % of GDP	11.0	Education spending, % of GDP	5.6
Doctors per 1,000 pop.	3.4	Enrolment, %: primary	110
Hospital beds per 1,000 pop.	7.3	secondary	113
Improved-water source access,		tertiary	56
% of pop.	100		

Society

No. of households	25.8m	Colour TVs per 100 households	95.4
Av. no. per household	2.4	Telephone lines per 100 pop.	56.5
Marriages per 1,000 pop.	4.0	Mobile telephone subscribers	
Divorces per 1,000 pop.	2.2	per 100 pop.	89.8
Cost of living, Feb. 2009		Computers per 100 pop.	65.2
New York = 100	132	Internet hosts per 1,000 pop.	224.1

GERMANY

Area	357,868 sq km	Capital	Berlin
Arable as % of total land	34	Currency	Euro (€)

People

Population	82.7m	Life expectancy: men	77.1 yrs
Pop. per sq km	231.0	women	82.4 yrs
Av. ann. growth		Adult literacy	...
in pop. 2010–15	-0.17%	Fertility rate (per woman)	1.3
Pop. under 15	13.5%	Urban population	73.5%
Pop. over 60	25.7%		per 1,000 pop.
No. of men per 100 women	96	Crude birth rate	9
Human Development Index	94.0	Crude death rate	10.3

The economy

GDP	€2,424bn	GDP per head	$40,320
GDP	$3,317bn	GDP per head in purchasing	
Av. ann. growth in real		power parity (USA=100)	75.5
GDP 2002–2007	1.5%	Economic freedom index	70.5

Origins of GDP		Components of GDP	
	% of total		% of total
Agriculture	0.9	Private consumption	56.7
Industry, of which:	30.4	Public consumption	18.0
manufacturing	...	Investment	18.3
Services	68.7	Exports	46.9
		Imports	-39.9

Structure of employment

	% of total		% of labour force
Agriculture	2	Unemployed 2007	8.6
Industry	28	Av. ann. rate 1995–2007	9.3
Services	70		

Energy

	m TOE		
Total output	136.8	Net energy imports as %	
Total consumption	348.6	of energy use	61
Consumption per head,			
kg oil equivalent	4,231		

Inflation and finance

Consumer price		av. ann. increase 2002–07	
inflation 2008	2.6%	Euro area:	
Av. ann. inflation 2003–08	2.0%	Narrow money (M1)	9.3%
Money market rate, 2008	3.82%	Broad money	8.4%
		Household saving rate, 2008	11.6%

Exchange rates

	end 2008		December 2008
€ per $	0.72	Effective rates	2000 = 100
€ per SDR	1.11	– nominal	115.70
		– real	90.80

Trade

Principal exports	$bn fob	Principal imports	$bn cif
Machinery & transport equip.	670.1	Machinery & transport equip.	397.0
Chemicals & related products	187.7	Chemicals & related products	137.5
Food, drink & tobacco	60.5	Mineral fuels & lubricants	115.9
Mineral fuels & lubricants	32.1	Food, drink & tobacco	70.5
Total incl. others	**1,327.3**	Total incl. others	**1,058.1**

Main export destinations	% of total	Main origins of imports	% of total
France	9.7	Netherlands	12.0
United States	7.5	France	8.6
United Kingdom	7.3	Belgium	7.8
Italy	6.7	China	6.2
Netherlands	6.4	Italy	5.8
Austria	5.4	United Kingdom	5.6
Belgium	5.3	United States	4.5
EU27	64.7	EU27	64.6

Balance of payments, reserves and aid, $bn

Visible exports fob	1,354.1	Overall balance	1.2
Visible imports fob	-1,075.4	Change in reserves	24.3
Trade balance	278.7	Level of reserves	
Invisibles inflows	535.1	end Dec.	135.9
Invisibles outflows	-519.4	No. months of import cover	1.0
Net transfers	-41.8	Official gold holdings, m oz	109.9
Current account balance	252.9	Aid given	12.29
– as % of GDP	7.8	– as % of GDP	0.37
Capital balance	-322.8		

Health and education

Health spending, % of GDP	10.6	Education spending, % of GDP	4.4
Doctors per 1,000 pop.	3.4	Enrolment, %: primary	104
Hospital beds per 1,000 pop.	8.3	secondary	100
Improved-water source access,		tertiary	46
% of pop.	100		

Society

No. of households	39.5m	Colour TVs per 100 households	97.9
Av. no. per household	2.1	Telephone lines per 100 pop.	64.7
Marriages per 1,000 pop.	4.9	Mobile telephone subscribers	
Divorces per 1,000 pop.	2.8	per 100 pop.	117.6
Cost of living, Feb. 2009		Computers per 100 pop.	65.6
New York = 100	104	Internet hosts per 1,000 pop.	281.8

GREECE

Area	131,957 sq km	Capital	Athens
Arable as % of total land	20	Currency	Euro (€)

People

Population	11.2m	Life expectancy: men	77.1 yrs
Pop. per sq km	84.9	women	81.3 yrs
Av. ann. growth		Adult literacy	97.1%
in pop. 2010–15	0.14%	Fertility rate (per woman)	1.4
Pop. under 15	14.2%	Urban population	60.7%
Pop. over 60	24.0%		per 1,000 pop.
No. of men per 100 women	98	Crude birth rate	10
Human Development Index	94.7	Crude death rate	10.2

The economy

GDP	€229bn	GDP per head	$28,000
GDP	$313bn	GDP per head in purchasing	
Av. ann. growth in real		power parity (USA=100)	62.5
GDP 2002–07	4.8%	Economic freedom index	60.8

Origins of GDP

	% of total
Agriculture	3.8
Industry, of which:	20.3
mining & manufacturing	...
Services	75.9

Components of GDP

	% of total
Private consumption	71.2
Public consumption	16.7
Investment	22.6
Exports	23.0
Imports	-33.5

Structure of employment

	% of total		% of labour force
Agriculture	12	Unemployed 2007	8.1
Industry	22	Av. ann. rate 1995–2007	10.0
Services	66		

Energy

	m TOE		
Total output	10.0	Net energy imports as %	
Total consumption	31.1	of energy use	68
Consumption per head,			
kg oil equivalent	2,792		

Inflation and finance

Consumer price			av. ann. increase 2002–07
inflation 2008	4.2%	Euro area:	
Av. ann. inflation 2003–08	3.4%	Narrow money (M1)	9.3%
Treasury bill rate, 2008	4.81%	Broad money	8.4%

Exchange rates

	end 2008		December 2008
€ per $	0.72	Effective rates	2000 = 100
€ per SDR	1.11	– nominal	115.50
		– real	138.50

Trade

Principal exports		Principal imports	
	$bn fob		*$bn cif*
Food, drink & tobacco	4.2	Machinery & transport equip.	23.0
Chemical & related products	3.3	Mineral fuels & lubricants	11.7
Machinery & transport equip.	3.2	Chemicals & related products	10.8
Mineral fuels & lubricants	2.9	Food, drink & tobacco	8.0
Total incl. others	**23.6**	Total incl. others	**76.2**

Main export destinations		Main origins of imports	
	% of total		*% of total*
Germany	11.4	Germany	12.8
Italy	10.6	Italy	11.6
Bulgaria	6.4	Russia	5.7
Romania	6.4	South Korea	5.5
United Kingdom	6.4	China	5.1
EU27	65.0	EU27	64.6

Balance of payments, reserves and debt, $bn

Visible exports fob	24.0	Overall balance	0.5
Visible imports fob	-81.0	Change in reserves	0.8
Trade balance	-57.1	Level of reserves	
Invisibles inflows	49.4	end Dec.	3.6
Invisibles outflows	-39.1	No. months of import cover	0.3
Net transfers	2.1	Official gold holdings, m oz	3.6
Current account balance	-44.6	Aid given	0.50
– as % of GDP	-14.2	– as % of GDP	0.16
Capital balance	44.0		

Health and education

Health spending, % of GDP	9.5	Education spending, % of GDP	3.5
Doctors per 1,000 pop.	5.0	Enrolment, %: primary	100
Hospital beds per 1,000 pop.	4.8	secondary	102
Improved-water source access,		tertiary	91
% of pop.	...		

Society

No. of households	3.9m	Colour TVs per 100 households	99.6
Av. no. per household	2.9	Telephone lines per 100 pop.	53.9
Marriages per 1,000 pop.	5.3	Mobile telephone subscribers	
Divorces per 1,000 pop.	1.2	per 100 pop.	110.3
Cost of living, Feb. 2009		Computers per 100 pop.	9.4
New York = 100	83	Internet hosts per 1,000 pop.	202.1

HONG KONG

Area	1,075 sq km	Capital	Victoria
Arable as % of total land	5	Currency	Hong Kong dollar (HK$)

People

Population	7.2m	Life expectancy: men	79.4 yrs
Pop. per sq km	6,697.7	women	85.1 yrs
Av. ann. growth		Adult literacy	...
in pop. 2010–15	0.91%	Fertility rate (per woman)	1.0
Pop. under 15	12.0%	Urban population	100.0%
Pop. over 60	17.7%		per 1,000 pop.
No. of men per 100 women	90	Crude birth rate	10
Human Development Index	94.2	Crude death rate	6.1

The economy

GDP	HK$1,616bn	GDP per head	$29,910
GDP	$207bn	GDP per head in purchasing	
Av. ann. growth in real		power parity (USA=100)	92.8
GDP 2002–07	7.2%	Economic freedom index	90.0

Origins of GDP		**Components of GDP**	
	% of total		% of total
Agriculture	0.1	Private consumption	60.2
Industry, of which:	7.6	Public consumption	8.1
manufacturing	2.5	Investment	20.9
Services	92.4	Exports	208.0
		Imports	-197.2

Structure of employment

	% of total		% of labour force
Agriculture	0	Unemployed 2007	4.0
Industry	15	Av. ann. rate 1995–2007	5.1
Services	85		

Energy

	m TOE		
Total output	0.0	Net energy imports as %	
Total consumption	18.2	of energy use	100
Consumption per head,			
kg oil equivalent	2,653		

Inflation and finance

Consumer price		av. ann. increase 2002-07	
inflation 2008	4.3%	Narrow money (M1)	10.7%
Av. ann. inflation 2003–08	1.8%	Broad money	10.3%
Money market rate, 2008	0.23%		

Exchange rates

	end 2008		December 2008
HK$ per $	7.75	Effective rates	2000 = 100
HK$ per SDR	11.94	– nominal	...
HK$ per €	10.79	– real	...

Trade

Principal exports[a]

	$bn fob
Clothing	5.0
Jewellery & related products	1.1
Office machinery	1.0
Telecommunications equipment	1.0
Textiles, yarns & related products	0.5
Total incl. others	**14.0**

Principal imports[a]

	$bn cif
Raw materials & semi-manufactures	35.4
Capital goods	21.1
Consumer goods	18.8
Fuel	10.8
Food	7.7
Total incl. others	**93.8**

Main export destinations

	% of total
China	48.7
United States	13.7
Japan	4.5
Germany	3.0

Main origins of imports

	% of total
China	46.3
Japan	10.0
Taiwan	7.2
Singapore	6.8

Balance of payments, reserves and debt, $bn

Visible exports fob	346.0	Change in reserves	19.5
Visible imports fob	-365.7	Level of reserves	
Trade balance	-19.7	end Dec.	152.7
Invisibles inflows	198.3	No. months of import cover	3.6
Invisibles outflows	-150.3	Official gold holdings, m oz	0.1
Net transfers	-2.6	Foreign debt[b]	72.3
Current account balance	25.7	– as % of GDP[b]	41
– as % of GDP	12.4	– as % of total exports[b]	17
Capital balance	-18.5	Debt service ratio[b]	2
Overall balance	14.7		

Health and education

Health spending, % of GDP	...	Education spending, % of GDP	3.5
Doctors per 1,000 pop.	1.4	Enrolment, %: primary	89
Hospital beds per 1,000 pop.	...	secondary	86
Improved-water source access, % of pop.	...	tertiary	33

Society

No. of households	2.2m	Colour TVs per 100 households	99.5
Av. no. per household	3.2	Telephone lines per 100 pop.	57.2
Marriages per 1,000 pop.	6.0	Mobile telephone subscribers	
Divorces per 1,000 pop.	2.5	per 100 pop.	149.2
Cost of living, Feb. 2009		Computers per 100 pop.	68.6
New York = 100	110	Internet hosts per 1,000 pop.	113.1

a Domestic, excluding re-exports.
b 2005
Note: Hong Kong became a Special Administrative Region of China on July 1 1997.

HUNGARY

Area	93,030 sq km	Capital	Budapest
Arable as % of total land	51	Currency	Forint (Ft)

People

Population	10.0m	Life expectancy: men	69.2 yrs
Pop. per sq km	107.5	women	77.4 yrs
Av. ann. growth		Adult literacy	98.9
in pop. 2010–15	-0.20%	Fertility rate (per woman)	1.4
Pop. under 15	14.8%	Urban population	67.1%
Pop. over 60	22.1%		per 1,000 pop.
No. of men per 100 women	90	Crude birth rate	10
Human Development Index	87.7	Crude death rate	13.4

The economy

GDP	Ft25,419bn	GDP per head	$13,770
GDP	$138bn	GDP per head in purchasing	
Av. ann. growth in real		power parity (USA=100)	41.1
GDP 2002–07	3.9%	Economic freedom index	66.8

Origins of GDP		**Components of GDP**	
	% of total		% of total
Agriculture	2.0	Private consumption	64.9
Industry, of which:	37.2	Public consumption	9.7
manufacturing	14.6	Investment	22.5
Services	60.8	Exports	80.4
		Imports	-78.8

Structure of employment

	% of total		% of labour force
Agriculture	5	Unemployed 2007	7.4
Industry	32	Av. ann. rate 1995–2007	7.3
Services	63		

Energy

	m TOE		
Total output	10.3	Net energy imports as %	
Total consumption	27.6	of energy use	63
Consumption per head,			
kg oil equivalent	2,740		

Inflation and finance

Consumer price			av. ann. increase 2002–07
inflation 2008	6.1%	Narrow money (M1)	14.0%
Av. ann. inflation 2003–08	5.6%	Broad money	11.6%
Treasury bill rate, 2008	8.90%		

Exchange rates

	end 2008		December 2008
Ft per $	187.91	Effective rates	2000 = 100
Ft per SDR	289.43	– nominal	142.80
Ft per €	261.57	– real	132.40

Trade

Principal exports		Principal imports	
	$bn fob		*$bn cif*
Machinery & equipment	58.5	Machinery & equipment	49.2
Other manufactures	25.0	Other manufactures	30.4
Food, drink & tobacco	5.8	Fuels	9.1
Raw materials	1.8	Food, drink & tobacco	4.0
Total incl. others	**94.5**	Total incl. others	**94.6**

Main export destinations		Main origins of imports	
	% of total		*% of total*
Germany	28.2	Germany	26.8
Italy	5.6	China	7.8
France	4.7	Russia	6.9
Slovakia	4.7	Austria	6.1
EU27	79.0	EU27	69.5

Balance of payments, reserves and debt, $bn

Visible exports fob	93.9	Change in reserves	2.5
Visible imports fob	-93.4	Level of reserves	
Trade balance	0.5	end Dec.	24.1
Invisibles inflows	28.6	No. months of import cover	2.2
Invisibles outflows	-37.0	Official gold holdings, m oz	0.1
Net transfers	-0.7	Foreign debt[a]	107.7
Current account balance	-8.6	– as % of GDP[a]	100
– as % of GDP	-6.2	– as % of total exports[a]	127
Capital balance	11.4	Debt service ratio[a]	33
Overall balance	0.2	Aid given	0.10
		% of GDP	0.07

Health and education

Health spending, % of GDP	8.3	Education spending, % of GDP	5.4
Doctors per 1,000 pop.	3.1	Enrolment, %: primary	97
Hospital beds per 1,000 pop.	7.1	secondary	96
Improved-water source access,		tertiary	69
% of pop.	99		

Society

No. of households	3.7m	Colour TVs per 100 households	97.9
Av. no. per household	2.7	Telephone lines per 100 pop.	32.4
Marriages per 1,000 pop.	4.4	Mobile telephone subscribers	
Divorces per 1,000 pop.	2.4	per 100 pop.	109.9
Cost of living, Feb. 2009		Computers per 100 pop.	25.6
New York = 100	63	Internet hosts per 1,000 pop.	216.8

a 2006

INDIA

Area	3,287,263 sq km	Capital	New Delhi
Arable as % of total land	54	Currency	Indian rupee (Rs)

People

Population	1,135.6m	Life expectancy: men	62.1 yrs
Pop. per sq km	345.5	women	65.0 yrs
Av. ann. growth		Adult literacy	66.0%
in pop. 2010–15	1.27%	Fertility rate (per woman)	2.5
Pop. under 15	31.3%	Urban population	29.2%
Pop. over 60	7.4%		per 1,000 pop.
No. of men per 100 women	107	Crude birth rate	24
Human Development Index	60.9	Crude death rate	8.5

The economy

GDP	Rs47,234bn	GDP per head	$1,050
GDP	$1,177bn	GDP per head in purchasing	
Av. ann. growth in real		power parity (USA=100)	6.0
GDP 2002–2007	10.2%	Economic freedom index	54.4

Origins of GDP[a]

	% of total
Agriculture	18.1
Industry, of which:	29.5
manufacturing	16.3
Services	52.4

Components of GDP[a]

	% of total
Private consumption	55.0
Public consumption	10.1
Investment	37.6
Exports	21.2
Imports	-24.7

Structure of employment

	% of total		% of labour force
Agriculture	...	Unemployed 2004	5.0
Industry	...	Av. ann. rate 1995–2004	3.3
Services	...		

Energy

	m TOE		
Total output	435.6	Net energy imports as %	
Total consumption	565.8	of energy use	23
Consumption per head,			
kg oil equivalent	510		

Inflation and finance

		av. ann. increase 2002–07	
Consumer price			
inflation 2008	8.3%	Narrow money (M1)	18.0%
Av. ann. inflation 2003–08	5.7%	Broad money	17.8%
Treasury bill rate, 2008	9.54%		

Exchange rates

	end 2008		December 2008
			2000 = 100
Rs per $	48.46	Effective rates	
Rs per SDR	74.63	– nominal	...
Rs per €	67.46	– real	...

Trade

Principal exports[a]

	$bn fob
Engineering goods	36.7
Petroleum & products	24.9
Gems & jewellery	19.7
Textiles	19.0
Agricultural goods	18.1
Total incl. others	**159.0**

Principal imports[a]

	$bn cif
Petroleum & products	79.6
Electronic goods	20.3
Machinery	19.7
Gold & silver	17.8
Gems	8.0
Total incl. others	**239.7**

Main export destinations

	% of total
United States	14.4
United Arab Emirates	8.4
China	7.9
United Kingdom	4.1

Main origins of imports

	% of total
China	10.8
United States	8.1
Germany	4.6
Singapore	4.6

Balance of payments, reserves and debt, $bn

Visible exports fob	149.7	Change in reserves	98.5
Visible imports fob	-231.2	Level of reserves	
Trade balance	-81.5	end Dec.	276.6
Invisibles inflows	99.4	No. months of import cover	11.1
Invisibles outflows	-68.0	Official gold holdings, m oz	11.5
Net transfers	36.3	Foreign debt	221.0
Current account balance	-13.8	– as % of GDP	20
– as % of GDP	-1.2	– as % of total exports	82
Capital balance	99.7	Debt service ratio[b]	8
Overall balance	87.6		

Health and education

Health spending, % of GDP	3.6	Education spending, % of GDP	3.2
Doctors per 1,000 pop.	0.6	Enrolment, %: primary	130
Hospital beds per 1,000 pop.	0.9	secondary	55
Improved-water source access,		tertiary	...
% of pop.	86		

Society

No. of households	213.5m	Colour TVs per 100 households	47.4
Av. no. per household	5.3	Telephone lines per 100 pop.	3.4
Marriages per 1,000 pop.	...	Mobile telephone subscribers	
Divorces per 1,000 pop.	...	per 100 pop.	20.0
Cost of living, Feb. 2009		Computers per 100 pop.	3.3
New York = 100	45	Internet hosts per 1,000 pop.	2.7

a Year ending March 31, 2008.
b 2006

INDONESIA

Area	1,904,443 sq km	Capital	Jakarta
Arable as % of total land	13	Currency	Rupiah (Rp)

People

Population	228.1m	Life expectancy: men	68.7 yrs
Pop. per sq km	119.8	women	72.7 yrs
Av. ann. growth		Adult literacy	92.0%
in pop. 2010–15	0.98%	Fertility rate (per woman)	2.0
Pop. under 15	27.0%	Urban population	50.4%
Pop. over 60	8.8%		per 1,000 pop.
No. of men per 100 women	100	Crude birth rate	21
Human Development Index	72.6	Crude death rate	6.3

The economy

GDP	Rp3,957trn	GDP per head	$1,920
GDP	$433bn	GDP per head in purchasing	
Av. ann. growth in real		power parity (USA=100)	8.1
GDP 2002–07	6.1%	Economic freedom index	53.4

Origins of GDP		**Components of GDP**	
	% of total		% of total
Agriculture	13.7	Private consumption	63.6
Industry, of which:	46.8	Public consumption	8.3
manufacturing	27.1	Investment	24.9
Services	39.5	Exports	29.4
		Imports	-25.4

Structure of employment

	% of total		% of labour force
Agriculture	45	Unemployed 2007	9.1
Industry	18	Av. ann. rate 1995–2007	7.4
Services	37		

Energy

	m TOE		
Total output	307.7	Net energy imports as %	
Total consumption	179.1	of energy use	-72
Consumption per head,			
kg oil equivalent	803		

Inflation and finance

		av. ann. increase 2002–07	
Consumer price			
inflation 2008	10.3%	Narrow money (M1)	19.8%
Av. ann. inflation 2003–08	9.3%	Broad money	13.4%
Money market rate, 2008	8.48%		

Exchange rates

	end 2008		December 2008
Rp per $	10,950	Effective rates	2000 = 100
Rp per SDR	16,866	– nominal	...
Rp per €	15,242	– real	...

Trade

Principal exports		Principal imports	
	$bn fob		*$bn cif*
Garments & textiles	9.8	Intermediate goods	57.4
Natural gas	9.8	Capital goods	11.2
Petroleum & products	9.2	Consumer goods	5.9
Total incl. others	**114.1**	Total incl. others	**74.5**

Main export destinations		Main origins of imports	
	% of total		*% of total*
Japan	20.6	Singapore	43.5
United States	12.1	China	18.8
Singapore	11.7	Japan	13.2
China	9.7	South Korea	8.6

Balance of payments, reserves and debt, $bn

Visible exports fob	118.0	Change in reserves	14.3
Visible imports fob	-82.3	Level of reserves	
Trade balance	32.8	end Dec.	56.9
Invisibles inflows	15.9	No. months of import cover	5.3
Invisibles outflows	-43.3	Official gold holdings, m oz	2.4
Net transfers	4.9	Foreign debt	140.8
Current account balance	10.3	– as % of GDP	43
– as % of GDP	2.4	– as % of total exports	120
Capital balance	3.5	Debt service ratio	11
Overall balance	12.7		

Health and education

Health spending, % of GDP	2.5	Education spending, % of GDP	3.5
Doctors per 1,000 pop.	0.1	Enrolment, %: primary	121
Hospital beds per 1,000 pop.	0.6	secondary	73
Improved-water source access,		tertiary	...
% of pop.	77		

Society

No. of households	60.6m	Colour TVs per 100 households	82.8
Av. no. per household	3.8	Telephone lines per 100 pop.	7.7
Marriages per 1,000 pop.	7.0	Mobile telephone subscribers	
Divorces per 1,000 pop.	0.8	per 100 pop.	35.3
Cost of living, Feb. 2009		Computers per 100 pop.	2.0
New York = 100	62	Internet hosts per 1,000 pop.	3.4

IRAN

Area	1,648,000 sq km	Capital	Tehran
Arable as % of total land	10	Currency	Rial (IR)

People

Population	71.2m	Life expectancy: men	70.0 yrs
Pop. per sq km	43.2	women	72.7 yrs
Av. ann. growth		Adult literacy	82.3%
in pop. 2010–15	1.13%	Fertility rate (per woman)	1.7
Pop. under 15	24.1%	Urban population	68.0%
Pop. over 60	7.1%		per 1,000 pop.
No. of men per 100 women	103	Crude birth rate	20
Human Development Index	77.7	Crude death rate	5.7

The economy

GDP	IR2,655trn	GDP per head	$4,030
GDP	$286bn	GDP per head in purchasing	
Av. ann. growth in real		power parity (USA=100)	24.0
GDP 2002–07	6.9%	Economic freedom index	44.6

Origins of GDP		Components of GDP	
	% of total		% of total
Agriculture	10.2	Private consumption	45.0
Industry, of which:	41.3	Public consumption	11.2
manufacturing	11.3	Investment	28.5
Services	48.5	Exports	32.2
		Imports	-21.5

Structure of employment

	% of total		% of labour force
Agriculture	25	Unemployed 2007	10.5
Industry	30	Av. ann. rate 2000–2007	12.5
Services	45		

Energy

	m TOE		
Total output	309.3	Net energy imports as %	
Total consumption	170.9	of energy use	-81
Consumption per head,			
kg oil equivalent	2,438		

Inflation and finance

		av. ann. increase 2002–07	
Consumer price			
inflation 2008	25.5%	Narrow money (M1)	22.5%
Av. ann. inflation 2003–08	16.5%	Broad money	25.9%
Deposit rate, 2007	11.60%		

Exchange rates

	end 2008		December 2008
IR per $	9,825	Effective rates	2000 = 100
IR per SDR	15,133	– nominal	70.15
IR per €	13,676	– real	188.75

Trade

Principal exports[a]

	$bn fob
Oil & gas	62.5
Chemicals & petrochemicals	2.9
Total incl. others	**76.1**

Principal imports[a]

	$bn cif
Raw materials &	
intermediate goods	27.3
Capital goods	8.2
Consumer goods	6.2
Total incl. others	**41.7**

Main export destinations

	% of total
China	14.5
Japan	13.3
Turkey	7.7
Italy	6.6
South Korea	6.2

Main origins of imports

	% of total
China	14.3
Germany	9.8
United Arab Emirates	8.4
South Korea	5.9
Russia	4.5

Balance of payments[b], reserves and debt, $bn

Visible exports fob	97.4	Change in reserves	...
Visible imports fob	-56.6	Level of reserves	
Trade balance	40.8	end Dec.	...
Net invisibles	-7.2	No. months of import cover	...
Net transfers	0.5	Official gold holdings, m oz	...
Current account balance	34.1	Foreign debt	20.1
– as % of GDP	11.9	– as % of GDP	8
Capital balance	-12.4	– as % of total exports	22
Overall balance	15.1	Debt service ratio[c]	4

Health and education

Health spending, % of GDP	6.8	Education spending, % of GDP	5.5
Doctors per 1,000 pop.	0.9	Enrolment, %: primary	108
Hospital beds per 1,000 pop.	1.7	secondary	81
Improved-water source access,		tertiary	27
% of pop.	94		

Society

No. of households	13.4m	Colour TVs per 100 households	...
Av. no. per household	5.3	Telephone lines per 100 pop.	33.5
Marriages per 1,000 pop.	11.0	Mobile telephone subscribers	
Divorces per 1,000 pop.	1.3	per 100 pop.	41.8
Cost of living, Feb. 2009		Computers per 100 pop.	10.6
New York = 100	43	Internet hosts per 1,000 pop.	0.2

a Iranian year ending March 20, 2007.
b Iranian year ending March 20, 2008.
c 2006

IRELAND

Area	70,282 sq km	Capital	Dublin
Arable as % of total land	18	Currency	Euro (€)

People

Population	4.3m	Life expectancy: men	77.5 yrs
Pop. per sq km	61.2	women	82.3 yrs
Av. ann. growth		Adult literacy	...
in pop. 2010–15	1.25%	Fertility rate (per woman)	1.9
Pop. under 15	20.7%	Urban population	61.0%
Pop. over 60	15.9%		per 1,000 pop.
No. of men per 100 women	100	Crude birth rate	16
Human Development Index	96.0	Crude death rate	6.4

The economy

GDP	€189bn	GDP per head	$59,320
GDP	$259bn	GDP per head in purchasing	
Av. ann. growth in real		power parity (USA=100)	97.9
GDP 2002–07	6.1%	Economic freedom index	82.2

Origins of GDP		Components of GDP	
	% of total		% of total
Agriculture	2	Private consumption	48.0
Industry, of which:	35	Public consumption	14.0
manufacturing	23	Investment	26.3
Services	63	Exports	79.4
		Imports	-68.7

Structure of employment

	% of total		% of labour force
Agriculture	6	Unemployed 2007	4.6
Industry	28	Av. ann. rate 1995–2007	6.3
Services	66		

Energy

	m TOE		
Total output	1.6	Net energy imports as %	
Total consumption	15.5	of energy use	90
Consumption per head,			
kg oil equivalent	3,628		

Inflation and finance

Consumer price		av. ann. increase 2002–07	
inflation 2008	4.1%	Euro area:	
Av. ann. inflation 2003–08	3.5%	Narrow money (M1)	9.3%
Money market rate, 2008	2.99%	Broad money	8.4%
		Household saving rate, 2008	10.6%

Exchange rates

	end 2008		December 2008
			2000 = 100
€ per $	0.72	Effective rates	
€ per SDR	1.11	– nominal	123.76
		– real	138.60

Trade

Principal exports

	$bn fob
Chemicals & related products	60.1
Machinery & transport equipment	29.8
Food, drink & tobacco	12.1
Raw materials	2.4
Total incl. others	**122.3**

Principal imports

	$bn cif
Machinery & transport equipment	32.9
Chemicals	11.3
Food, drink & tobacco	7.6
Minerals, fuels & lubricants	7.4
Total incl. others	**86.6**

Main export destinations

	% of total
United Kingdom	18.5
United States	17.6
Belgium	14.6
Germany	7.3
France	5.8
Netherlands	3.8
EU27	63.5

Main origins of imports

	% of total
United Kingdom	36.1
United States	10.8
Germany	9.1
Netherlands	4.7
France	4.0
China	3.2
EU27	70.0

Balance of payments, reserves and aid, $bn

Visible exports fob	115.5	Overall balance	0.0
Visible imports fob	-84.2	Change in reserves	0.1
Trade balance	31.3	Level of reserves	
Invisibles inflows	193.0	end Dec.	0.9
Invisibles outflows	-235.3	No. months of import cover	0.0
Net transfers	-1.7	Official gold holdings, m oz	0.2
Current account balance	-12.7	Aid given	1.19
– as % of GDP	-4.9	– as % of GDP	0.46
Capital balance	14.2		

Health and education

Health spending, % of GDP	7.5	Education spending, % of GDP	4.9
Doctors per 1,000 pop.	2.9	Enrolment, %: primary	98
Hospital beds per 1,000 pop.	5.6	secondary	113
Improved-water source access, % of pop.	...	tertiary	61

Society

No. of households	1.4m	Colour TVs per 100 households	99.6
Av. no. per household	3.0	Telephone lines per 100 pop.	52.0
Marriages per 1,000 pop.	4.9	Mobile telephone subscribers	
Divorces per 1,000 pop.	0.8	per 100 pop.	115.9
Cost of living, Feb. 2009		Computers per 100 pop.	58.2
New York = 100	108	Internet hosts per 1,000 pop.	291.6

ISRAEL

Area	20,770 sq km	Capital	Jerusalem[a]
Arable as % of total land	15	Currency	New Shekel (NIS)

People

Population	7.0m	Life expectancy: men	78.6 yrs
Pop. per sq km	337.0	women	82.8 yrs
Av. ann. growth		Adult literacy	97.1%
in pop. 2010–15	1.43%	Fertility rate (per woman)	2.6
Pop. under 15	27.7%	Urban population	91.7%
Pop. over 60	14.2%		per 1,000 pop.
No. of men per 100 women	98	Crude birth rate	21
Human Development Index	93.0	Crude death rate	5.5

The economy

GDP	NIS674bn	GDP per head	$22,840
GDP	$164bn	GDP per head in purchasing	
Av. ann. growth in real		power parity (USA=100)	57.7
GDP 2002–2007	4.9%	Economic freedom index	67.6

Origins of GDP[b]		Components of GDP	
	% of total		% of total
Agriculture	2.8	Private consumption	56.4
Industry, of which:	32.0	Public consumption	25.2
manufacturing	22.1	Investment	20.1
Services	63.7	Exports	43.2
		Imports	-44.9

Structure of employment

	% of total		% of labour force
Agriculture	2	Unemployed 2007	7.3
Industry	21	Av. ann. rate 1995–2007	8.6
Services	77		

Energy

	m TOE		
Total output	2.7	Net energy imports as %	
Total consumption	21.3	of energy use	88
Consumption per head,			
kg oil equivalent	3,017		

Inflation and finance

		av. ann. increase 2002–06	
Consumer price			
inflation 2008	4.6%	Narrow money (M1)	14.1%
Av. ann. inflation 2003–08	1.6%	Broad money	4.9%
Treasury bill rate, 2008	4.07%		

Exchange rates

	end 2008		December 2008
NIS per $	3.80	Effective rates	2000 = 100
NIS per SDR	5.86	– nominal	92.43
NIS per €	5.29	– real	88.87

Trade

Principal exports		Principal imports	
	$bn fob		$bn fob
Diamonds	14.6	Diamonds	9.6
Chemicals	9.6	Fuel	8.9
Communications, medical &		Machinery & equipment	6.5
scientific equipment	8.0	Chemicals	3.6
Electronics	2.5		
Total incl. others	**45.9**	Total incl. others	**56.1**

Main export destinations		Main origins of imports	
	% of total		% of total
United States	41.1	United States	14.0
Belgium	8.9	Belgium	7.9
Hong Kong	6.8	China	6.2
United Kingdom	4.3	Germany	6.2
Germany	4.2	Switzerland	5.1

Balance of payments, reserves and debt, $bn

Visible exports fob	49.8	Change in reserves	-0.6
Visible imports fob	-55.8	Level of reserves	
Trade balance	-6.0	end Dec.	28.5
Invisibles inflows	31.6	No. months of import cover	4.1
Invisibles outflows	-28.4	Official gold holdings, m oz	0.0
Net transfers	7.3	Foreign debt	89.1
Current account balance	4.5	– as % of GDP	54
– as % of GDP	2.8	– as % of total exports	105
Capital balance	-1.1	Debt service ratio	13
Overall balance	0.4	Aid given	0.11
		% of GDP	0.07

Health and education

Health spending, % of GDP	8.0	Education spending, % of GDP	6.2
Doctors per 1,000 pop.	3.7	Enrolment, %: primary	96
Hospital beds per 1,000 pop.	6.0	secondary	92
Improved-water source access,		tertiary	60
% of pop.	100		

Society

No. of households	2.1m	Colour TVs per 100 households	94.7
Av. no. per household	3.4	Telephone lines per 100 pop.	44.4
Marriages per 1,000 pop.	5.1	Mobile telephone subscribers	
Divorces per 1,000 pop.	1.6	per 100 pop.	128.5
Cost of living, Feb. 2009		Computers per 100 pop.	...
New York = 100	96	Internet hosts per 1,000 pop.	217.5

a Sovereignty over the city is disputed.
b 2006

ITALY

Area	301,245 sq km	Capital	Rome
Arable as % of total land	26	Currency	Euro (€)

People

Population	58.2m	Life expectancy: men	78.1 yrs
Pop. per sq km	193.2	women	84.1 yrs
Av. ann. growth		Adult literacy	98.9%
in pop. 2010–15	0.17%	Fertility rate (per woman)	1.4
Pop. under 15	14.2%	Urban population	67.9%
Pop. over 60	26.4%		per 1,000 pop.
No. of men per 100 women	95	Crude birth rate	9
Human Development Index	94.5	Crude death rate	9.9

The economy

GDP	€1,536bn	GDP per head	$35,400
GDP	$2,102bn	GDP per head in purchasing	
Av. ann. growth in real		power parity (USA=100)	66.6
GDP 2002–2007	1.2%	Economic freedom index	61.4

Origins of GDP		Components of GDP	
	% of total		% of total
Agriculture	2.0	Private consumption	58.4
Industry, of which:	27.0	Public consumption	20.1
manufacturing	...	Investment	21.8
Services	70.9	Exports	29.0
		Imports	-29.2

Structure of employment

	% of total		% of labour force
Agriculture	4	Unemployed 2007	6.1
Industry	29	Av. ann. rate 1995–2007	9.5
Services	67		

Energy

	m TOE		
Total output	27.4	Net energy imports as %	
Total consumption	184.2	of energy use	85
Consumption per head,			
kg oil equivalent	3,125		

Inflation and finance

Consumer price		av. ann. increase 2002–07	
inflation 2008	3.3%	Euro area:	
Av. ann. inflation 2003–08	2.3%	Narrow money (M1)	9.3%
Money market rate, 2008	4.67%	Broad money	8.4%
		Household saving rate, 2008	9.2%

Exchange rates

	end 2008		December 2008
			2000 = 100
€ per $	0.72	Effective rates	
€ per SDR	1.11	– nominal	116.10
		– real	143.90

Trade

Principal exports

	$bn fob
Machinery & transport equip.	191.0
Chemicals & related products	51.2
Food, drink & tobacco	29.9
Mineral fuels & lubricants	19.7
Total incl. others	**499.4**

Principal imports

	$bn cif
Machinery & transport equip.	147.4
Mineral fuels & lubricants	84.2
Chemicals & related products	65.7
Food, drink & tobacco	38.5
Total incl. others	**509.1**

Main export destinations

	% of total
Germany	12.9
France	11.4
Spain	7.4
United States	6.8
United Kingdom	5.8
EU27	60.1

Main origins of imports

	% of total
Germany	16.9
France	9.0
Netherlands	5.5
Belgium	4.3
United States	3.0
EU27	57.0

Balance of payments, reserves and aid, $bn

Visible exports fob	502.4	Overall balance	1.9
Visible imports fob	-498.1	Change in reserves	18.3
Trade balance	4.2	Level of reserves	
Invisibles inflows	200.1	end Dec.	94.1
Invisibles outflows	-236.4	No. months of import cover	1.5
Net transfers	-18.9	Official gold holdings, m oz	78.8
Current account balance	-51.0	Aid given	3.97
– as % of GDP	-2.4	– as % of GDP	0.19
Capital balance	41.3		

Health and education

Health spending, % of GDP	9.0	Education spending, % of GDP	4.8
Doctors per 1,000 pop.	3.7	Enrolment, %: primary	105
Hospital beds per 1,000 pop.	4.0	secondary	101
Improved-water source access,		tertiary	68
% of pop.	...		

Society

No. of households	22.7m	Colour TVs per 100 households	96.4
Av. no. per household	2.6	Telephone lines per 100 pop.	46.3
Marriages per 1,000 pop.	4.4	Mobile telephone subscribers	
Divorces per 1,000 pop.	0.8	per 100 pop.	150.7
Cost of living, Feb. 2009		Computers per 100 pop.	36.7
New York = 100	98	Internet hosts per 1,000 pop.	334.8

JAPAN

Area	377,727 sq km	Capital	Tokyo
Arable as % of total land	12	Currency	Yen (¥)

People

Population	128.3m	Life expectancy:	men	79.0 yrs
Pop. per sq km	339.7		women	86.2 yrs
Av. ann. growth		Adult literacy		...
in pop. 2010–15	-0.19%	Fertility rate (per woman)		1.3
Pop. under 15	13.3%	Urban population		66.3%
Pop. over 60	29.7%			per 1,000 pop.
No. of men per 100 women	95	Crude birth rate		9
Human Development Index	95.6	Crude death rate		9.1

The economy

GDP	¥516trn	GDP per head	$34,310
GDP	$4,384bn	GDP per head in purchasing	
Av. ann. growth in real		power parity (USA=100)	73.8
GDP 2002–2007	2.2%	Economic freedom index	72.8

Origins of GDP		Components of GDP	
	% of total		% of total
Agriculture	1.4	Private consumption	56.3
Industry, of which:	26.8	Public consumption	17.9
manufacturing	...	Investment	24.1
Services	71.7	Exports	17.6
		Imports	-15.9

Structure of employment

	% of total		% of labour force
Agriculture	4	Unemployed 2007	3.9
Industry	27	Av. ann. rate 1995–2007	4.3
Services	69		

Energy

	m TOE		
Total output	101.1	Net energy imports as %	
Total consumption	527.6	of energy use	81
Consumption per head,			
kg oil equivalent	4,129		

Inflation and finance

		av. ann. increase 2002–07	
Consumer price			
inflation 2008	1.4%	Narrow money (M1)	5.6%
Av. ann. inflation 2003–08	0.3%	Broad money	0.3%
Money market rate, 2008	0.46%	Household saving rate, 2008	3.3%

Exchange rates

	end 2008		December 2008
¥ per $	90.75	Effective rates	2000 = 100
¥ per SDR	139.78	– nominal	102.50
¥ per €	126.32	– real	85.60

Trade

Principal exports		Principal imports	
	$bn fob		*$bn cif*
Capital equipment	368.0	Industrial supplies	318.0
Industrial supplies	159.4	Capital equipment	152.9
Consumer durable goods	137.9	Food & direct consumer goods	51.1
Consumer nondurable goods	4.3	Consumer durable goods	44.9
Total incl. others	**714.1**	Total incl. others	**622.0**

Main export destinations		Main origins of imports	
	% of total		*% of total*
United States	20.0	China	20.4
China	15.4	United States	11.5
South Korea	7.6	Saudi Arabia	5.3
Hong Kong	5.5	United Arab Emirates	5.0
Thailand	3.6	Australia	4.9
EU27	14.8	EU27	10.5

Balance of payments, reserves and aid, $bn

Visible exports fob	678.1	Overall balance	36.5
Visible imports fob	-573.3	Change in reserves	78.0
Trade balance	104.8	Level of reserves	
Invisibles inflows	328.6	end Dec.	973.3
Invisibles outflows	-211.3	No. months of import cover	14.9
Net transfers	-11.5	Official gold holdings, m oz	24.6
Current account balance	210.5	Aid given	7.68
– as % of GDP	4.8	– as % of GDP	0.18
Capital balance	-191.1		

Health and education

Health spending, % of GDP	8.8	Education spending, % of GDP	3.5
Doctors per 1,000 pop.	2.2	Enrolment, %: primary	100
Hospital beds per 1,000 pop.	14.0	secondary	101
Improved-water source access,		tertiary	57
% of pop.	100		

Society

No. of households	49.0m	Colour TVs per 100 households	99.6
Av. no. per household	2.6	Telephone lines per 100 pop.	40.0
Marriages per 1,000 pop.	5.5	Mobile telephone subscribers	
Divorces per 1,000 pop.	2.0	per 100 pop.	83.9
Cost of living, Feb. 2009		Computers per 100 pop.	...
New York = 100	152	Internet hosts per 1,000 pop.	338.7

KENYA

Area	582,646 sq km	Capital	Nairobi
Arable as % of total land	9	Currency	Kenyan shilling (KSh)

People

Population	36.0m	Life expectancy: men	53.7 yrs
Pop. per sq km	61.8	women	54.5 yrs
Av. ann. growth		Adult literacy	73.6%
in pop. 2010–15	2.56%	Fertility rate (per woman)	4.5
Pop. under 15	42.8%	Urban population	21.3%
Pop. over 60	4.1%		per 1,000 pop.
No. of men per 100 women	100	Crude birth rate	40
Human Development Index	53.2	Crude death rate	11.7

The economy

GDP	KSh1,814bn	GDP per head	$650
GDP	$24.2bn	GDP per head in purchasing	
Av. ann. growth in real		power parity (USA=100)	3.4
GDP 2002–07	5.9%	Economic freedom index	58.7

Origins of GDP		**Components of GDP**	
	% of total		% of total
Agriculture	23.0	Private consumption	76.8
Industry, of which:	15.8	Public consumption	16.8
manufacturing	9.7	Investment	21.2
Other	60.1	Exports	25.7
		Imports	-40.6

Structure of employment

	% of total		% of labour force
Agriculture	...	Unemployed 2007	...
Industry	...	Av. ann. rate 1995–2007	...
Services	...		

Energy

	m TOE		
Total output	14.3	Net energy imports as %	
Total consumption	17.9	of energy use	21
Consumption per head,			
kg oil equivalent	491		

Inflation and finance

Consumer price		av. ann. increase 2002–07	
inflation 2008	26.2%	Narrow money (M1)	20.0%
Av. ann. inflation 2003–08	14.3%	Broad money	14.4%
Deposit bill rate, 2008	5.30%		

Exchange rates

	end 2008		December 2008
KSh per $	77.71	Effective rates	2000 = 100
KSh per SDR	119.70	– nominal	...
KSh per €	108.17	– real	...

Trade

Principal exports		Principal imports	
	$bn fob		*$bn cif*
Horticultural products	0.8	Industrial supplies	2.9
Tea	0.7	Machinery & other equip.	1.4
Coffee	0.2	Transport equipment	1.4
Fish products	0.1	Consumer goods	0.7
		Food & drink	0.6
Total incl. others	**4.1**	Total incl. others	**8.0**

Main export destinations		Main origins of imports	
	% of total		*% of total*
Uganda	16.6	United Arab Emirates	11.0
United Kingdom	9.8	China	10.1
Netherlands	8.3	India	8.6
Tanzania	8.0	Saudi Arabia	7.7

Balance of payments, reserves and debt, $bn

Visible exports fob	4.1	Change in reserves	0.9
Visible imports fob	-8.4	Level of reserves	
Trade balance	-4.3	end Dec.	3.4
Invisibles inflows	2.8	No. months of import cover	4.0
Invisibles outflows	-1.8	Official gold holdings, m oz	0.0
Net transfers	2.1	Foreign debt	7.3
Current account balance	-1.1	– as % of GDP	26
– as % of GDP	-4.6	– as % of total exports	85
Capital balance	2.2	Debt service ratio	6
Overall balance	0.8		

Health and education

Health spending, % of GDP	4.6	Education spending, % of GDP	7.1
Doctors per 1,000 pop.	0.1	Enrolment, %: primary	110
Hospital beds per 1,000 pop.	1.9	secondary	53
Improved-water source access,		tertiary	...
% of pop.	61		

Society

No. of households	8.0m	Colour TVs per 100 households	...
Av. no. per household	4.7	Telephone lines per 100 pop.	0.7
Marriages per 1,000 pop.	...	Mobile telephone subscribers	
Divorces per 1,000 pop.	...	per 100 pop.	30.2
Cost of living, Feb. 2009		Computers per 100 pop.	1.4
New York = 100	62	Internet hosts per 1,000 pop.	0.8

LATVIA

Area	63,700 sq km	Capital	Riga
Arable as % of total land	18	Currency	Lats (LVL)

People

Population	2.3m	Life expectancy: men	67.3 yrs
Pop. per sq km	36.1	women	77.2 yrs
Av. ann. growth		Adult literacy	99.8%
in pop. 2010–15	-0.39%	Fertility rate (per woman)	1.5
Pop. under 15	13.8%	Urban population	68.0%
Pop. over 60	22.5%		per 1,000 pop.
No. of men per 100 women	85	Crude birth rate	10
Human Development Index	86.3	Crude death rate	13.8

The economy

GDP	LVL14.0bn	GDP per head	$11,930
GDP	$27.2bn	GDP per head in purchasing	
Av. ann. growth in real		power parity (USA=100)	35.9
GDP 2002–07	11.8%	Economic freedom index	66.6

Origins of GDP		Components of GDP	
	% of total		% of total
Agriculture	3.6	Private consumption	62.3
Industry, of which:	23.3	Public consumption	17.4
manufacturing	11.4	Investment	40.4
Services	73.2	Exports	44.2
		Imports	-62.4

Structure of employment

	% of total		% of labour force
Agriculture	11	Unemployed 2007	6.0
Industry	26	Av. ann. rate 1996–2007	12.2
Services	63		

Energy

			m TOE
Total output	1.8	Net energy imports as %	
Total consumption	4.6	of energy use	60
Consumption per head,			
kg oil equivalent	2,017		

Inflation and finance

Consumer price		av. ann. increase 2002–07	
inflation 2008	15.4%	Narrow money (M1)	30.3%
Av. ann. inflation 2003–08	9.0%	Broad money	27.5%
Money market rate, 2008	4.09%		

Exchange rates

	end 2008		December 2008
LVL per $	0.50	Effective rates	2000 = 100
LVL per SDR	0.76	– nominal	...
LVL per €	0.70	– real	...

Trade

Principal exports		Principal imports	
	$bn fob		*$bn cif*
Wood & wood products	1.8	Machinery & equipment	3.2
Metals	1.2	Transport equipment	2.2
Machinery & equipment	0.9	Mineral products	1.7
Chemicals	0.6	Base metals	1.5
Total incl. others	**7.9**	Total incl. others	**15.2**

Main export destinations		Main origins of imports	
	% of total		*% of total*
Lithuania	15.8	Germany	15.2
Estonia	14.4	Lithuania	13.9
Russia	9.6	Russia	8.4
Germany	8.7	Estonia	8.1
Sweden	7.7	Finland	5.1
EU27	72.5	EU27	77.4

Balance of payments, reserves and debt, $bn

Visible exports fob	8.2	Change in reserves	1.2
Visible imports fob	-15.1	Level of reserves	
Trade balance	-6.9	end Dec.	5.8
Invisibles inflows	5.2	No. months of import cover	3.4
Invisibles outflows	-5.1	Official gold holdings, m oz	0.2
Net transfers	0.4	Foreign debt	39.3
Current account balance	-6.2	– as % of GDP	192
– as % of GDP	-23.9	– as % of total exports	373
Capital balance	7.6	Debt service ratio	73
Overall balance	1.0		

Health and education

Health spending, % of GDP	6.6	Education spending, % of GDP	5.1
Doctors per 1,000 pop.	3.1	Enrolment, %: primary	95
Hospital beds per 1,000 pop.	7.5	secondary	98
Improved-water source access,		tertiary	71
% of pop.	99		

Society

No. of households	0.8m	Colour TVs per 100 households	95.3
Av. no. per household	2.9	Telephone lines per 100 pop.	28.3
Marriages per 1,000 pop.	4.8	Mobile telephone subscribers	
Divorces per 1,000 pop.	2.4	per 100 pop.	97.4
Cost of living, Feb. 2009		Computers per 100 pop.	32.7
New York = 100	...	Internet hosts per 1,000 pop.	109.9

LITHUANIA

Area	65,200 sq km	Capital	Vilnius
Arable as % of total land	30	Currency	Litas (LTL)

People

Population	3.4m	Life expectancy: men		65.8 yrs
Pop. per sq km	52.1	women		77.7 yrs
Av. ann. growth		Adult literacy		99.7%
in pop. 2010–15	-0.70%	Fertility rate (per woman)		1.4
Pop. under 15	14.9%	Urban population		66.8%
Pop. over 60	21.3%			per 1,000 pop.
No. of men per 100 women	88	Crude birth rate		10
Human Development Index	86.9	Crude death rate		13.1

The economy

GDP	LTL96.7bn	GDP per head	$11,360
GDP	$38.3bn	GDP per head in purchasing	
Av. ann. growth in real		power parity (USA=100)	38.5
GDP 2002–07	10.0%	Economic freedom index	70.0

Origins of GDP		**Components of GDP**	
	% of total		% of total
Agriculture	4.5	Private consumption	64.7
Industry, of which:	32.8	Public consumption	18.2
manufacturing	19.0	Investment	30.5
Services	62.7	Exports	54.4
		Imports	-67.8

Structure of employment

	% of total		% of labour force
Agriculture	12	Unemployed 2007	4.3
Industry	29	Av. ann. rate 1995–2007	12.8
Services	59		

Energy

		m TOE	
Total output	3.5	Net energy imports as %	
Total consumption	8.5	of energy use	59
Consumption per head,			
kg oil equivalent	2,517		

Inflation and finance

Consumer price		av. ann. increase 2002–07	
inflation 2008	10.9%	Narrow money (M1)	27.4%
Av. ann. inflation 2003–08	4.8%	Broad money	24.4%
Money market rate, 2008	3.95%		

Exchange rates

	end 2008		December 2008
			2000 = 100
LTL per $	2.45	Effective rates	
LTL per SDR	3.78	– nominal	...
LTL per €	3.41	– real	...

Trade

Principal exports		Principal imports	
	$bn fob		$bn cif
Mineral products	2.4	Machinery & equipment	4.3
Machinery & equipment	2.2	Mineral products	4.2
Transport equipment	1.8	Transport equipment	4.0
Chemicals	1.4	Chemicals	2.3
Total incl. others	**17.1**	Total incl. others	**24.4**

Main export destinations		Main origins of imports	
	% of total		% of total
Russia	15.0	Russia	18.0
Latvia	12.9	Germany	14.8
Germany	10.5	Poland	10.5
Poland	6.3	Latvia	5.4
United Kingdom	4.6	Netherlands	4.2
EU27	64.8	EU25	68.3

Balance of payments, reserves and debt, $bn

Visible exports fob	17.2	Change in reserves	1.9
Visible imports fob	-23.0	Level of reserves	
Trade balance	-5.9	end Dec.	7.7
Invisibles inflows	4.8	No. months of import cover	3.2
Invisibles outflows	-5.8	Official gold holdings, m oz	0.2
Net transfers	1.2	Foreign debt[a]	19.0
Current account balance	-5.7	– as % of GDP[a]	79
– as % of GDP	-14.9	– as % of total exports[a]	121
Capital balance	7.0	Debt service ratio[a]	22
Overall balance	1.2		

Health and education

Health spending, % of GDP	6.2	Education spending, % of GDP	4.9
Doctors per 1,000 pop.	4.0	Enrolment, %: primary	96
Hospital beds per 1,000 pop.	8.1	secondary	98
Improved-water source access, % of pop.	...	tertiary	76

Society

No. of households	1.4m	Colour TVs per 100 households	97.0
Av. no. per household	2.5	Telephone lines per 100 pop.	23.6
Marriages per 1,000 pop.	6.3	Mobile telephone subscribers	
Divorces per 1,000 pop.	3.4	per 100 pop.	145.2
Cost of living, Feb. 2009		Computers per 100 pop.	18.3
New York = 100	...	Internet hosts per 1,000 pop.	251.4

a 2006

MALAYSIA

Area	332,665 sq km	Capital	Kuala Lumpur
Arable as % of total land	5	Currency	Malaysian dollar/ringgit (M$)

People

Population	26.2m	Life expectancy: men	72.0 yrs
Pop. per sq km	78.8	women	76.7 yrs
Av. ann. growth		Adult literacy	91.9%
in pop. 2010–15	1.47%	Fertility rate (per woman)	2.4
Pop. under 15	29.5%	Urban population	69.6%
Pop. over 60	7.5%		per 1,000 pop.
No. of men per 100 women	103	Crude birth rate	21
Human Development Index	82.3	Crude death rate	4.5

The economy

GDP	M$642bn	GDP per head	$7,030
GDP	$187bn	GDP per head in purchasing	
Av. ann. growth in real		power parity (USA=100)	29.6
GDP 2002–2007	6.8%	Economic freedom index	64.6

Origins of GDP		**Components of GDP**	
	% of total		% of total
Agriculture	10.0	Private consumption	45.6
Industry, of which:	45.3	Public consumption	12.2
manufacturing	27.4	Investment	21.7
Services	44.8	Exports	110.2
		Imports	-89.9

Structure of employment

	% of total		% of labour force
Agriculture	15	Unemployed 2007	3.2
Industry	30	Av. ann. rate 1995–2007	3.2
Services	55		

Energy

	m TOE		
Total output	97.9	Net energy imports as %	
Total consumption	68.3	of energy use	-43
Consumption per head,			
kg oil equivalent	2,617		

Inflation and finance

		av. ann. increase 2002–07	
Consumer price			
inflation 2008	5.4%	Narrow money (M1)	13.3%
Av. ann. inflation 2003–08	3.1%	Broad money	9.6%
Money market rate, 2008	3.48%		

Exchange rates

	end 2008		December 2008
M$ per $	3.46	Effective rates	2000 = 100
M$ per SDR	5.34	– nominal	98.90
M$ per €	4.82	– real	103.20

Trade

Principal exports		Principal imports	
	$bn fob		*$bn cif*
Electronics	62.0	Machinery	15.1
Electrical machinery	21.7	Transport equipment	6.4
Chemicals & products	10.9	Metal products	5.9
Palm oil	9.3	Foodstuffs	3.6
Total incl. others	**176.2**	Total incl. others	**147.0**

Main export destinations		Main origins of imports	
	% of total		*% of total*
United States	15.9	Singapore	13.1
Singapore	14.9	Japan	12.9
Japan	9.1	China	12.8
China	8.7	United States	10.7
Thailand	4.9	Thailand	5.4

Balance of payments, reserves and debt, $bn

Visible exports fob	176.4	Change in reserves	19.1
Visible imports fob	-139.1	Level of reserves	
Trade balance	37.3	end Dec.	102.0
Invisibles inflows	39.6	No. months of import cover	6.7
Invisibles outflows	-43.3	Official gold holdings, m oz	1.2
Net transfers	-4.7	Foreign debt	53.7
Current account balance	28.9	– as % of GDP	34
– as % of GDP	15.5	– as % of total exports	28
Capital balance	-10.9	Debt service ratio	5
Overall balance	13.1		

Health and education

Health spending, % of GDP	4.3	Education spending, % of GDP	4.6
Doctors per 1,000 pop.	0.8	Enrolment, %: primary	99
Hospital beds per 1,000 pop.	1.8	secondary	69
Improved-water source access,		tertiary	...
% of pop.	99		

Society

No. of households	5.8m	Colour TVs per 100 households	95.5
Av. no. per household	4.7	Telephone lines per 100 pop.	16.4
Marriages per 1,000 pop.	5.8	Mobile telephone subscribers	
Divorces per 1,000 pop.	...	per 100 pop.	87.9
Cost of living, Feb. 2009		Computers per 100 pop.	23.1
New York = 100	67	Internet hosts per 1,000 pop.	14.4

MEXICO

Area	1,972,545 sq km	Capital	Mexico city
Arable as % of total land	13	Currency	Mexican peso (PS)

People

Population	109.6m	Life expectancy: men	73.8 yrs
Pop. per sq km	55.6	women	78.7 yrs
Av. ann. growth		Adult literacy	92.8%
in pop. 2010–15	0.86%	Fertility rate (per woman)	2.0
Pop. under 15	28.5%	Urban population	76.9%
Pop. over 60	9.1%		per 1,000 pop.
No. of men per 100 women	97	Crude birth rate	20
Human Development Index	84.2	Crude death rate	4.7

The economy

GDP	PS11,178bn	GDP per head	$9,720
GDP	$1,023bn	GDP per head in purchasing	
Av. ann. growth in real		power parity (USA=100)	30.9
GDP 2002–2007	3.7%	Economic freedom index	65.8

Origins of GDP		Components of GDP	
	% of total		% of total
Agriculture	3.7	Private consumption	65.2
Industry, of which:	34.3	Public consumption	10.5
manufacturing & mining	18.6	Investment	25.8
Services	62.1	Exports	28.2
		Imports	-29.8

Structure of employment

	% of total		% of labour force
Agriculture	14	Unemployed 2007	3.4
Industry	27	Av. ann. rate 1995–2007	2.9
Services	59		

Energy

	m TOE		
Total output	256.0	Net energy imports as %	
Total consumption	177.4	of energy use	-44
Consumption per head,			
kg oil equivalent	1,702		

Inflation and finance

Consumer price		av. ann. increase 2002–07	
inflation 2008	5.1%	Narrow money (M1)	13.4%
Av. ann. inflation 2003–08	4.3%	Broad money	11.5%
Money market rate, 2008	8.28%		

Exchange rates

	end 2008		December 2008
			2000 = 100
PS per $	13.54	Effective rates	
PS per SDR	20.85	– nominal	...
PS per €	18.85	– real	...

Trade

Principal exports		**Principal imports**	
	$bn fob		*$bn fob*
Manufactured products	219.4	Intermediate goods	205.5
(Maquiladora[a]	*121.0)*	*(Maquiladora[a]*	*95.9)*
Crude oil & products	43.0	Consumer goods	41.8
Agricultural products	7.7	Capital goods	34.7
Total incl. others	**271.9**	Total	**282.0**

Main export destinations		**Main origins of imports**	
	% of total		*% of total*
United States	82.1	United States	49.6
Canada	2.4	South Korea	10.5
Spain	1.5	China	5.8
Germany	1.3	Japan	4.5

Balance of payments, reserves and debt, $bn

Visible exports fob	271.9	Change in reserves	10.9
Visible imports fob	-281.9	Level of reserves	
Trade balance	-10.1	end Dec.	87.2
Invisibles inflows	25.5	No. months of import cover	3.2
Invisibles outflows	-50.0	Official gold holdings, m oz	0.1
Net transfers	26.4	Foreign debt	178.1
Current account balance	-8.1	– as % of GDP	20
– as % of GDP	-0.8	– as % of total exports	62
Capital balance	20.7	Debt service ratio	13
Overall balance	10.3		

Health and education

Health spending, % of GDP	6.6	Education spending, % of GDP	5.5
Doctors per 1,000 pop.	1.6	Enrolment, %: primary	111
Hospital beds per 1,000 pop.	1.0	secondary	89
Improved-water source access,		tertiary	...
% of pop.	97		

Society

No. of households	25.5m	Colour TVs per 100 households	93.9
Av. no. per household	4.2	Telephone lines per 100 pop.	18.5
Marriages per 1,000 pop.	5.6	Mobile telephone subscribers	
Divorces per 1,000 pop.	0.6	per 100 pop.	62.5
Cost of living, Feb. 2009		Computers per 100 pop.	14.4
New York = 100	64	Internet hosts per 1,000 pop.	114.2

a Manufacturing assembly plants near the Mexican-US border where goods for
processing may be imported duty-free and all output is exported.

MOROCCO

Area	446,550 sq km	Capital	Rabat
Arable as % of total land	19	Currency	Dirham (Dh)

People

Population	32.4m	Life expectancy: men	69.0 yrs
Pop. per sq km	72.6	women	73.4 yrs
Av. ann. growth		Adult literacy	55.6%
in pop. 2010–15	1.17%	Fertility rate (per woman)	2.3
Pop. under 15	28.4%	Urban population	55.7%
Pop. over 60	7.9%		per 1,000 pop.
No. of men per 100 women	97	Crude birth rate	21
Human Development Index	64.6	Crude death rate	5.8

The economy

GDP	Dh615bn	GDP per head	$2,430
GDP	$75.1bn	GDP per head in purchasing	
Av. ann. growth in real		power parity (USA=100)	9.0
GDP 2002–07	5.4%	Economic freedom index	57.7

Origins of GDP		**Components of GDP**	
	% of total		% of total
Agriculture	13.7	Private consumption	58.4
Industry, of which:	27.7	Public consumption	18.2
manufacturing	15.0	Investment	32.5
Services	58.6	Exports	35.8
		Imports	-44.9

Structure of employment

	% of total		% of labour force
Agriculture	44	Unemployed 2007	9.5
Industry	20	Av. ann. rate 1995–2007	13.9
Services	36		

Energy

	m TOE		
Total output	0.7	Net energy imports as %	
Total consumption	14.0	of energy use	95
Consumption per head,			
kg oil equivalent	458		

Inflation and finance

Consumer price		av. ann. increase 2002–07	
inflation 2008	3.9%	Narrow money (M1)	13.8%
Av. ann. inflation 2003–08	2.3%	Broad money	12.7%
Money market rate, July 2008	3.30%		

Exchange rates

	end 2008		December 2008
			2000 = 100
Dh per $	8.10	Effective rates	
Dh per SDR	12.47	– nominal	100.70
Dh per €	11.28	– real	98.80

Trade

Principal exports	$bn fob	Principal imports	$bn cif
Textiles	2.5	Semi-finished goods	7.2
Phosphoric acid	1.1	Capital goods	6.8
Electrical components	0.8	Energy & lubricants	6.3
Phosphate rock	0.7	Consumer goods	5.9
Citrus fruits	0.3	Food, drink & tobacco	3.2
Total incl. others	**13.8**	Total incl. others	**30.0**

Main export destinations	% of total	Main origins of imports	% of total
Spain	21.4	Spain	16.5
France	19.2	France	13.9
Italy	4.9	China	7.4
United Kingdom	4.9	Italy	6.9

Balance of payments, reserves and debt, $bn

Visible exports fob	15.1	Change in reserves	3.9
Visible imports fob	-29.3	Level of reserves	
Trade balance	-14.2	end Dec.	24.7
Invisibles inflows	13.2	No. months of import cover	8.2
Invisibles outflows	-6.8	Official gold holdings, m oz	0.7
Net transfers	7.6	Foreign debt	20.3
Current account balance	-0.2	– as % of GDP	29
– as % of GDP	-0.3	– as % of total exports	66
Capital balance	-0.7	Debt service ratio	11
Overall balance	-0.8		

Health and education

Health spending, % of GDP	5.3	Education spending, % of GDP	...
Doctors per 1,000 pop.	0.6	Enrolment, %: primary	114
Hospital beds per 1,000 pop.	0.9	secondary	56
Improved-water source access,		tertiary	...
% of pop.	81		

Society

No. of households	6.3m	Colour TVs per 100 households	78.4
Av. no. per household	5.0	Telephone lines per 100 pop.	3.7
Marriages per 1,000 pop.	...	Mobile telephone subscribers	
Divorces per 1,000 pop.	...	per 100 pop.	64.2
Cost of living, Feb. 2009		Computers per 100 pop.	3.6
New York = 100	73	Internet hosts per 1,000 pop.	8.5

NETHERLANDS

Area[a]	41,526 sq km	Capital	Amsterdam
Arable as % of total land	27	Currency	Euro (€)

People

Population	16.4m	Life expectancy: men	77.8 yrs
Pop. per sq km	394.9	women	82.0 yrs
Av. ann. growth		Adult literacy	...
in pop. 2010–15	0.31%	Fertility rate (per woman)	1.8
Pop. under 15	17.8%	Urban population	81.3%
Pop. over 60	21.4%		per 1,000 pop.
No. of men per 100 women	98	Crude birth rate	11
Human Development Index	95.8	Crude death rate	8.4

The economy

GDP	€560bn	GDP per head	$46,750
GDP	$766bn	GDP per head in purchasing	
Av. ann. growth in real		power parity (USA=100)	84.9
GDP 2002–07	2.4%	Economic freedom index	77.0

Origins of GDP		Components of GDP	
	% of total		% of total
Agriculture	2.0	Private consumption	46.6
Industry, of which:	24.4	Public consumption	25.1
manufacturing	...	Investment	19.7
Services	73.6	Exports	74.9
		Imports	-66.3

Structure of employment

	% of total		% of labour force
Agriculture	3	Unemployed 2007	3.5
Industry	19	Av. ann. rate 1995–2007	4.5
Services	78		

Energy

	m TOE		
Total output	60.8	Net energy imports as %	
Total consumption	80.1	of energy use	24
Consumption per head,			
kg oil equivalent	4,901		

Inflation and finance

Consumer price		av. ann. increase 2002–07	
inflation 2008	2.5%	Euro area:	
Av. ann. inflation 2003–08	1.6%	Narrow money (M1)	9.3%
Deposit rate, households, 2008	4.42%	Broad money	8.4%
		Household saving rate, 2008	5.8%

Exchange rates

	end 2008		December 2008
€ per $	0.72	Effective rates	2000 = 100
€ per SDR	1.11	– nominal	114.50
		– real	119.00

Trade

Principal exports		Principal imports	
	$bn fob		*$bn cif*
Machinery & transport equipment	183.4	Machinery & transport equipment	166.5
Chemicals & related products	86.8	Mineral fuels & lubricants	84.2
Mineral fuels & lubricants	74.0	Chemicals & related products	61.9
Food, drink & tobacco	65.1	Food, drink & tobacco	40.3
Total incl. others	**472.8**	Total incl. others	**421.2**

Main export destinations		Main origins of imports	
	% of total		*% of total*
Germany	28.5	Germany	20.6
Belgium	15.8	China	12.3
United Kingdom	10.6	Belgium	10.9
France	9.9	United States	8.6
EU27	78.1	EU27	50.1

Balance of payments, reserves and aid, $bn

Visible exports fob	462.2	Overall balance	-1.4
Visible imports fob	-407.3	Change in reserves	3.0
Trade balance	54.9	Level of reserves	
Invisibles inflows	256.4	end Dec.	26.9
Invisibles outflows	-239.4	No. months of import cover	0.5
Net transfers	-12.3	Official gold holdings, m oz	20.0
Current account balance	59.6	Aid given	6.22
– as % of GDP	7.8	– as % of GDP	0.81
Capital balance	-32.3		

Health and education

Health spending, % of GDP	9.4	Education spending, % of GDP	5.6
Doctors per 1,000 pop.	3.7	Enrolment, %: primary	102
Hospital beds per 1,000 pop.	4.8	secondary	120
Improved-water source access, % of pop.	100	tertiary	60

Society

No. of households	7.2m	Colour TVs per 100 households	98.5
Av. no. per household	2.3	Telephone lines per 100 pop.	44.7
Marriages per 1,000 pop.	4.2	Mobile telephone subscribers	
Divorces per 1,000 pop.	1.8	per 100 pop.	117.5
Cost of living, Feb. 2009		Computers per 100 pop.	91.2
New York = 100	99	Internet hosts per 1,000 pop.	712.3

a Includes water.

NEW ZEALAND

Area	270,534 sq km	Capital	Wellington
Arable as % of total land	6	Currency	New Zealand dollar (NZ$)

People

Population	4.1m	Life expectancy:	men	78.2 yrs
Pop. per sq km	15.2		women	82.2 yrs
Av. ann. growth		Adult literacy		...
in pop. 2010–15	0.86%	Fertility rate (per woman)		2.0
Pop. under 15	20.4%	Urban population		86.4%
Pop. over 60	17.8%			*per 1,000 pop.*
No. of men per 100 women	98	Crude birth rate		15
Human Development Index	94.4	Crude death rate		7.0

The economy

GDP	NZ$179bn	GDP per head	$32,090
GDP	$136bn	GDP per head in purchasing	
Av. ann. growth in real		power parity (USA=100)	60.0
GDP 2002–07	3.5%	Economic freedom index	82.0

Origins of GDP		**Components of GDP**	
	% of total		*% of total*
Agriculture & mining	4.4	Private consumption	58.6
Industry	26.6	Public consumption	18.6
Services	69.0	Investment	24.0
		Exports	28.4
		Imports	-29.6

Structure of employment

	% of total		*% of labour force*
Agriculture	7	Unemployed 2007	3.6
Industry	22	Av. ann. rate 1995–2007	5.3
Services	71		

Energy

	m TOE		
Total output	13.1	Net energy imports as %	
Total consumption	17.5	of energy use	26
Consumption per head,			
kg oil equivalent	4,192		

Inflation and finance

		av. ann. increase 2002–07	
Consumer price			
inflation 2008	4.0%	Narrow money (M1)	9.3%
Av. ann. inflation 2003–08	3.0%	Broad money	10.2%
Money market rate, 2008	7.55%		

Exchange rates

	end 2008		*December 2008*
NZ$ per $	1.73	Effective rates	*2000 = 100*
NZ$ per SDR	2.66	– nominal	108.00
NZ$ per €	2.41	– real	115.10

Trade

Principal exports		Principal imports	
	$bn fob		*$bn cif*
Dairy produce	5.4	Machinery & electrical	
Meat	3.2	equipment	6.7
Forestry products	1.5	Mineral fuels & lubricants	4.4
Wool	0.4	Transport equipment	3.8
Total incl. others	**26.6**	Total incl. others	**30.7**

Main export destinations		Main origins of imports	
	% of total		*% of total*
Australia	22.1	Australia	20.6
United States	11.6	China	13.3
Japan	9.3	United States	9.7
China	5.4	Japan	9.4

Balance of payments, reserves and aid, $bn

Visible exports fob	27.3	Overall balance	3.1
Visible imports fob	-29.1	Change in reserves	3.2
Trade balance	-1.8	Level of reserves	
Invisibles inflows	12.0	end Dec.	17.2
Invisibles outflows	-21.3	No. months of import cover	4.1
Net transfers	0.4	Official gold holdings, m oz	0.0
Current account balance	-10.6	Aid given	0.32
– as % of GDP	-7.8	– as % of GDP	0.24
Capital balance	13.9		

Health and education

Health spending, % of GDP	9.3	Education spending, % of GDP	6.3
Doctors per 1,000 pop.	2.1	Enrolment, %: primary	104
Hospital beds per 1,000 pop.	6.0	secondary	121
Improved-water source access,		tertiary	80
% of pop.	...		

Society

No. of households	1.5m	Colour TVs per 100 households	98.6
Av. no. per household	2.7	Telephone lines per 100 pop.	41.8
Marriages per 1,000 pop.	4.9	Mobile telephone subscribers	
Divorces per 1,000 pop.	2.6	per 100 pop.	101.7
Cost of living, Feb. 2009		Computers per 100 pop.	52.6
New York = 100	71	Internet hosts per 1,000 pop.	432.3

NIGERIA

Area	923,768 sq km	Capital	Abuja
Arable as % of total land	35	Currency	Naira (N)

People

Population	137.2m	Life expectancy: men	47.3 yrs
Pop. per sq km	148.5	women	48.3 yrs
Av. ann. growth		Adult literacy	72.0%
in pop. 2010–15	2.12%	Fertility rate (per woman)	4.8
Pop. under 15	42.5%	Urban population	47.6%
Pop. over 60	4.9%		per 1,000 pop.
No. of men per 100 women	100	Crude birth rate	43
Human Development Index	49.9	Crude death rate	16.5

The economy

GDP	N20,817bn	GDP per head	$1,120
GDP	$165bn	GDP per head in purchasing	
Av. ann. growth in real		power parity (USA=100)	4.3
GDP 2002–07	9.1%	Economic freedom index	55.1

Origins of GDP		**Components of GDP**a	
	% of total		% of total
Agriculture	33	Private and public consumption	56
Industry, of which:	39	Investment	22
manufacturing	3	Exports	56
Services	28	Imports	-35

Structure of employment

	% of total		% of labour force
Agriculture	...	Unemployed 2001	3.9
Industry	...	Av. ann. rate 1995–2001	3.7
Services	...		

Energy

	m TOE		
Total output	235.3	Net energy imports as %	
Total consumption	105.1	of energy use	-124
Consumption per head,			
kg oil equivalent	726		

Inflation and finance

		av. ann. increase 2002–07	
Consumer price			
inflation 2008	11.6%	Narrow money (M1)	22.0%
Av. ann. inflation 2003–08	11.5%	Broad money	24.6%
Treasury bill rate Aug. 2008	9.13%		

Exchange rates

	end 2008		December 2008
N per $	132.56	Effective rates	2000 = 100
N per SDR	204.18	– nominal	75.20
N per €	184.52	– real	167.80

Trade

Principal exports	$bn fob	Principal imports	$bn cif
Crude oil	58.5	Manufactured goods	12.2
Gas	5.2	Chemicals	9.0
		Machinery & transport equip.	8.4
		Food & live animals	2.3
Total incl. others	**65.1**	Total incl. others	**37.3**

Main export destinations	% of total	Main origins of imports	% of total
United States	47.1	China	10.9
Spain	7.0	Netherlands	8.2
Brazil	6.9	United States	8.1
France	2.6	United Kingdom	5.4

Balance of payments, reserves and debt, $bn

Visible exports fob	65.1	Change in reserves	9.2
Visible imports fob	-31.9	Level of reserves	
Trade balance	33.1	end Dec.	51.9
Invisibles inflows	4.3	No. months of import cover	9.5
Invisibles outflows	-33.4	Official gold holdings, m oz	0.7
Net transfers	18.0	Foreign debt	9.0
Current account balance	22.0	– as % of GDP	6
– as % of GDP	13.3	– as % of total exports	12
Capital balance	5.2	Debt service ratio[b]	1
Overall balance	9.0		

Health and education

Health spending, % of GDP	3.8	Education spending, % of GDP	...
Doctors per 1,000 pop.	0.3	Enrolment, %: primary	108
Hospital beds per 1,000 pop.	...	secondary	32
Improved-water source access,		tertiary	...
% of pop.	48		

Society

No. of households	28.1m	Colour TVs per 100 households	30.5
Av. no. per household	5.3	Telephone lines per 100 pop.	1.1
Marriages per 1,000 pop.	...	Mobile telephone subscribers	
Divorces per 1,000 pop.	...	per 100 pop.	27.3
Cost of living, Feb. 2009		Computers per 100 pop.	0.8
New York = 100	70	Internet hosts per 1,000 pop.	...

a   2006
b   2005

NORWAY

Area	323,878 sq km	Capital	Oslo
Arable as % of total land	3	Currency	Norwegian krone (Nkr)

People

Population	4.7m	Life expectancy: men		78.3 yrs
Pop. per sq km	14.5		women	82.8 yrs
Av. ann. growth		Adult literacy		...
in pop. 2010–15	0.73%	Fertility rate (per woman)		1.9
Pop. under 15	19.0%	Urban population		77.5%
Pop. over 60	20.8%			per 1,000 pop.
No. of men per 100 women	99	Crude birth rate		12
Human Development Index	96.8	Crude death rate		8.7

The economy

GDP	Nkr2,277bn	GDP per head	$82,480
GDP	$388bn	GDP per head in purchasing	
Av. ann. growth in real		power parity (USA=100)	117.2
GDP 2002–2007	2.7%	Economic freedom index	70.2

Origins of GDP		Components of GDP	
	% of total		% of total
Agriculture	2.4	Private consumption	41.4
Industry, of which:	41.3	Public consumption	19.6
manufacturing	...	Investment	23.1
Services	56.4	Exports	45.8
		Imports	-29.8

Structure of employment

	% of total		% of labour force
Agriculture	3	Unemployed 2007	2.5
Industry	20	Av. ann. rate 1995–2007	3.9
Services	77		

Energy

	m TOE		
Total output	222.9	Net energy imports as %	
Total consumption	26.1	of energy use	-754
Consumption per head,			
kg oil equivalent	5,598		

Inflation and finance

Consumer price		av. ann. increase 2002–07	
inflation 2008	3.8%	Narrow money (M1)	...
Av. ann. inflation 2003–08	1.8%	Broad money	10.3%
Money market rate, 2008	6.06%	Household saving rate, 2008	2.0%

Exchange rates

	end 2008		December 2008
Nkr per $	7.00	Effective rates	2000 = 100
Nkr per SDR	10.78	– nominal	102.40
Nkr per €	9.74	– real	130.10

Trade

Principal exports[a]	$bn fob	Principal imports[a]	$bn cif
Oil, gas & products	82.9	Machinery & transport equip.	24.5
Metals	9.7	Metals	4.1
Machinery & transport equip.	8.0	Chemicals	3.6
Food, drink & tobacco	5.9	Refined petroleum products	3.0
Total incl. others	**122.1**	Total incl. others	**64.3**

Main export destinations	% of total	Main origins of imports	% of total
United Kingdom	25.3	Sweden	15.9
Germany	13.9	Germany	13.6
Netherlands	9.8	United Kingdom	7.0
France	7.9	Denmark	6.7
Sweden	7.0	China	5.6
United States	5.9	United States	4.6
EU27	80.8	EU27	68.8

Balance of payments, reserves and aid, $bn

Visible exports fob	137.3	Overall balance	1.0
Visible imports fob	-77.0	Change in reserves	4.0
Trade balance	60.3	Level of reserves	
Invisibles inflows	79.9	end Dec.	60.8
Invisibles outflows	-77.0	No. months of import cover	4.7
Net transfers	-2.6	Official gold holdings, m oz	0.0
Current account balance	60.5	Aid given	3.73
– as % of GDP	15.6	– as % of GDP	0.98
Capital balance	-30.5		

Health and education

Health spending, % of GDP	8.7	Education spending, % of GDP	6.6
Doctors per 1,000 pop.	3.7	Enrolment, %: primary	100
Hospital beds per 1,000 pop.	4.0	secondary	113
Improved-water source access,		tertiary	76
% of pop.	100		

Society

No. of households	2.0m	Colour TVs per 100 households	98.3
Av. no. per household	2.3	Telephone lines per 100 pop.	42.4
Marriages per 1,000 pop.	4.8	Mobile telephone subscribers	
Divorces per 1,000 pop.	2.5	per 100 pop.	110.5
Cost of living, Feb. 2009		Computers per 100 pop.	62.9
New York = 100	123	Internet hosts per 1,000 pop.	662.4

a 2006

PAKISTAN

Area	803,940 sq km	Capital	Islamabad
Arable as % of total land	28	Currency	Pakistan rupee (PRs)

People

Population	164.6m	Life expectancy: men	66.0 yrs
Pop. per sq km	204.7	women	66.7 yrs
Av. ann. growth		Adult literacy	54.2%
in pop. 2010–15	2.13%	Fertility rate (per woman)	3.6
Pop. under 15	36.9%	Urban population	35.7%
Pop. over 60	6.1%		per 1,000 pop.
No. of men per 100 women	106	Crude birth rate	31
Human Development Index	56.2	Crude death rate	7.0

The economy

GDP	PRs8,723bn	GDP per head	$880
GDP	$143bn	GDP per head in purchasing	
Av. ann. growth in real		power parity (USA=100)	5.5
GDP 2002–07	7.3%	Economic freedom index	57.0

Origins of GDP[a]		Components of GDP[a]	
	% of total		% of total
Agriculture	20.4	Private consumption	79.7
Industry, of which:	26.6	Public consumption	8.8
manufacturing	17.5	Investment	21.6
Services	53.0	Exports	12.1
		Imports	-22.1

Structure of employment

	% of total		% of labour force
Agriculture	44	Unemployed 2007	5.3
Industry	20	Av. ann. rate 1995–2007	6.4
Services	36		

Energy

	m TOE		
Total output	61.3	Net energy imports as %	
Total consumption	79.3	of energy use	23
Consumption per head,			
kg oil equivalent	499		

Inflation and finance

Consumer price		av. ann. increase 2002–07	
inflation 2008	20.3%	Narrow money (M1)	23.6%
Av. ann. inflation 2003–08	10.4%	Broad money	17.7%
Money market rate, 2008	11.93%		

Exchange rates

	end 2008		December 2008
PRs per $	79.10	Effective rates	2000 = 100
PRs per SDR	121.83	– nominal	59.99
PRs per €	110.11	– real	95.99

Trade[b]

Principal exports		Principal imports	
	$bn fob		*$bn fob*
Cotton fabrics	1.8	Machinery & transport equip.	8.5
Cotton yarn & thread	1.3	Mineral fuels	7.9
Rice	1.0	Chemicals	4.7
Raw cotton	0.1	Palm oil	1.2
Total incl. others	**17.8**	Total incl. others	**32.6**

Main export destinations		Main origins of imports	
	% of total		*% of total*
United States	19.5	China	19.8
United Arab Emirates	11.3	Saudi Arabia	12.4
Afghanistan	8.8	United Arab Emirates	11.5
China	5.7	United States	6.9
United Kingdom	5.2	Kuwait	5.6

Balance of payments, reserves and debt, $bn

Visible exports fob	18.1	Change in reserves	2.9
Visible imports fob	-28.8	Level of reserves	
Trade balance	-10.6	end Dec.	15.8
Invisibles inflows	5.1	No. months of import cover	4.4
Invisibles outflows	-13.8	Official gold holdings, m oz	2.1
Net transfers	11.1	Foreign debt	40.7
Current account balance	-8.3	– as % of GDP	25
– as % of GDP	-5.8	– as % of total exports	123
Capital balance	10.2	Debt service ratio	9
Overall balance	2.1		

Health and education

Health spending, % of GDP	2.0	Education spending, % of GDP	2.9
Doctors per 1,000 pop.	0.8	Enrolment, %: primary	118
Hospital beds per 1,000 pop.	1.0	secondary	33
Improved-water source access,		tertiary	...
% of pop.	91		

Society

No. of households	23.2m	Colour TVs per 100 households	34.2
Av. no. per household	7.1	Telephone lines per 100 pop.	2.9
Marriages per 1,000 pop.	...	Mobile telephone subscribers	
Divorces per 1,000 pop.	...	per 100 pop.	38.4
Cost of living, Feb. 2009		Computers per 100 pop.	...
New York = 100	37	Internet hosts per 1,000 pop.	1.2

a Fiscal year ending June 30, 2008.
b Fiscal year ending June 30, 2007.

PERU

Area	1,285,216 sq km	Capital	Lima
Arable as % of total land	3	Currency	Nuevo Sol (New Sol)

People

Population	28.8m	Life expectancy:	men	70.5 yrs
Pop. per sq km	22.4		women	75.9 yrs
Av. ann. growth		Adult literacy		89.6%
in pop. 2010–15	1.12%	Fertility rate (per woman)		2.4
Pop. under 15	30.3%	Urban population		71.3%
Pop. over 60	8.5%			per 1,000 pop.
No. of men per 100 women	100	Crude birth rate		21
Human Development Index	78.8	Crude death rate		5.4

The economy

GDP	New Soles 336bn	GDP per head	$3,850
GDP	$107bn	GDP per head in purchasing	
Av. ann. growth in real		power parity (USA=100)	17.2
GDP 2002–2007	7.4%	Economic freedom index	64.6

Origins of GDP		**Components of GDP**	
	% of total		% of total
Agriculture	7	Private consumption	61.5
Industry, of which:	37	Public consumption	9.1
manufacturing	16	Investment	22.9
Services	56	Exports	28.9
		Imports	-22.4

Structure of employment

	% of total		% of labour force
Agriculture	1	Unemployed 2007	7.0
Industry	24	Av. ann. rate 1996–2007	8.6
Services	75		

Energy

	m TOE		
Total output	11.5	Net energy imports as %	
Total consumption	13.6	of energy use	15
Consumption per head,			
kg oil equivalent	491		

Inflation and finance

Consumer price		av. ann. increase 2002–07	
inflation 2008	6.6%	Narrow money (M1)	14.8%
Av. ann. inflation 2003–08	3.1%	Broad money	10.1%
Money market rate, 2008	6.54%		

Exchange rates

	end 2008		December 2008
New Soles per $	3.14	Effective rates	2000 = 100
New Soles per SDR	4.84	– nominal	...
New Soles per €	4.37	– real	...

Trade

Principal exports		Principal imports	
	$bn fob		*$bn fob*
Copper	7.2	Intermediate goods	10.4
Gold	4.2	Capital goods	5.9
Zinc	2.5	Consumer goods	3.2
Fishmeal	1.5	Other goods	0.1
Total incl. others	**27.9**	Total incl. others	**19.6**

Main export destinations		Main origins of imports	
	% of total		*% of total*
United States	18.5	United States	21.7
China	11.5	China	11.5
Switzerland	7.9	Brazil	10.4
Canada	6.8	Ecuador	6.3

Balance of payments, reserves and debt, $bn

Visible exports fob	28.0	Change in reserves	10.3
Visible imports fob	-19.6	Level of reserves	
Trade balance	8.4	end Dec.	27.8
Invisibles inflows	4.9	No. months of import cover	9.8
Invisibles outflows	-14.3	Official gold holdings, m oz	1.1
Net transfers	2.5	Foreign debt	32.2
Current account balance	1.5	– as % of GDP	42
– as % of GDP	1.4	– as % of total exports	125
Capital balance	9.2	Debt service ratio	25
Overall balance	10.3		

Health and education

Health spending, % of GDP	4.4	Education spending, % of GDP	...
Doctors per 1,000 pop.	1.2	Enrolment, %: primary	109
Hospital beds per 1,000 pop.	1.2	secondary	98
Improved-water source access,		tertiary	...
% of pop.	83		

Society

No. of households	5.9m	Colour TVs per 100 households	53.3
Av. no. per household	4.7	Telephone lines per 100 pop.	9.6
Marriages per 1,000 pop.	2.9	Mobile telephone subscribers	
Divorces per 1,000 pop.	...	per 100 pop.	55.3
Cost of living, Feb. 2009		Computers per 100 pop.	10.3
New York = 100	60	Internet hosts per 1,000 pop.	9.6

PHILIPPINES

Area	300,000 sq km	Capital	Manila
Arable as % of total land	19	Currency	Philippine peso (P)

People

Population	85.9m	Life expectancy: men	69.5 yrs
Pop. per sq km	286.3	women	74.0 yrs
Av. ann. growth		Adult literacy	93.4%
in pop. 2010–15	1.66%	Fertility rate (per woman)	2.9
Pop. under 15	33.9%	Urban population	64.2%
Pop. over 60	6.5%		per 1,000 pop.
No. of men per 100 women	101	Crude birth rate	26
Human Development Index	74.5	Crude death rate	4.8

The economy

GDP	P6,648bn	GDP per head	$1,640
GDP	$144bn	GDP per head in purchasing	
Av. ann. growth in real		power parity (USA=100)	7.5
GDP 2002–2007	6.5%	Economic freedom index	56.8

Origins of GDP		**Components of GDP**	
	% of total		% of total
Agriculture	14.1	Private consumption	69.4
Industry, of which:	31.8	Public consumption	9.7
manufacturing	22.0	Investment	15.3
Services	54.2	Exports	42.5
		Imports	-42.3

Structure of employment

	% of total		% of labour force
Agriculture	37	Unemployed 2007	7.3
Industry	14	Av. ann. rate 1995–2007	8.9
Services	47		

Energy

	m TOE		
Total output	24.7	Net energy imports as %	
Total consumption	43.0	of energy use	43
Consumption per head,			
kg oil equivalent	498		

Inflation and finance

Consumer price		av. ann. increase 2002–07	
inflation 2008	9.3%	Narrow money (M1)	13.0%
Av. ann. inflation 2003–08	6.4%	Broad money	8.8%
Money market rate, 2008	5.48%		

Exchange rates

	end 2008		December 2008
P per $	47.49	Effective rates	2000 = 100
P per SDR	73.14	– nominal	83.30
P per €	66.11	– real	112.20

Trade

Principal exports		Principal imports	
	$bn fob		*$bn fob*
Electrical & electronic equipment	31.0	Electronic products	25.1
		Fuels	9.7
Mineral products	2.6	Transport equipment	2.2
Clothing	2.3	Industrial machinery	2.1
Agricultural products	1.8	Textile fabrics	1.1
Total incl. others	**50.3**	Total incl. others	**57.7**

Main export destinations		Main origins of imports	
	% of total		*% of total*
United States	17.1	United States	13.6
Japan	14.5	Japan	11.9
Hong Kong	11.5	Singapore	10.8
China	11.4	China	6.9
Netherlands	8.3	Saudi Arabia	6.1

Balance of payments, reserves and debt, $bn

Visible exports fob	49.5	Change in reserves	-0.6
Visible imports fob	-57.7	Level of reserves	
Trade balance	-8.2	end Dec.	22.4
Invisibles inflows	13.9	No. months of import cover	3.8
Invisibles outflows	-13.4	Official gold holdings, m oz	4.2
Net transfers	14.0	Foreign debt	65.8
Current account balance	6.3	– as % of GDP	51
– as % of GDP	4.4	– as % of total exports	97
Capital balance	3.0	Debt service ratio	14
Overall balance	8.7		

Health and education

Health spending, % of GDP	3.8	Education spending, % of GDP	2.5
Doctors per 1,000 pop.	1.1	Enrolment, %: primary	126
Hospital beds per 1,000 pop.	1.2	secondary	83
Improved-water source access, % of pop.	85	tertiary	…

Society

No. of households	17.8m	Colour TVs per 100 households	86.0
Av. no. per household	5.0	Telephone lines per 100 pop.	4.5
Marriages per 1,000 pop.	6.5	Mobile telephone subscribers	
Divorces per 1,000 pop.	…	per 100 pop.	55.9
Cost of living, Feb. 2009		Computers per 100 pop.	7.3
New York = 100	50	Internet hosts per 1,000 pop.	3.3

POLAND

Area	312,683 sq km	Capital	Warsaw
Arable as % of total land	40	Currency	Zloty (Zl)

People

Population	38.5m	Life expectancy: men	71.3 yrs
Pop. per sq km	123.1	women	79.8 yrs
Av. ann. growth		Adult literacy	99.3
in pop. 2010–15	-0.13%	Fertility rate (per woman)	1.3
Pop. under 15	15.0%	Urban population	61.3%
Pop. over 60	18.8%		*per 1,000 pop.*
No. of men per 100 women	93	Crude birth rate	10
Human Development Index	87.5	Crude death rate	10.0

The economy

GDP	Zl1,168bn	GDP per head	$11,070
GDP	$422bn	GDP per head in purchasing	
Av. ann. growth in real		power parity (USA=100)	35.1
GDP 2002–2007	5.7%	Economic freedom index	60.3

Origins of GDP

Components of GDP

	% of total		*% of total*
Agriculture	4.3	Private consumption	60.6
Industry, of which:	31.8	Public consumption	18.0
manufacturing	18.9	Investment	24.3
Services	63.8	Exports	40.8
		Imports	-43.6

Structure of employment

	% of total		*% of labour force*
Agriculture	15	Unemployed 2007	9.6
Industry	29	Av. ann. rate 1995–2007	15.0
Services	56		

Energy

	m TOE		
Total output	77.9	Net energy imports as %	
Total consumption	97.7	of energy use	20
Consumption per head,			
kg oil equivalent	2,562		

Inflation and finance

Consumer price		*av. ann. increase 2002–07*	
inflation 2008	4.3%	Narrow money (M1)	24.3%
Av. ann. inflation 2003–08	2.7%	Broad money	10.7%
Money market rate, 2008	5.75%	Household saving rate, 2008	8.1%

Exchange rates

	end 2008		*December 2008*
Zl per $	2.96	Effective rates	*2000 = 100*
Zl per SDR	4.56	– nominal	137.20
Zl per €	4.12	– real	140.40

Trade

Principal exports	$bn fob	Principal imports	$bn cif
Machinery & transport equipment	55.1	Machinery & transport equipment	56.6
Manufactured goods	48.8	Manufactured goods	33.8
Foodstuffs & live animals	11.3	Chemicals & products	20.7
		Mineral fuels & lubricants	15.8
Total incl. others	**134.8**	Total incl. others	**157.6**

Main export destinations	% of total	Main origins of imports	% of total
Germany	26.7	Germany	29.8
Italy	7.1	Russia	9.1
France	6.2	Italy	6.7
United Kingdom	6.1	China	5.4
EU27	78.9	EU27	73.3

Balance of payments, reserves and debt, $bn

Visible exports fob	144.6	Change in reserves	17.3
Visible imports fob	-160.2	Level of reserves	
Trade balance	-15.6	end Dec.	65.7
Invisibles inflows	38.8	No. months of import cover	3.7
Invisibles outflows	-50.4	Official gold holdings, m oz	3.3
Net transfers	8.5	Foreign debt	195.4
Current account balance	-18.6	– as % of GDP	53
– as % of GDP	-4.4	– as % of total exports	121
Capital balance	45.6	Debt service ratio	26
Overall balance	13.0	Aid given	0.36
		% of GDP	0.09

Health and education

Health spending, % of GDP	6.2	Education spending, % of GDP	5.5
Doctors per 1,000 pop.	2.0	Enrolment, %: primary	97
Hospital beds per 1,000 pop.	5.2	secondary	100
Improved-water source access, % of pop.	...	tertiary	67

Society

No. of households	13.7m	Colour TVs per 100 households	98.7
Av. no. per household	2.8	Telephone lines per 100 pop.	27.1
Marriages per 1,000 pop.	5.2	Mobile telephone subscribers	
Divorces per 1,000 pop.	1.6	per 100 pop.	108.7
Cost of living, Feb. 2009		Computers per 100 pop.	16.9
New York = 100	69	Internet hosts per 1,000 pop.	216.9

PORTUGAL

Area	88,940 sq km	Capital	Lisbon
Arable as % of total land	14	Currency	Euro (€)

People

Population	10.6m	Life expectancy: men	75.4 yrs
Pop. per sq km	119.2	women	81.9 yrs
Av. ann. growth		Adult literacy	94.9%
in pop. 2010–15	0.10%	Fertility rate (per woman)	1.4
Pop. under 15	15.3%	Urban population	58.9%
Pop. over 60	23.3%		per 1,000 pop.
No. of men per 100 women	94	Crude birth rate	10
Human Development Index	90.0	Crude death rate	10.1

The economy

GDP	€163bn	GDP per head	$21,000
GDP	$223bn	GDP per head in purchasing	
Av. ann. growth in real		power parity (USA=100)	49.9
GDP 2002–2007	1.0%	Economic freedom index	64.9

Origins of GDP		Components of GDP	
	% of total		% of total
Agriculture	2.9	Private consumption	64.9
Industry, of which:	25.5	Public consumption	20.3
manufacturing	...	Investment	22.1
Services	71.8	Exports	32.7
		Imports	-40.2

Structure of employment

	% of total		% of labour force
Agriculture	12	Unemployed 2007	8.0
Industry	31	Av. ann. rate 1995–2007	6.2
Services	57		

Energy

	m TOE		
Total output	4.3	Net energy imports as %	
Total consumption	25.4	of energy use	83
Consumption per head,			
kg oil equivalent	2,402		

Inflation and finance

Consumer price		av. ann. increase 2002–07
inflation 2008	2.6%	Euro area:
Av. ann. inflation 2003–08	2.6%	Narrow money (M1) 9.3%
Deposit rate, h'holds, 2008	3.58%	Broad money 8.4%
		Household saving rate[a], 2008 6.9%

Exchange rates

	end 2008		December 2008
€ per $	0.72	Effective rates	2000 = 100
€ per SDR	1.11	– nominal	109.10
		– real	114.40

Trade

Principal exports

	$bn fob
Machinery & transport equip.	16.6
Food, drink & tobacco	4.4
Chemicals & related products	3.8
Raw materials	2.5
Total incl. others	**51.5**

Principal imports

	$bn cif
Machinery & transport equip.	24.5
Mineral fuels & lubricants	11.1
Chemicals & related products	8.8
Food, drink & tobacco	8.8
Total incl. others	**78.1**

Main export destinations

	% of total
Spain	26.8
Germany	12.8
France	12.2
United Kingdom	5.8
United States	4.7
EU27	76.7

Main origins of imports

	% of total
Spain	29.3
Germany	12.8
France	8.4
Italy	5.2
Netherlands	4.5
EU27	75.4

Balance of payments, reserves and debt, $bn

Visible exports fob	51.7	Overall balance	-1.0
Visible imports fob	-75.9	Change in reserves	1.6
Trade balance	-24.1	Level of reserves	
Invisibles inflows	40.5	end Dec.	11.5
Invisibles outflows	-41.5	No. months of import cover	1.2
Net transfers	3.6	Official gold holdings, m oz	12.3
Current account balance	-21.4	Aid given	0.47
– as % of GDP	-9.6	– as % of GDP	0.21
Capital balance	22.0		

Health and education

Health spending, % of GDP	10.2	Education spending, % of GDP	5.3
Doctors per 1,000 pop.	3.4	Enrolment, %: primary	109
Hospital beds per 1,000 pop.	3.7	secondary[b]	101
Improved-water source access,		tertiary	56
% of pop.	...		

Society

No. of households	3.9m	Colour TVs per 100 households	98.9
Av. no. per household	2.7	Telephone lines per 100 pop.	39.5
Marriages per 1,000 pop.	4.9	Mobile telephone subscribers	
Divorces per 1,000 pop.	2.4	per 100 pop.	126.6
Cost of living, Feb. 2009		Computers per 100 pop.	17.2
New York = 100	83	Internet hosts per 1,000 pop.	181.0

a Gross.
b Includes training for unemployed.

ROMANIA

Area	237,500 sq km	Capital	Bucharest
Arable as % of total land	40	Currency	Leu (RON)

People

Population	21.5m	Life expectancy: men	69.1 yrs
Pop. per sq km	90.5	women	76.2 yrs
Av. ann. growth		Adult literacy	97.6%
in pop. 2010–15	-0.38%	Fertility rate (per woman)	1.4
Pop. under 15	15.2%	Urban population	54.0%
Pop. over 60	20.0%		per 1,000 pop.
No. of men per 100 women	95	Crude birth rate	10
Human Development Index	82.5	Crude death rate	12.3

The economy

GDP	RON405bn	GDP per head	$7,700
GDP	$166bn	GDP per head in purchasing	
Av. ann. growth in real		power parity (USA=100)	27.1
GDP 2002–07	7.3%	Economic freedom index	63.2

Origins of GDP		Components of GDP	
	% of total		% of total
Agriculture	10.0	Private consumption	75.3
Industry, of which:	36.7	Public consumption	7.6
manufacturing	26.4	Investment	29.6
Services	55.9	Exports	29.5
		Imports	-43.5

Structure of employment

	% of total		% of labour force
Agriculture	30	Unemployed 2007	6.4
Industry	31	Av. ann. rate 1995–2007	7.1
Services	39		

Energy

	m TOE		
Total output	28.0	Net energy imports as %	
Total consumption	40.1	of energy use	30
Consumption per head,			
kg oil equivalent	1,859.8		

Inflation and finance

		av. ann. increase 2002–07	
Consumer price			
inflation 2008	7.8%	Narrow money (M1)	47.6%
Av. ann. inflation 2003–08	8.0%	Broad money	27.6%
Money market rate, 2008	11.37%		

Exchange rates

	end 2008		December 2008
			2000 = 100
RON per $	2.83	Effective rates	
RON per SDR	4.37	– nominal	55.46
RON per €	3.94	– real	128.29

Trade

Principal exports		Principal imports	
	$bn fob		*$bn cif*
Machinery & equipment		Machinery & equipment	
(incl. transport)	13.9	(incl. transport)	25.2
Textiles & apparel	7.2	Chemical & plastic products	8.8
Basic metals & products	6.6	Mineral products	7.8
Chemical & plastic products	3.5	Base metals	7.2
Total incl. others	**40.2**	Total incl. others	**69.8**

Main export destinations		Main origins of imports	
	% of total		*% of total*
Italy	17.2	Germany	17.2
Germany	17.0	Italy	12.8
France	7.7	Hungary	7.0
EU27	72.0	EU27	71.3

Balance of payments, reserves and debt, $bn

Visible exports fob	40.6	Change in reserves	9.8
Visible imports fob	-65.1	Level of reserves	
Trade balance	-24.6	end Dec.	40.0
Invisibles inflows	12.8	No. months of import cover	5.8
Invisibles outflows	-17.9	Official gold holdings, m oz	3.3
Net transfers	6.6	Foreign debt	85.4
Current account balance	-23.0	– as % of GDP	67
– as % of GDP	-13.9	– as % of total exports	175
Capital balance	30.4	Debt service ratio	19
Overall balance	6.3		

Health and education

Health spending, % of GDP	4.5	Education spending, % of GDP	3.5
Doctors per 1,000 pop.	1.9	Enrolment, %: primary	97
Hospital beds per 1,000 pop.	6.5	secondary	87
Improved-water source access,		tertiary	58
% of pop.	57		

Society

No. of households	7.7m	Colour TVs per 100 households	88.3
Av. no. per household	2.8	Telephone lines per 100 pop.	19.9
Marriages per 1,000 pop.	6.4	Mobile telephone subscribers	
Divorces per 1,000 pop.	1.8	per 100 pop.	95.2
Cost of living, Feb. 2009		Computers per 100 pop.	19.2
New York = 100	53	Internet hosts per 1,000 pop.	101.6

RUSSIA

| Area | 17,075,400 sq km | Capital | Moscow |
| Arable as % of total land | 7 | Currency | Rouble (Rb) |

People

Population	141.9m	Life expectancy: men	60.3 yrs
Pop. per sq km	8.3	women	73.1 yrs
Av. ann. growth		Adult literacy	99.5%
in pop. 2010–15	-0.34%	Fertility rate (per woman)	1.5
Pop. under 15	14.8%	Urban population	72.8%
Pop. over 60	17.8%		per 1,000 pop.
No. of men per 100 women	86	Crude birth rate	12
Human Development Index	80.6	Crude death rate	15.1

The economy

GDP	Rb32,987bn	GDP per head	$9,080
GDP	$1,290bn	GDP per head in purchasing	
Av. ann. growth in real		power parity (USA=100)	32.2
GDP 2002–2007	8.5%	Economic freedom index	50.8

Origins of GDP		**Components of GDP**	
	% of total		% of total
Agriculture	4.6	Private consumption	48.8
Industry, of which:	38.4	Public consumption	17.2
manufacturing	19.3	Investment	24.3
Services	57.0	Exports	30.3
		Imports	-21.7

Structure of employment

	% of total		% of labour force
Agriculture	10	Unemployed 2007	6.1
Industry	28	Av. ann. rate 1995–2007	9.3
Services	62		

Energy

	m TOE		
Total output	1,220	Net energy imports as %	
Total consumption	676.2	of energy use	-80
Consumption per head,			
kg oil equivalent	4,745		

Inflation and finance

Consumer price		av. ann. increase 2002–07	
inflation 2008	14.1%	Narrow money (M1)	38.4%
Av. ann. inflation 2003–08	11.3%	Broad money	38.6%
Money market rate, 2008	5.48%		

Exchange rates

	end 2008		December 2008
Rb per $	29.38	Effective rates	2000 = 100
Rb per SDR	45.25	– nominal	95.71
Rb per 7	40.90	– real	181.70

Trade

Principal exports		Principal imports	
	$bn fob		*$bn fob*
Fuels	231.0	Machinery & equipment	98.1
Metals	47.9	Chemicals	26.7
Chemicals	19.6	Food & agricultural products	26.1
Machinery & equipment	17.9	Metals	14.8
Total incl. others	**354.4**	Total incl. others	**223.5**

Main export destinations		Main origins of imports	
	% of total		*% of total*
Netherlands	12.1	Germany	11.9
Germany	9.6	China	10.9
Italy	7.8	Ukraine	6.0
China	5.0	United States	4.2

Balance of payments, reserves and debt, $bn

Visible exports fob	354.4	Change in reserves	172.7
Visible imports fob	-223.5	Level of reserves	
Trade balance	130.9	end Dec.	476.5
Invisibles inflows	86.2	No. months of import cover	15.8
Invisibles outflows	-137.4	Official gold holdings, m oz	14.5
Net transfers	-3.5	Foreign debt	370.2
Current account balance	76.2	– as % of GDP	39
– as % of GDP	5.9	– as % of total exports	105
Capital balance	85.9	Debt service ratio	9
Overall balance	148.9		

Health and education

Health spending, % of GDP	5.3	Education spending, % of GDP	3.9
Doctors per 1,000 pop.	4.3	Enrolment, %: primary	100
Hospital beds per 1,000 pop.	9.7	secondary	84
Improved-water source access,		tertiary	75
% of pop.	97		

Society

No. of households	53.0m	Colour TVs per 100 households	95.1
Av. no. per household	2.7	Telephone lines per 100 pop.	31.0
Marriages per 1,000 pop.	7.7	Mobile telephone subscribers	
Divorces per 1,000 pop.	4.0	per 100 pop.	114.6
Cost of living, Feb. 2009		Computers per 100 pop.	13.3
New York = 100	79	Internet hosts per 1,000 pop.	42.4

SAUDI ARABIA

Area	2,200,000 sq km	Capital	Riyadh
Arable as % of total land	2	Currency	Riyal (SR)

People

Population	25.8m	Life expectancy: men		70.9 yrs
Pop. per sq km	11.7		women	75.3 yrs
Av. ann. growth		Adult literacy		85.0%
in pop. 2010–15	1.95%	Fertility rate (per woman)		2.8
Pop. under 15	32.4%	Urban population		81.4%
Pop. over 60	4.5%			per 1,000 pop.
No. of men per 100 women	121	Crude birth rate		29
Human Development Index	83.5	Crude death rate		3.6

The economy

GDP	SR1,431bn	GDP per head	$15,800
GDP	$382bn	GDP per head in purchasing	
Av. ann. growth in real		power parity (USA=100)	50.3
GDP 2002–07	5.5%	Economic freedom index	64.3

Origins of GDP		**Components of GDP**	
	% of total		% of total
Agriculture	2.8	Private consumption	28.3
Industry, of which:	64.7	Public consumption	22.5
manufacturing	9.6	Investment	21.8
Services	32.5	Exports	65.5
		Imports	-38.1

Structure of employment

	% of total		% of labour force
Agriculture	4	Unemployed 2007	5.6
Industry	22	Av. ann. rate 1995–2007	4.7
Services	74		

Energy

	m TOE		
Total output	570.7	Net energy imports as %	
Total consumption	146.1	of energy use	-291
Consumption per head,			
kg oil equivalent	6,170		

Inflation and finance

		av. ann. increase 2002–07	
Consumer price			
inflation 2008	9.9%	Narrow money (M1)	13.7%
Av. ann. inflation 2003–08	3.4%	Broad money	15.8%
Deposit rate, 2008	3.28%		

Exchange rates

	end 2008		December 2008
			2000 = 100
SR per $	3.75	Effective rates	
SR per SDR	5.78	– nominal	89.20
SRE per €	5.22	– real	87.80

Trade

Principal exports		Principal imports	
	$bn fob		*$bn cif*
Crude oil	177.6	Machinery & transport equip.	42.5
Refined petroleum products	28.7	Foodstuffs	12.0
Total incl. others	**234.1**	Total incl. others	**90.2**

Main export destinations		Main origins of imports	
	% of total		*% of total*
United States	17.4	United States	12.7
Japan	15.4	China	9.4
South Korea	10.1	Germany	8.9
China	8.0	Japan	8.2

Balance of payments, reserves and aid, $bn

Visible exports fob	234.1	Overall balance	6.2
Visible imports fob	-82.6	Change in reserves	7.1
Trade balance	151.5	Level of reserves	
Invisibles inflows	22.9	end Dec.	37.6
Invisibles outflows	-45.6	No. months of import cover	3.5
Net transfers	-33.8	Official gold holdings, m oz	4.6
Current account balance	95.1	Aid given	2.08
– as % of GDP	24.9	– as % of GDP	0.54
Capital balance	-88.9		

Health and education

Health spending, % of GDP	3.3	Education spending, % of GDP	6.8
Doctors per 1,000 pop.	0.5	Enrolment, %: primary	...
Hospital beds per 1,000 pop.	2.2	secondary	94
Improved-water source access,		tertiary	...
% of pop.	96		

Society

No. of households	4.4m	Colour TVs per 100 households	97.7
Av. no. per household	5.6	Telephone lines per 100 pop.	16.2
Marriages per 1,000 pop.	4.4	Mobile telephone subscribers	
Divorces per 1,000 pop.	1.0	per 100 pop.	114.7
Cost of living, Feb. 2009		Computers per 100 pop.	14.8
New York = 100	68	Internet hosts per 1,000 pop.	5.4

SINGAPORE

Area	639 sq km	Capital	Singapore
Arable as % of total land	1	Currency	Singapore dollar (S$)

People

Population	4.4m	Life expectancy: men	77.9 yrs
Pop. per sq km	6,885.8	women	82.8 yrs
Av. ann. growth		Adult literacy	94.4%
in pop. 2010–15	0.90%	Fertility rate (per woman)	1.3
Pop. under 15	16.3%	Urban population	100.0%
Pop. over 60	15.2%		per 1,000 pop.
No. of men per 100 women	101	Crude birth rate	11
Human Development Index	91.8	Crude death rate	5.1

The economy

GDP	S$243bn	GDP per head	$35,160
GDP	$161bn	GDP per head in purchasing	
Av. ann. growth in real		power parity (USA=100)	109.0
GDP 2002–2007	8.4%	Economic freedom index	87.1

Origins of GDP

	% of total
Agriculture	0
Industry, of which:	30.6
manufacturing	...
Services	69.4

Components of GDP

	% of total
Private consumption	38.6
Public consumption	9.7
Investment	20.7
Exports	230.2
Imports	-198.5

Structure of employment

	% of total		% of labour force
Agriculture	0	Unemployed 2007	4.0
Industry	30	Av. ann. rate 1995–2007	3.9
Services	70		

Energy

	m TOE		
Total output	0.0	Net energy imports as %	
Total consumption	30.7	of energy use	100
Consumption per head,			
kg oil equivalent	6,968		

Inflation and finance

		av. ann. increase 2002–07	
Consumer price			
inflation 2008	6.5%	Narrow money (M1)	12.3%
Av. ann. inflation 2003–08	2.3%	Broad money	10.5%
Money market rate, 2008	1.31%		

Exchange rates

	end 2008		December 2008
S$ per $	1.44	Effective rates	2000 = 100
S$ per SDR	2.22	– nominal	108.90
S$ per 7	2.00	– real	103.40

Trade

Principal exports	$bn fob	Principal imports	$bn cif
Electronic components & parts	76.4	Machinery & transport equip.	138.7
Mineral fuels	52.9	Mineral fuels	53.6
Chemicals & products	36.8	Manufactured products	20.4
Manufactured products	19.4	Misc. manufacture articles	19.6
Total incl. others	**299.4**	Total incl. others	**263.3**

Main export destinations	% of total	Main origins of imports	% of total
Malaysia	12.9	Malaysia	13.1
Hong Kong	10.4	United States	12.3
China	9.7	China	12.1
United States	8.8	Japan	8.2
Japan	4.8	Taiwan	5.9
Thailand	4.1	Saudi Arabia	3.3
Australia	3.7	Thailand	3.2

Balance of payments, reserves and debt, $bn

Visible exports fob	303.1	Change in reserves	26.7
Visible imports fob	-254.0	Level of reserves	
Trade balance	49.1	end Dec.	163.0
Invisibles inflows	112.8	No. months of import cover	5.2
Invisibles outflows	-121.1	Official gold holdings, m oz	...
Net transfers	-1.7	Foreign debt	25.6
Current account balance	39.1	– as % of GDP	15
– as % of GDP	24.2	– as % of total exports	6
Capital balance	-18.6	Debt service ratio	1
Overall balance	19.6		

Health and education

Health spending, % of GDP	3.3	Education spending, % of GDP	...
Doctors per 1,000 pop.	1.6	Enrolment, %: primary	...
Hospital beds per 1,000 pop.	3.2	secondary	...
Improved-water source access,		tertiary	...
% of pop.	100		

Society

No. of households	1.0m	Colour TVs per 100 households	99.4
Av. no. per household	4.3	Telephone lines per 100 pop.	42.0
Marriages per 1,000 pop.	5.1	Mobile telephone subscribers	
Divorces per 1,000 pop.	1.7	per 100 pop.	133.5
Cost of living, Feb. 2009		Computers per 100 pop.	74.3
New York = 100	112	Internet hosts per 1,000 pop.	191.5

SLOVAKIA

Area	49,035 sq km	Capital	Bratislava
Arable as % of total land	29	Currency	Koruna (Sk)

People

Population	5.4m	Life expectancy:	men	70.7 yrs
Pop. per sq km	110.1		women	78.5 yrs
Av. ann. growth		Adult literacy		...
in pop. 2010–15	0.09%	Fertility rate (per woman)		1.4
Pop. under 15	15.4%	Urban population		56.4%
Pop. over 60	17.3%			per 1,000 pop.
No. of men per 100 women	94	Crude birth rate		10.0
Human Development Index	87.2	Crude death rate		10.0

The economy

GDP	Sk1,853bn	GDP per head	$13,890
GDP	$75.0bn	GDP per head in purchasing	
Av. ann. growth in real		power parity (USA=100)	44.0
GDP 2002–2007	8.1%	Economic freedom index	69.4

Origins of GDP		Components of GDP	
	% of total		% of total
Agriculture	3.7	Private consumption	55.9
Industry, of which:	41.1	Public consumption	17.3
Manufacturing	25.9	Investment	27.8
Services	55.1	Exports	86.5
		Imports	-87.5

Structure of employment

	% of total		% of labour force
Agriculture	4	Unemployed 2007	11.0
Industry	39	Av. ann. rate 1995–2007	15.2
Services	57		

Energy

	m TOE		
Total output	6.6	Net energy imports as %	
Total consumption	18.7	of energy use	65
Consumption per head,			
kg oil equivalent	3,465		

Inflation and finance

Consumer price		av. ann. increase 2002–07	
inflation 2008	4.6%	Narrow money	19.6%
Av. ann. inflation 2003–08	4.4%	Broad money	9.1%
Interbank rate, 2008	3.90%	Household saving rate, 2008	2.0%

Exchange rates

	end 2008		December 2008
Sk per $	21.39	Effective rates	2000 = 100
Sk per SDR	32.94	– nominal	160.19
Sk per €	29.77	– real	201.31

Trade

Principal exports		Principal imports	
	$bn fob		*$bn fob*
Machinery & transport equipment	34.8	Machinery & transport equipment	25.6
Semi-manufactures	13.9	Semi-manufactures	10.2
Other manufactured goods	6.0	Fuels	6.6
Chemicals	3.2	Chemicals	5.1
Total incl. others	**64.8**	Total incl. others	**58.5**

Main export destinations		Main origins of imports	
	% of total		*% of total*
Germany	19.2	Germany	22.8
Czech Republic	11.3	Czech Republic	17.8
France	6.1	Russia	9.5
Italy	5.7	Hungary	6.9
EU27	86.7	EU27	74.2

Balance of payments, reserves and debt, $bn

Visible exports fob	57.8	Change in reserves	5.6
Visible imports fob	-58.7	Level of reserves	
Trade balance	-0.9	end Dec.	19.0
Invisibles inflows	9.4	No. months of import cover	3.2
Invisibles outflows	-12.2	Official gold holdings, m oz	1.1
Net transfers	-0.4	Foreign debt	36.8
Current account balance	-4.1	– as % of GDP	49
– as % of GDP	-5.5	– as % of total exports	55
Capital balance	7.5	Debt service ratio	8
Overall balance	3.7	Aid given	0.07
		% of GDP	0.09

Health and education

Health spending, % of GDP	7.1	Education spending, % of GDP	3.8
Doctors per 1,000 pop.	3.1	Enrolment, %: primary	101
Hospital beds per 1,000 pop.	6.8	secondary	94
Improved-water source access, % of pop.	100	tertiary	51

Society

No. of households	2.2m	Colour TVs per 100 households	98.3
Av. no. per household	2.5	Telephone lines per 100 pop.	21.4
Marriages per 1,000 pop.	5.0	Mobile telephone subscribers	
Divorces per 1,000 pop.	2.2	per 100 pop.	112.6
Cost of living, Feb. 2009		Computers per 100 pop.	51.4
New York = 100	...	Internet hosts per 1,000 pop.	140.6

SLOVENIA

Area	20,253 sq km	Capital	Ljubljana
Arable as % of total land	9	Currency	Euro (€)

People

Population	2.0m	Life expectancy: men	74.6 yrs
Pop. per sq km	98.8	women	81.9 yrs
Av. ann. growth		Adult literacy	99.7%
in pop. 2010–15	0.19%	Fertility rate (per woman)	1.5
Pop. under 15	13.8%	Urban population	48.9%
Pop. over 60	21.9%		*per 1,000 pop.*
No. of men per 100 women	95	Crude birth rate	10
Human Development Index	92.3	Crude death rate	9.5

The economy

GDP	€34.5bn	GDP per head	$23,380
GDP	$47.2bn	GDP per head in purchasing	
Av. ann. growth in real		power parity (USA=100)	58.7
GDP 2002–2007	5.3%	Economic freedom index	62.9

Origins of GDP		**Components of GDP**	
	% of total		*% of total*
Agriculture	2.4	Private consumption	52.2
Industry, of which:	34.4	Public consumption	17.7
manufacturing	23.4	Investment	29.7
Services	63.3	Exports	70.2
		Imports	-71.5

Structure of employment

	% of total		*% of labour force*
Agriculture	10	Unemployed 2007	4.6
Industry	36	Av. ann. rate 1995–2007	6.5
Services	54		

Energy

	m TOE		
Total output	3.3	Net energy imports as %	
Total consumption	7.3	of energy use	54
Consumption per head,			
kg oil equivalent	3,618		

Inflation and finance

Consumer price		*av. ann. increase 2000–05*	
inflation 2008	5.7%	Narrow money (M1)	15.9%
Av. ann. inflation 2003–08	3.6%	Broad money	11.9%
Money market rate, 2008	4.27%		

Exchange rates

	end 2008		*December 2008*
€ per $	0.72	Effective rates	*2000 = 100*
€ per SDR	1.11	– nominal	...
		– real	...

Trade

Principal exports		**Principal imports**	
	$bn fob		*$bn fob*
Machinery & transport equip.	10.7	Machinery & transport equip.	10.1
Manufactures	6.6	Manufactures	6.6
Chemicals	3.7	Chemicals	3.5
Miscellaneous manufactures	3.3	Miscellaneous manufactures	2.8
Total incl. others	**26.5**	Total incl. others	**29.5**

Main export destinations		**Main origins of imports**	
	% of total		*% of total*
Germany	21.2	Germany	19.5
Italy	14.1	Italy	18.3
Croatia	9.0	Austria	12.5
Austria	8.4	France	5.4
France	6.6	Croatia	5.0
Russia	5.0	Netherlands	3.6
EU27	69.3	EU27	73.7

Balance of payments, reserves and debt, $bn

Visible exports fob	27.1	Change in reserves	-6.1
Visible imports fob	-29.4	Level of reserves	
Trade balance	-2.3	end Dec.	1.1
Invisibles inflows	7.1	No. months of import cover	0.4
Invisibles outflows	-6.6	Official gold holdings, m oz	0.1
Net transfers	-0.4	Foreign debt[a]	21.4
Current account balance	-2.3	– as % of GDP[a]	55
– as % of GDP	-4.9	– as % of total exports[a]	80
Capital balance	2.6	Debt service ratio[a]	19
Overall balance	-0.2		

Health and education

Health spending, % of GDP	8.4	Education spending, % of GDP	5.8
Doctors per 1,000 pop.	2.4	Enrolment, %: primary	96
Hospital beds per 1,000 pop.	4.8	secondary	94
Improved-water source access,		tertiary	86
% of pop.	...		

Society

No. of households	0.7m	Colour TVs per 100 households	97.0
Av. no. per household	2.9	Telephone lines per 100 pop.	42.8
Marriages per 1,000 pop.	3.2	Mobile telephone subscribers	
Divorces per 1,000 pop.	1.2	per 100 pop.	96.4
Cost of living, Feb. 2009		Computers per 100 pop.	42.5
New York = 100	...	Internet hosts per 1,000 pop.	40.3

a 2006

SOUTH AFRICA

Area	1,225,815 sq km	Capital	Pretoria
Arable as % of total land	12	Currency	Rand (R)

People

Population	47.7m	Life expectancy: men	49.9 yrs
Pop. per sq km	38.9	women	53.2 yrs
Av. ann. growth		Adult literacy	88.0
in pop. 2010–15	0.47%	Fertility rate (per woman)	2.4
Pop. under 15	30.5%	Urban population	60.2%
Pop. over 60	7.1%		per 1,000 pop.
No. of men per 100 women	97	Crude birth rate	23
Human Development Index	67.0	Crude death rate	15.1

The economy

GDP	R1,994bn	GDP per head	$5,910
GDP	$283bn	GDP per head in purchasing	
Av. ann. growth in real		power parity (USA=100)	21.4
GDP 2002–2007	5.1%	Economic freedom index	63.8

Origins of GDP		Components of GDP	
	% of total		% of total
Agriculture	3.2	Private consumption	61.4
Industry, of which:	31.9	Public consumption	19.7
manufacturing	18.4	Investment	21.9
Services	64.9	Exports	31.5
		Imports	-34.6

Structure of employment

	% of total		% of labour force
Agriculture	8	Unemployed 2007	23.0
Industry	25	Av. ann. rate 1995–2007	24.3
Services	67		

Energy

	m TOE		
Total output	158.7	Net energy imports as %	
Total consumption	129.8	of energy use	-22
Consumption per head,			
kg oil equivalent	2,739		

Inflation and finance

Consumer price		av. ann. increase 2002–07	
inflation 2008	9.8%	Narrow money (M1)	15.1%
Av. ann. inflation 2003–08	4.0%	Broad money	16.9%
Money market rate, 2008	11.32%		

Exchange rates

	end 2008		December 2008
R per $	9.31	Effective rates	2000 = 100
R per SDR	14.33	– nominal	75.90
R per €	12.96	– real	65.60

Trade

Principal exports		Principal imports	
	$bn fob		*$bn cif*
Platinum	9.9	Petrochemicals	10.9
Gold	5.6	Equipment components for cars	5.7
Ferro-alloys	3.7	Cars & other components	4.4
Coal	3.4	Petroleum oils & other	3.2
Cars & other components	2.9	Telecoms components	1.8
Total incl. others	**69.9**	Total incl. others	**79.9**

Main export destinations		Main origins of imports	
	% of total		*% of total*
United States	12.1	Germany	13.4
Japan	10.0	China	10.4
China	8.5	United States	7.6
United Kingdom	8.3	Japan	6.4

Balance of payments, reserves and debt, $bn

Visible exports fob	75.9	Change in reserves	7.3
Visible imports fob	-81.7	Level of reserves	
Trade balance	-5.7	end Dec.	32.9
Invisibles inflows	20.4	No. months of import cover	3.5
Invisibles outflows	-32.6	Official gold holdings, m oz	4.0
Net transfers	-3.0	Foreign debt	43.4
Current account balance	-20.8	– as % of GDP	19
– as % of GDP	-7.3	– as % of total exports	58
Capital balance	22.1	Debt service ratio	6
Overall balance	5.7		

Health and education

Health spending, % of GDP	8.0	Education spending, % of GDP	5.4
Doctors per 1,000 pop.	0.8	Enrolment, %: primary	113
Hospital beds per 1,000 pop.	...	secondary	97
Improved-water source access,		tertiary	...
% of pop.	88		

Society

No. of households	13.0m	Colour TVs per 100 households	64.5
Av. no. per household	3.9	Telephone lines per 100 pop.	9.6
Marriages per 1,000 pop.	3.8	Mobile telephone subscribers	
Divorces per 1,000 pop.	1.0	per 100 pop.	87.1
Cost of living, Feb. 2009		Computers per 100 pop.	8.5
New York = 100	53	Internet hosts per 1,000 pop.	27.4

SOUTH KOREA

Area	99,274 sq km	Capital	Seoul
Arable as % of total land	16	Currency	Won (W)

People

Population	48.1m	Life expectancy: men		75.9 yrs
Pop. per sq km	482.3	women		82.5 yrs
Av. ann. growth		Adult literacy		...
in pop. 2010–15	0.27%	Fertility rate (per woman)		1.3
Pop. under 15	16.8%	Urban population		81.2%
Pop. over 60	15.1%			*per 1,000 pop.*
No. of men per 100 women	98	Crude birth rate		10
Human Development Index	92.8	Crude death rate		5.5

The economy

GDP	W901trn	GDP per head	$20,010
GDP	$970bn	GDP per head in purchasing	
Av. ann. growth in real		power parity (USA=100)	54.4
GDP 2002–2007	4.7%	Economic freedom index	68.1

Origins of GDP		**Components of GDP**	
	% of total		*% of total*
Agriculture	3.0	Private consumption	54.4
Industry, of which:	39.4	Public consumption	14.7
manufacturing	...	Investment	29.4
Services	57.6	Exports	41.9
		Imports	-40.4

Structure of employment

	% of total		*% of labour force*
Agriculture	7	Unemployed 2007	3.2
Industry	27	Av. ann. rate 1995–2007	3.7
Services	66		

Energy

	m TOE		
Total output	43.7	Net energy imports as %	
Total consumption	216.5	of energy use	80
Consumption per head,			
kg oil equivalent	4,483		

Inflation and finance

		av. ann. increase 2002–07	
Consumer price			
inflation 2008	4.7%	Narrow money (M1)	6.5%
Av. ann. inflation 2003–08	3.2%	Broad money	2.7%
Money market rate, 2008	4.78%	Household saving rate, 2008	3.7%

Exchange rates

	end 2008		*December 2008*
W per $	1,260	Effective rates	*2000 = 100*
W per SDR	1,940	– nominal	...
W per €	1,753	– real	...

Trade

Principal exports		Principal imports	
	$bn fob		*$bn cif*
Information & communications		Crude petroleum	60.3
products	50.7	Machinery & equipment	39.3
Semiconductors	39.0	Semiconductors	30.8
Chemicals	36.8	Chemicals	29.2
Machinery & equipment	36.2		
Total incl. others	**371.5**	Total incl. others	**356.9**

Main export destinations		Main origins of imports	
	% of total		*% of total*
China	22.1	China	17.7
United States	12.3	Japan	15.8
Japan	7.1	United States	10.4
Hong Kong	5.0	Germany	3.8

Balance of payments, reserves and debt, $bn

Visible exports fob	379.0	Change in reserves	23.4
Visible imports fob	-349.6	Level of reserves	
Trade balance	29.4	end Dec.	262.5
Invisibles inflows	82.4	No. months of import cover	7.0
Invisibles outflows	-102.2	Official gold holdings, m oz	0.5
Net transfers	-3.6	Foreign debt	268.8
Current account balance	6.0	– as % of GDP	26
– as % of GDP	0.6	– as % of total exports	58
Capital balance	6.2	Debt service ratio	6
Overall balance	15.1	Aid given	0.70
		% of GDP	0.07

Health and education

Health spending, % of GDP	6.4	Education spending, % of GDP	4.4
Doctors per 1,000 pop.	1.4	Enrolment, %: primary	107
Hospital beds per 1,000 pop.	7.1	secondary	98
Improved-water source access,		tertiary	95
% of pop.	92		

Society

No. of households	17.8m	Colour TVs per 100 households	99.6
Av. no. per household	2.7	Telephone lines per 100 pop.	46.4
Marriages per 1,000 pop.	6.8	Mobile telephone subscribers	
Divorces per 1,000 pop.	4.2	per 100 pop.	90.2
Cost of living, Feb. 2009		Computers per 100 pop.	57.6
New York = 100	78	Internet hosts per 1,000 pop.	6.9

SPAIN

Area	504,782 sq km	Capital	Madrid
Arable as % of total land	27	Currency	Euro (€)

People

Population	43.6m	Life expectancy: men	77.6 yrs
Pop. per sq km	86.4	women	84.1 yrs
Av. ann. growth		Adult literacy	97.9
in pop. 2010–15	0.82%	Fertility rate (per woman)	1.6
Pop. under 15	14.8%	Urban population	77.0%
Pop. over 60	22.2%		per 1,000 pop.
No. of men per 100 women	97	Crude birth rate	11
Human Development Index	94.9	Crude death rate	8.7

The economy

GDP	€1,050bn	GDP per head	$32,020
GDP	$1,437bn	GDP per head in purchasing	
Av. ann. growth in real		power parity (USA=100)	69.2
GDP 2002–2007	3.8%	Economic freedom index	70.1

Origins of GDP		**Components of GDP**	
	% of total		% of total
Agriculture	3.6	Private consumption	57.3
Industry, of which:	29.8	Public consumption	18.3
manufacturing	...	Investment	31.2
Services	66.6	Exports	26.5
		Imports	-33.3

Structure of employment

	% of total		% of labour force
Agriculture	5	Unemployed 2007	8.3
Industry	30	Av. ann. rate 1995–2007	14.4
Services	65		

Energy

	m TOE		
Total output	31.4	Net energy imports as %	
Total consumption	144.6	of energy use	78
Consumption per head,			
kg oil equivalent	3,277		

Inflation and finance

Consumer price		av. ann. increase 2002–07	
inflation 2008	4.1%	Euro area:	
Av. ann. inflation 2003–08	3.4%	Narrow money (M1)	9.3%
Money market rate, 2008	3.85%	Broad money	8.4%
		Household saving rate[a], 2008	11.2%

Exchange rates

	end 2008		December 2008
€ per $	0.72	Effective rates	2000 = 100
€ per SDR	1.11	– nominal	110.10
		– real	135.80

Trade

Principal exports	$bn fob	Principal imports	$bn cif
Machinery & transport equip.	99.4	Machinery & transport equip.	144.6
Chemicals & related products	32.2	Mineral fuels & lubricants	59.1
Food, drink & tobacco	31.7	Chemicals & related products	44.1
Mineral fuels & lubricants	14.1	Food, drink & tobacco	31.9
Total incl. others	**248.9**	Total incl. others	**385.1**

Main export destinations	% of total	Main origins of imports	% of total
France	18.1	Germany	15.2
Germany	10.4	France	12.3
Portugal	8.3	Italy	8.1
EU27	70.8	EU27	63.0

Balance of payments, reserves and aid, $bn

Visible exports fob	256.7	Overall balance	0.2
Visible imports fob	-380.2	Change in reserves	-0.3
Trade balance	-123.5	Level of reserves	
Invisibles inflows	202.0	end Dec.	19.0
Invisibles outflows	-214.8	No. months of import cover	0.4
Net transfers	-9.0	Official gold holdings, m oz	9.1
Current account balance	-145.4	Aid given	5.14
– as % of GDP	-10.1	– as % of GDP	0.36
Capital balance	140.3		

Health and education

Health spending, % of GDP	8.4	Education spending, % of GDP	4.3
Doctors per 1,000 pop.	3.1	Enrolment, %: primary	104
Hospital beds per 1,000 pop.	3.5	secondary	120
Improved-water source access,		tertiary	69
% of pop.	100		

Society

No. of households	15.5m	Colour TVs per 100 households	99.5
Av. no. per household	2.9	Telephone lines per 100 pop.	45.6
Marriages per 1,000 pop.	4.9	Mobile telephone subscribers	
Divorces per 1,000 pop.	1.1	per 100 pop.	109.4
Cost of living, Feb. 2009		Computers per 100 pop.	39.3
New York = 100	102	Internet hosts per 1,000 pop.	76.3

a Gross.

SWEDEN

Area	449,964 sq km	Capital	Stockholm
Arable as % of total land	7	Currency	Swedish krona (Skr)

People

Population	9.1m	Life expectancy: men	78.7 yrs
Pop. per sq km	20.2	women	83.0 yrs
Av. ann. growth		Adult literacy	...
in pop. 2010–15	0.44%	Fertility rate (per woman)	1.9
Pop. under 15	16.6%	Urban population	84.5%
Pop. over 60	24.7%		per 1,000 pop.
No. of men per 100 women	95	Crude birth rate	12
Human Development Index	95.8	Crude death rate	10.1

The economy

GDP	Skr3,071bn	GDP per head	$49,660
GDP	$454bn	GDP per head in purchasing	
Av. ann. growth in real		power parity (USA=100)	80.5
GDP 2002–2007	3.4%	Economic freedom index	70.5

Origins of GDP

	% of total
Agriculture	1.4
Industry, of which:	28.3
manufacturing	...
Services	70.3

Components of GDP

	% of total
Private consumption	46.7
Public consumption	25.9
Investment	19.7
Exports	52.6
Imports	-44.9

Structure of employment

	% of total		% of labour force
Agriculture	2	Unemployed 2007	6.1
Industry	22	Av. ann. rate 1995–2007	6.3
Services	76		

Energy

	m TOE		
Total output	32.8	Net energy imports as %	
Total consumption	51.3	of energy use	36
Consumption per head,			
kg oil equivalent	5,650		

Inflation and finance

		av. ann. increase 2002–07	
Consumer price			
inflation 2008	3.5%	Narrow money	13.7%
Av. ann. inflation 2003–08	1.6%	Broad money	8.3%
Repurchase rate, 2008	2.00%	Household saving rate, 2008	9.2%

Exchange rates

	end 2008		December 2008
			2000 = 100
Skr per $	7.81	Effective rates	
Skr per SDR	12.03	– nominal	89.80
Skr per €	10.87	– real	77.10

Trade

Principal exports		Principal imports	
	$bn fob		*$bn cif*
Machinery & transport equipment	75.6	Machinery & transport equipment	60.1
Chemicals & related products	19.0	Fuels & lubricants	17.1
Raw materials	10.7	Chemicals & related products	16.6
Mineral fuels & lubricants	9.5	Food, drink & tobacco	10.9
Total incl. others	**169.3**	Total incl. others	**151.5**

Main export destinations		Main origins of imports	
	% of total		*% of total*
Germany	10.4	Germany	18.4
Norway	9.4	Denmark	9.2
United States	7.6	Norway	8.3
Denmark	7.5	United Kingdom	6.8
United Kingdom	7.1	Finland	6.1
EU27	61.2	EU27	70.9

Balance of payments, reserves and aid, $bn

Visible exports fob	170.5	Overall balance	-0.4
Visible imports fob	-152.2	Change in reserves	3.0
Trade balance	18.2	Level of reserves	
Invisibles inflows	126.1	end Dec.	31.0
Invisibles outflows	-100.9	No. months of import cover	1.5
Net transfers	-5.0	Official gold holdings, m oz	4.8
Current account balance	38.4	Aid given	4.34
– as % of GDP	8.3	– as % of GDP	0.93
Capital balance	-22.5		

Health and education

Health spending, % of GDP	9.2	Education spending, % of GDP	7.0
Doctors per 1,000 pop.	3.2	Enrolment, %: primary	95
Hospital beds per 1,000 pop.	...	secondary	104
Improved-water source access, % of pop.	100	tertiary	95

Society

No. of households	4.3m	Colour TVs per 100 households	97.5
Av. no. per household	2.1	Telephone lines per 100 pop.	60.4
Marriages per 1,000 pop.	4.9	Mobile telephone subscribers	
Divorces per 1,000 pop.	2.2	per 100 pop.	113.7
Cost of living, Feb. 2009		Computers per 100 pop.	88.1
New York = 100	90	Internet hosts per 1,000 pop.	425.1

SWITZERLAND

Area	41,293 sq km	Capital	Berne
Arable as % of total land	10	Currency	Swiss franc (SFr)

People

Population	7.3m	Life expectancy: men	79.3 yrs
Pop. per sq km	176.8	women	84.1 yrs
Av. ann. growth		Adult literacy	...
in pop. 2010–15	0.37%	Fertility rate (per woman)	1.5
Pop. under 15	15.3%	Urban population	73.4%
Pop. over 60	23.0%		per 1,000 pop.
No. of men per 100 women	95	Crude birth rate	10
Human Development Index	95.5	Crude death rate	8.3

The economy

GDP	SFr509bn	GDP per head	$56,210
GDP	$424bn	GDP per head in purchasing	
Av. ann. growth in real		power parity (USA=100)	89.2
GDP 2002–2007	2.4%	Economic freedom index	79.4

Origins of GDP		Components of GDP	
	% of total		% of total
Agriculture	1	Private consumption	57.8
Industry, of which:	28	Public consumption	10.8
manufacturing	...	Investment	22.1
Services	71	Exports	55.9
		Imports	-46.7

Structure of employment

	% of total		% of labour force
Agriculture	4	Unemployed 2007	3.6
Industry	22	Av. ann. rate 1995–2007	3.6
Services	74		

Energy

	m TOE		
Total output	12.1	Net energy imports as %	
Total consumption	28.2	of energy use	57
Consumption per head,			
kg oil equivalent	3,770		

Inflation and finance

		av. ann. increase 2002–07	
Consumer price inflation 2008	2.4%	Narrow money (M1)	4.8%
Av. ann. inflation 2003–08	1.2%	Broad money	5.2%
Money market rate, 2008	0.01%	Household saving rate, 2008	12.6%

Exchange rates

	end 2008		December 2008
SFr per $	1.06	Effective rates	2000 = 100
SFr per SDR	1.64	– nominal	110.10
SFr per €	1.48	– real	128.70

Trade

Principal exports	$bn	Principal imports	$bn
Chemicals	57.3	Chemicals	34.4
Machinery , equipment & electronics	35.9	Machinery, equipment & electronics	29.3
Watches & jewellery	29.5	Metals	15.4
Metals & metal manufactures	12.9	Motor vehicles	14.2
Total incl. others	**164.9**	Total incl. others	**153.2**

Main export destinations	% of total	Main origins of imports	% of total
Germany	22.1	Germany	36.0
Italy	8.5	Italy	13.2
France	8.4	United States	12.2
United States	8.4	France	10.2
United Kingdom	5.3	Belgium	5.4
Austria	4.5	Austria	5.1
China	3.1	United Kingdom	5.1
EU27	62.0	EU27	79.5

Balance of payments, reserves and aid, $bn

Visible exports fob	200.5	Overall balance	3.5
Visible imports fob	-187.7	Change in reserves	10.7
Trade balance	12.8	Level of reserves	
Invisibles inflows	192.6	end Dec.	75.2
Invisibles outflows	-152.0	No. months of import cover	2.7
Net transfers	-9.4	Official gold holdings, m oz	36.8
Current account balance	43.9	Aid given	1.69
– as % of GDP	18.1	– as % of GDP	0.40
Capital balance	-32.1		

Health and education

Health spending, % of GDP	10.8	Education spending, % of GDP	5.6
Doctors per 1,000 pop.	3.9	Enrolment, %: primary	90
Hospital beds per 1,000 pop.	5.5	secondary	93
Improved-water source access,		tertiary	...
% of pop.	100		

Society

No. of households	3.3m	Colour TVs per 100 households	98.4
Av. no. per household	2.2	Telephone lines per 100 pop.	65.9
Marriages per 1,000 pop.	5.2	Mobile telephone subscribers	
Divorces per 1,000 pop.	2.6	per 100 pop.	109.7
Cost of living, Feb. 2009		Computers per 100 pop.	91.8
New York = 100	115	Internet hosts per 1,000 pop.	474.6

TAIWAN

Area	36,179 sq km	Capital	Taipei
Arable as % of total land	25	Currency	Taiwan dollar (T$)

People

Population	22.9m	Life expectancy:[a] men	75.1 yrs
Pop. per sq km	633.0	women	81.1 yrs
Av. ann. growth		Adult literacy	96.1%
in pop. 2010–15	0.12%	Fertility rate (per woman)	1.6
Pop. under 15	16.7%	Urban population	...
Pop. over 60	14.5%		per 1,000 pop.
No. of men per 100 women	101	Crude birth rate	13.0
Human Development Index	...	Crude death rate[a]	6.7

The economy

GDP	T$12,589bn	GDP per head	$16,730
GDP	$383bn	GDP per head in purchasing	
Av. ann. growth in real		power parity (USA=100)	75.4
GDP 2002–2007	5.4%	Economic freedom index	69.5

Origins of GDP		Components of GDP	
	% of total		% of total
Agriculture	1.5	Private consumption	58.9
Industry, of which:	27.8	Public consumption	12.1
manufacturing	24.0	Investment	21.5
Services	70.7	Exports	73.5
		Imports	-66.0

Structure of employment

	% of total		% of labour force
Agriculture	5	Unemployed 2007	5.1
Industry	37	Av. ann. rate 1995–2007	3.4
Services	59		

Energy

	m TOE		
Total output	...	Net energy imports as %	
Total consumption	...	of energy use	...
Consumption per head,			
kg oil equivalent	...		

Inflation and finance

Consumer price		av. ann. increase 2002–07	
inflation 2008	3.5%	Narrow money (M1)	8.7%
Av. ann. inflation 2003–08	2.0%	Broad money	5.2%
Money market rate, 2008	2.62%		

Exchange rates

	end 2008		December 2008
			2000 = 100
T$ per $	32.82	Effective rates	
T$ per SDR	50.54	– nominal	...
T$ per €	45.69	– real	...

Trade

Principal exports		Principal imports	
	$bn fob		$bn cif
Electronic products	40.9	Intermediate goods	166.7
Base metals	27.8	Capital goods	35.6
Information & communications products	21.2	Consumer goods	16.9
Textiles & clothing	11.6		
Total incl. others	**235.1**	Total incl. others	**218.2**

Main export destinations		Main origins of imports	
	% of total		% of total
China	26.6	Japan	21.0
Hong Kong	16.2	China	12.8
United States	13.6	United States	12.1
Japan	6.8	South Korea	6.9

Balance of payments, reserves and debt, $bn

Visible exports fob	246.6	Change in reserves	4.2
Visible imports fob	-217.2	Level of reserves	
Trade balance	29.4	end Dec.	271.1
Invisibles inflows	55.5	No. months of import cover	12.2
Invisibles outflows	-49.4	Official gold holdings, m oz	0.0
Net transfers	-3.8	Foreign debt	98.4
Current account balance	31.7	– as % of GDP	26
– as % of GDP	8.3	– as % of total exports	33
Capital balance	-39.0	Debt service ratio	3
Overall balance	-4.0	Aid given	0.51
		% of GDP	0.13

Health and education

Health spending, % of GDP	...	Education spending, % of GDP	...
Doctors per 1,000 pop.	1.7	Enrolment, %: primary	...
Hospital beds per 1,000 pop.	...	secondary	...
Improved-water source access, % of pop.	...	tertiary	...

Society

No. of households	7.4m	Colour TVs per 100 households	99.6
Av. no. per household	3.1	Telephone lines per 100 pop.	62.3
Marriages per 1,000 pop.	7.4	Mobile telephone subscribers	
Divorces per 1,000 pop.	3.4	per 100 pop.	106.1
Cost of living, Feb. 2009		Computers per 100 pop.	...
New York = 100	80	Internet hosts per 1,000 pop.	238.6

a 2002 estimate.

THAILAND

Area	513,115 sq km	Capital	Bangkok
Arable as % of total land	28	Currency	Baht (Bt)

People

Population	65.3m	Life expectancy: men	65.7 yrs
Pop. per sq km	127.3	women	72.0 yrs
Av. ann. growth		Adult literacy	94.1%
in pop. 2010–15	0.52%	Fertility rate (per woman)	1.9
Pop. under 15	21.7%	Urban population	32.9%
Pop. over 60	11.2%		per 1,000 pop.
No. of men per 100 women	97	Crude birth rate	13
Human Development Index	78.6	Crude death rate	8.9

The economy

GDP	Bt8,469bn	GDP per head	$3,840
GDP	$245bn	GDP per head in purchasing	
Av. ann. growth in real		power parity (USA=100)	17.8
GDP 2002–07	6.3%	Economic freedom index	63.0

Origins of GDP		Components of GDP	
	% of total		% of total
Agriculture	10.8	Private consumption	53.7
Industry, of which:	44.7	Public consumption	12.2
manufacturing	35.6	Investment	26.6
Services	44.6	Exports	73.2
		Imports	-65.3

Structure of employment

	% of total		% of labour force
Agriculture	42	Unemployed 2007	1.2
Industry	20	Av. ann. rate 1995–2007	1.8
Services	38		

Energy

	m TOE		
Total output	56.2	Net energy imports as %	
Total consumption	103.4	of energy use	46
Consumption per head,			
kg oil equivalent	1,630		

Inflation and finance

Consumer price		av. ann. increase 2002–07	
inflation 2008	5.4%	Narrow money (M1)	8.9%
Av. ann. inflation 2003–08	3.9%	Broad money	6.0%
Money market rate, 2008	3.28%		

Exchange rates

	end 2008		December 2008
Bt per $	34.90	Effective rates	2000 = 100
Bt per SDR	53.75	– nominal	...
Bt per €	48.58	– real	...

Trade

Principal exports	$bn fob	Principal imports	$bn cif
Machinery & mech. appliances	23.5	Fuel & lubricants	25.7
Integrated circuits & parts	15.7	Minerals & metal products	19.8
Vehicle parts & accessories	12.8	Electronic parts	15.9
Electrical appliances	11.3	Industry machinery,	
		tools & parts	9.5
Total incl. others	**152.1**	Total incl. others	**141.3**

Main export destinations	% of total	Main origins of imports	% of total
United States	12.7	Japan	20.3
Japan	11.9	China	11.6
China	9.8	United States	6.8
Singapore	6.3	Malaysia	6.2

Balance of payments, reserves and debt, $bn

Visible exports fob	150.0	Change in reserves	20.5
Visible imports fob	-124.5	Level of reserves	
Trade balance	25.5	end Dec.	87.5
Invisibles inflows	37.2	No. months of import cover	6.0
Invisibles outflows	-50.9	Official gold holdings, m oz	2.7
Net transfers	3.9	Foreign debt	63.1
Current account balance	15.8	– as % of GDP	29
– as % of GDP	6.4	– as % of total exports	37
Capital balance	-3.0	Debt service ratio	8
Overall balance	17.1		

Health and education

Health spending, % of GDP	3.5	Education spending, % of GDP	3.9
Doctors per 1,000 pop.	0.3	Enrolment, %: primary	77
Hospital beds per 1,000 pop.	...	secondary	83
Improved-water source access,		tertiary	46
% of pop.	99		

Society

No. of households	17.8m	Colour TVs per 100 households	95.5
Av. no. per household	3.6	Telephone lines per 100 pop.	11.0
Marriages per 1,000 pop.	4.5	Mobile telephone subscribers	
Divorces per 1,000 pop.	1.1	per 100 pop.	123.8
Cost of living, Feb. 2009		Computers per 100 pop.	7.0
New York = 100	74	Internet hosts per 1,000 pop.	18.2

TURKEY

Area	779,452 sq km	Capital	Ankara
Arable as % of total land	31	Currency	Turkish Lira (YTL)

People

Population	75.2m	Life expectancy: men	69.4 yrs
Pop. per sq km	96.5	women	74.3 yrs
Av. ann. growth		Adult literacy	88.7%
in pop. 2010–15	1.10%	Fertility rate (per woman)	2.0
Pop. under 15	26.8%	Urban population	68.3%
Pop. over 60	8.8%		per 1,000 pop.
No. of men per 100 women	101	Crude birth rate	19
Human Development Index	79.8	Crude death rate	6.0

The economy

GDP	YTL854bn	GDP per head	$8,880
GDP	$656bn	GDP per head in purchasing	
Av. ann. growth in real		power parity (USA=100)	28.4
GDP 2002–2007	7.9%	Economic freedom index	61.6

Origins of GDP		**Components of GDP**	
	% of total		% of total
Agriculture	8.7	Private consumption	70.9
Industry, of which:	28.3	Public consumption	12.8
manufacturing	19.1	Investment	21.5
Services	63.1	Exports	22.3
		Imports	-27.5

Structure of employment

	% of total		% of labour force
Agriculture	26	Unemployed 2007	9.9
Industry	25	Av. ann. rate 1995–2007	8.6
Services	49		

Energy

	m TOE		
Total output	26.3	Net energy imports as %	
Total consumption	94.0	of energy use	72
Consumption per head,			
kg oil equivalent	1,288		

Inflation and finance

Consumer price		av. ann. increase 2002–07	
inflation 2008	10.4%	Narrow money (M1)	36.5%
Av. ann. inflation 2003–08	10.1%	Broad money	21.4%
Money market rate, 2008	16.00%		

Exchange rates

	end 2008		December 2008
			2000 = 100
YTL per $	1.53	Effective rates	
YTL per SDR	2.35	– nominal	...
YTL per €	2.13	– real	...

Trade

Principal exports		Principal imports	
	$bn fob		*$bn cif*
Textiles & clothing	22.6	Fuels	33.9
Transport equipment	17.0	Chemicals	23.6
Agricultural products	8.9	Mechanical machinery	22.6
Iron & steel	8.4	Transport equipment	15.1
Total incl. others	**107.3**	Total incl. others	**170.1**

Main export destinations		Main origins of imports	
	% of total		*% of total*
Germany	11.2	Russia	13.8
United Kingdom	8.0	Germany	10.3
Italy	7.0	China	7.8
France	5.6	Italy	5.9
EU27	56.4	EU27	40.4

Balance of payments, reserves and debt, $bn

Visible exports fob	115.4	Change in reserves	13.2
Visible imports fob	-162.0	Level of reserves	
Trade balance	-46.7	end Dec.	76.5
Invisibles inflows	35.3	No. months of import cover	4.8
Invisibles outflows	-28.5	Official gold holdings, m oz	3.7
Net transfers	2.2	Foreign debt	251.5
Current account balance	-37.7	– as % of GDP	47
– as % of GDP	-5.8	– as % of total exports	200
Capital balance	48.5	Debt service ratio	32
Overall balance	12.1	Aid given	0.60
		% of GDP	0.09

Health and education

Health spending, % of GDP	4.8	Education spending, % of GDP	4.0
Doctors per 1,000 pop.	1.5	Enrolment, %: primary	94
Hospital beds per 1,000 pop.	2.7	secondary	80
Improved-water source access,		tertiary	35
% of pop.	96		

Society

No. of households	15.9m	Colour TVs per 100 households	92.4
Av. no. per household	4.6	Telephone lines per 100 pop.	24.3
Marriages per 1,000 pop.	6.5	Mobile telephone subscribers	
Divorces per 1,000 pop.	0.8	per 100 pop.	82.8
Cost of living, Feb. 2009		Computers per 100 pop.	6.0
New York = 100	84	Internet hosts per 1,000 pop.	34.5

UKRAINE

Area	603,700 sq km	Capital	Kiev
Arable as % of total land	56	Currency	Hryvnya (UAH)

People

Population	45.5m	Life expectancy: men	62.8 yrs
Pop. per sq km	75.4	women	73.8 yrs
Av. ann. growth		Adult literacy	99.7%
in pop. 2010–15	-0.57%	Fertility rate (per woman)	1.5
Pop. under 15	13.9%	Urban population	67.9%
Pop. over 60	20.8%		per 1,000 pop.
No. of men per 100 women	86	Crude birth rate	10
Human Development Index	78.6	Crude death rate	16.0

The economy

GDP	UAH713bn	GDP per head	$3,040
GDP	$141bn	GDP per head in purchasing	
Av. ann. growth in real		power parity (USA=100)	15.2
GDP 2002–2007	9.2%	Economic freedom index	48.8

Origins of GDP

Components of GDP

	% of total		% of total
Agriculture	8	Private consumption	70.7
Industry, of which:	37	Public consumption	6.8
manufacturing	23	Investment	28.2
Services	55	Exports	44.8
		Imports	-50.6

Structure of employment

	% of total		% of labour force
Agriculture	17	Unemployed 2007	6.4
Industry	24	Av. ann. rate 1995–2007	9.0
Services	59		

Energy

	m TOE		
Total output	82.8	Net energy imports as %	
Total consumption	137.4	of energy use	40
Consumption per head,			
kg oil equivalent	2,937		

Inflation and finance

			av. ann. increase 2002–07
Consumer price			
inflation 2007	12.8%	Narrow money (M1)	45.7%
Av. ann. inflation 2003–07	11.1%	Broad money	57.0%
Money market rate, 2008	13.71%		

Exchange rates

	end 2008		December 2008
UAH per $	7.70	Effective rates	2000 = 100
UAH per SDR	11.86	– nominal	96.46
UAH per €	10.72	– real	141.51

Trade

Principal exports		**Principal imports**	
	$bn fob		*$bn cif*
Metals	20.8	Machinery & equipment	19.8
Machinery & equipment	8.5	Fuels, mineral products	17.3
Food & agricultural produce	6.2	Chemicals	5.3
Fuels & mineral products	4.3	Food & agricultural produce	4.1
Chemicals	4.0		
Total incl. others	**49.3**	Total incl. others	**60.6**

Main export destinations		**Main origins of imports**	
	% of total		*% of total*
Russia	25.7	Russia	27.9
Turkey	7.4	Germany	9.7
Italy	5.4	Poland	5.5
Germany	3.3	China	4.8

Balance of payments, reserves and debt, $bn

Visible exports fob	49.8	Change in reserves	10.1
Visible imports fob	-60.4	Level of reserves	
Trade balance	-10.6	end Dec.	32.5
Invisibles inflows	17.8	No. months of import cover	5.1
Invisibles outflows	-16.2	Official gold holdings, m oz	0.8
Net transfers	3.5	Foreign debt	73.6
Current account balance	-5.9	– as % of GDP	66
– as % of GDP	-3.7	– as % of total exports	131
Capital balance	15.1	Debt service ratio	17
Overall balance	9.4		

Health and education

Health spending, % of GDP	6.9	Education spending, % of GDP	5.4
Doctors per 1,000 pop.	3.2	Enrolment, %: primary	100
Hospital beds per 1,000 pop.	8.7	secondary	94
Improved-water source access,		tertiary	76
% of pop.	96		

Society

No. of households	19.9m	Colour TVs per 100 households	96.9
Av. no. per household	2.3	Telephone lines per 100 pop.	27.8
Marriages per 1,000 pop.	5.8	Mobile telephone subscribers	
Divorces per 1,000 pop.	3.5	per 100 pop.	119.6
Cost of living, Feb. 2009		Computers per 100 pop.	4.5
New York = 100	52	Internet hosts per 1,000 pop.	13.6

UNITED ARAB EMIRATES

Area	83,600 sq km	Capital	Abu Dhabi
Arable as % of total land	1	Currency	Dirham (AED)

People

Population	4.8m	Life expectancy: men	76.6 yrs
Pop. per sq km	57.4	women	78.8 yrs
Av. ann. growth		Adult literacy	90.0%
in pop. 2010–15	1.97%	Fertility rate (per woman)	1.9
Pop. under 15	19.2%	Urban population	77.8%
Pop. over 60	1.9%		per 1,000 pop.
No. of men per 100 women	205	Crude birth rate	15
Human Development Index	90.3	Crude death rate	1.5

The economy

GDP[a]	AED600bn	GDP per head[a]	$38,440
GDP[a]	$163bn	GDP per head in purchasing	
Av. ann. growth in real		power parity (USA=100)[a]	116.7
GDP 2002–07	10.9%	Economic freedom index	64.7

Origins of GDP		**Components of GDP**	
	% of total		% of total
Agriculture	1.8	Private consumption	43.8
Industry, of which:	60.6	Public consumption	10.4
manufacturing	12.4	Investment	21.4
Services	37.6	Exports	91.0
		Imports	-72.0

Structure of employment

	% of total		% of labour force
Agriculture	8	Unemployed 2001	2.3
Industry	22	Av. ann. rate 1995–2001	2.1
Services	70		

Energy

			m TOE
Total output	177.3	Net energy imports as %	
Total consumption	46.9	of energy use	-278
Consumption per head,			
kg oil equivalent	11,036		

Inflation and finance

		av. ann. increase 2002–07	
Consumer price			
inflation 2007	11.1%	Narrow money (M1)	31.0%
Av. ann. inflation 2003–07	8.9%	Broad money	26.6%
Interbank rate, 2007	5.14%		

Exchange rates

	end 2008		December 2008
		Effective rates	2000 = 100
AED per $	3.67	– nominal	91.50
AED per SDR	5.66		
AED per €	5.11	– real	...

Trade

Principal exports
	$bn fob
Crude oil	71.2
Re-exports	62.3
Gas	7.8
Total incl. others	**180.9**

Principal imports[a]
	$bn cif
Machinery & electrical equip.	18.1
Precious stones & metals	14.3
Transport equipment	10.0
Total incl. others	**100.1**

Main export destinations
	% of total
Japan	23.6
South Korea	10.2
Thailand	5.2
India	4.8

Main origins of imports
	% of total
China	13.2
India	10.3
United States	9.0
Germany	6.1

Balance of payments, reserves and debt, $bn

Visible exports fob	180.9	Change in reserves	49.6
Visible imports fob	-116.6	Level of reserves	
Trade balance	64.3	end Dec.	77.2
Invisibles, net	-18.0	No. months of import cover	3.3
Net transfers	-9.3	Official gold holdings, m oz	0.0
Current account balance	37.0	Foreign debt	105.9
– as % of GDP	18.6	– as % of GDP	53
Capital balance	11.3	– as % of total exports	51
Overall balance	49.9	Debt service ratio	4
		Aid given	0.43
		% of GDP	0.22

Health and education

Health spending, % of GDP	2.5	Education spending, % of GDP	1.4
Doctors per 1,000 pop.	1.4	Enrolment, %: primary	107
Hospital beds per 1,000 pop.	2.2	secondary	92
Improved-water source access,		tertiary	...
% of pop.	100		

Society

No. of households	0.7m	Colour TVs per 100 households	99.8
Av. no. per household	6.0	Telephone lines per 100 pop.	31.6
Marriages per 1,000 pop.	3.5	Mobile telephone subscribers	
Divorces per 1,000 pop.	1.0	per 100 pop.	176.5
Cost of living, Feb. 2009		Computers per 100 pop.	33.0
New York = 100	71	Internet hosts per 1,000 pop.	78.9

a 2006

UNITED KINGDOM

Area	242,534 sq km	Capital	London
Arable as % of total land	24	Currency	Pound (£)

People

Population	60.0m	Life expectancy: men	77.2 yrs
Pop. per sq km	247.4	women	81.6 yrs
Av. ann. growth		Adult literacy	...
in pop. 2010–15	0.52%	Fertility rate (per woman)	1.9
Pop. under 15	17.4%	Urban population	89.9%
Pop. over 60	22.4%		per 1,000 pop.
No. of men per 100 women	96	Crude birth rate	13.0
Human Development Index	94.2	Crude death rate	9.9

The economy

GDP	£1,385bn	GDP per head	$45,440
GDP	$2,772bn	GDP per head in purchasing	
Av. ann. growth in real		power parity (USA=100)	77.1
GDP 2002–2007	2.8%	Economic freedom index	79.0

Origins of GDP		Components of GDP	
	% of total		% of total
Agriculture	1.3	Private consumption	63.9
Industry, of which:	24.9	Public consumption	21.1
manufacturing	...	Investment	18.2
Services	73.8	Exports	26.4
		Imports	-29.8

Structure of employment

	% of total		% of labour force
Agriculture	1	Unemployed 2007	5.3
Industry	22	Av. ann. rate 1995–2007	5.9
Services	77		

Energy

	m TOE		
Total output	186.6	Net energy imports as %	
Total consumption	231.1	of energy use	19
Consumption per head,			
kg oil equivalent	3,814		

Inflation and finance

Consumer price		av. ann. increase 2001–07	
inflation 2008	4.0%	Narrow money (M0)	5.5%
Av. ann. inflation 2002–07	3.5%	Broad money (M4)	10.6%
Money market rate, 2008	4.65%	Household saving rate[a], 2008	-0.2%

Exchange rates

	end 2008		December 2008
			2000 = 100
£ per $	0.69	Effective rates	
£ per SDR	0.95	– nominal	79.20
£ per €	0.96	– real	73.80

Trade

Principal exports	$bn fob	Principal imports	$bn fob
Machinery & transport equip.	153.3	Machinery & transport equip.	221.4
Chemicals & related products	79.3	Chemicals & related products	72.4
Mineral fuels & lubricants	47.5	Mineral fuels & lubricants	59.8
Food, drink & tobacco	23.6	Food, drink & tobacco	53.2
Total incl. others	**441.9**	Total incl. others	**621.5**

Main export destinations	% of total	Main origins of imports	% of total
United States	13.8	Germany	14.0
Germany	10.7	United States	8.5
France	7.7	Netherlands	7.4
Ireland	7.4	France	7.0
Netherlands	6.3	Belgium	6.0
EU27	58.2	EU27	54.7

Balance of payments, reserves and aid, $bn

Visible exports fob	442.2	Overall balance	2.6
Visible imports fob	-620.7	Change in reserves	10.2
Trade balance	-178.7	Level of reserves	
Invisibles inflows	866.6	end Dec.	57.3
Invisibles outflows	-739.6	No. months of import cover	0.5
Net transfers	-27.1	Official gold holdings, m oz	10.0
Current account balance	-78.8	Aid given	9.85
– as % of GDP	-2.8	– as % of GDP	0.36
Capital balance	70.4		

Health and education

Health spending, % of GDP	8.2	Education spending, % of GDP	5.5
Doctors per 1,000 pop.	2.1	Enrolment, %: primary	105
Hospital beds per 1,000 pop.	3.9	secondary	97
Improved-water source access,		tertiary	55
% of pop.	100		

Society

No. of households	26.4m	Colour TVs per 100 households	99.6
Av. no. per household	2.3	Telephone lines per 100 pop.	55.4
Marriages per 1,000 pop.	5.1	Mobile telephone subscribers	
Divorces per 1,000 pop.	2.9	per 100 pop.	118.5
Cost of living, Feb. 2009		Computers per 100 pop.	80.2
New York = 100	99	Internet hosts per 1,000 pop.	149.7

a Gross.

UNITED STATES

Area	9,372,610 sq km	Capital	Washington DC
Arable as % of total land	19	Currency	US dollar ($)

People

Population	303.9m	Life expectancy:	men	76.9 yrs
Pop. per sq km	32.4		women	81.4 yrs
Av. ann. growth		Adult literacy		...
in pop. 2010–15	0.90%	Fertility rate (per woman)		2.0
Pop. under 15	20.3%	Urban population		81.4%
Pop. over 60	17.9%			per 1,000 pop.
No. of men per 100 women	97	Crude birth rate		14.0
Human Development Index	95.0	Crude death rate		7.8

The economy

GDP	$13,751bn	GDP per head	$45,592
Av. ann. growth in real		GDP per head in purchasing	
GDP 2002–2007	2.9%	power parity (USA=100)	100
		Economic freedom index	80.7

Origins of GDP		**Components of GDP**	
	% of total		% of total
Agriculture	1.2	Private consumption	70.3
Industry, of which:	19.8	Public consumption	19.4
manufacturing	...	Non-government investment	15.4
Services[a]	79.0	Exports	12.0
		Imports	-17.2

Structure of employment

	% of total		% of labour force
Agriculture	2	Unemployed 2007	4.6
Industry	22	Av. ann. rate 1995–2007	5.0
Services	76		

Energy

	m TOE		
Total output	1,654.2	Net energy imports as %	
Total consumption	2,320.7	of energy use	29
Consumption per head,			
kg oil equivalent	7,770		

Inflation and finance

Consumer price		av. ann. increase 2002-07	
inflation 2008	3.8%	Narrow money	2.5%
Av. ann. inflation 2003–08	3.2%	Broad money	7.9%
Money market rate, 2008	1.93%	Household saving rate, 2008	1.6%

Exchange rates

	end 2008		December 2008
$ per SDR	1.54	Effective rates	2000 = 100
$ per €	1.39	– nominal	90.50
		– real	80.50

Trade

Principal exports	$bn fob	Principal imports	$bn fob
Capital goods, excl. vehicles	445.9	Industrial supplies	630.7
Industrial supplies	315.5	Consumer goods, excl. vehicles	474.9
Consumer goods, excl. vehicles	146.4	Capital goods, excl. vehicles	444.7
Vehicles & products	120.9	Vehicles & products	258.9
Food & beverages	84.2	Food & beverages	81.7
Total incl. others	**1,162.5**	**Total incl. others**	**1,957.0**

Main export destinations	% of total	Main origins of imports	% of total
Canada	21.4	China	17.4
Mexico	11.7	Canada	16.2
China	5.6	Mexico	10.9
Japan	5.4	Japan	7.6
Germany	4.3	Germany	4.9
United Kingdom	4.3	United Kingdom	3.0
EU27	21.3	EU27	18.0

Balance of payments, reserves and aid, $bn

Visible exports fob	1,152.6	Overall balance	0.1
Visible imports fob	-1,967.9	Change in reserves	56.5
Trade balance	-815.3	Level of reserves	
Invisibles inflows	1,310.9	end Dec.	277.5
Invisibles outflows	-1,114.1	No. months of import cover	1.1
Net transfers	-112.7	Official gold holdings, m oz	261.5
Current account balance	-731.2	Aid given	21.79
– as % of GDP	-5.3	– as % of GDP	0.16
Capital balance	772.6		

Health and education

Health spending, % of GDP	15.3	Education spending, % of GDP	5.7
Doctors per 1,000 pop.	2.9	Enrolment, %: primary	104
Hospital beds per 1,000 pop.	3.3	secondary	94
Improved-water source access,		tertiary	82
% of pop.	100		

Society

No. of households	115.2m	Colour TVs per 100 households	98.8
Av. no. per household	2.6	Telephone lines per 100 pop.	53.4
Marriages per 1,000 pop.	7.7	Mobile telephone subscribers	
Divorces per 1,000 pop.	3.4	per 100 pop.	83.5
Cost of living, Feb. 2009		Computers per 100 pop.	80.5
New York = 100	100	Internet hosts per 1,000 pop.[b]	1,093.2

---

a Including utilities.
b Includes all hosts ending ".com", ".net" and ".org" which exaggerates the numbers.

VENEZUELA

Area	912,050 sq km	Capital	Caracas
Arable as % of total land	3	Currency	Bolivar (Bs)

People

Population	27.7m	Life expectancy:	men	70.9 yrs
Pop. per sq km	30.4		women	76.8 yrs
Av. ann. growth		Adult literacy		95.2%
in pop. 2010–15	1.49%	Fertility rate (per woman)		2.4
Pop. under 15	29.8%	Urban population		93.1%
Pop. over 60	8.4%			per 1,000 pop.
No. of men per 100 women	101	Crude birth rate		25
Human Development Index	82.6	Crude death rate		5.1

The economy

GDP	Bs490bn	GDP per head	$8,300
GDP	$228bn	GDP per head in purchasing	
Av. ann. growth in real		power parity (USA=100)	26.7
GDP 2002–07	8.8%	Economic freedom index	39.9

Origins of GDP		**Components of GDP**	
	% of total		% of total
Agriculture	3.8	Private consumption	53.8
Industry, of which:	38.4	Public consumption	11.9
manufacturing	16.5	Investment	28.0
Services	57.8	Exports	31.0
		Imports	-24.7

Structure of employment

	% of total		% of labour force
Agriculture	9	Unemployed 2003	16.8
Industry	21	Av. ann. rate 1995–2003	13.2
Services	70		

Energy

	m TOE		
Total output	195.5	Net energy imports as %	
Total consumption	62.2	of energy use	-214
Consumption per head,			
kg oil equivalent	2,302		

Inflation and finance

		av. ann. increase 2002–07	
Consumer price			
inflation 2008	30.6%	Narrow money	64.2%
Av. ann. inflation 2003–08	20.0%	Broad money	51.2%
Money market rate, 2008	11.09%		

Exchange rates

	end 2008		December 2008
			2000 = 100
Bs per $	2.15	Effective rates	
Bs per SDR	3.31	– nominal	30.80
Bs per €	2.99	– real	118.40

Trade

Principal exports		Principal imports	
	$bn fob		*$bn fob*
Oil	62.6	Intermediate goods	20.5
Non-oil	6.6	Capital goods	14.3
		Consumer goods	11.3
Total incl. others	**69.2**	Total incl. others	**46.1**

Main export destinations[a]		Main origins of imports[a]	
	% of total		*% of total*
United States	53.5	United States	29.2
Netherlands Antilles	8.8	Colombia	9.6
China	3.7	Brazil	7.9
Spain	3.0	Mexico	6.1

Balance of payments, reserves and debt, $bn

Visible exports fob	69.2	Change in reserves	-3.0
Visible imports fob	-45.5	Level of reserves	
Trade balance	23.7	end Dec.	33.8
Invisibles inflows	11.8	No. months of import cover	6.7
Invisibles outflows	-15.1	Official gold holdings, m oz	11.5
Net transfers	-0.4	Foreign debt	43.1
Current account balance	20.0	– as % of GDP	26
– as % of GDP	8.8	– as % of total exports	66
Capital balance	-22.9	Debt service ratio	23
Overall balance	-5.4		

Health and education

Health spending, % of GDP	4.9	Education spending, % of GDP	3.7
Doctors per 1,000 pop.	1.4	Enrolment, %: primary	105
Hospital beds per 1,000 pop.	0.9	secondary	81
Improved-water source access,		tertiary	52
% of pop.	83		

Society

No. of households	6.0m	Colour TVs per 100 households	90.8
Av. no. per household	4.5	Telephone lines per 100 pop.	18.4
Marriages per 1,000 pop.	2.7	Mobile telephone subscribers	
Divorces per 1,000 pop.	0.9	per 100 pop.	86.1
Cost of living, Feb. 2009		Computers per 100 pop.	9.3
New York = 100	101	Internet hosts per 1,000 pop.	5.4

a 2006

VIETNAM

Area	331,114 sq km	Capital	Hanoi
Arable as % of total land	21	Currency	Dong (D)

People

Population	86.4m	Life expectancy: men	72.3 yrs
Pop. per sq km	260.9	women	76.2 yrs
Av. ann. growth		Adult literacy	...
in pop. 2010–15	1.01%	Fertility rate (per woman)	2.0
Pop. under 15	25.7%	Urban population	27.3%
Pop. over 60	8.6%		per 1,000 pop.
No. of men per 100 women	98	Crude birth rate	17
Human Development Index	71.8	Crude death rate	5.4

The economy

GDP	D1,111trn	GDP per head	$810
GDP	$68.6bn	GDP per head in purchasing	
Av. ann. growth in real		power parity (USA=100)	5.7
GDP 2002–07	9.5%	Economic freedom index	51.0

Origins of GDP		**Components of GDP**	
	% of total		% of total
Agriculture	20.3	Private consumption	64.9
Industry, of which:	41.6	Public consumption	6.1
manufacturing	24.9	Investment	41.6
Services	38.1	Exports	76.8
		Imports	-90.2

Structure of employment

	% of total		% of labour force
Agriculture	52	Unemployed 2004	2.1
Industry	18	Av. ann. rate 2003–2004	2.2
Services	30		

Energy

	m TOE		
Total output	71.9	Net energy imports as %	
Total consumption	52.3	of energy use	-38
Consumption per head,			
kg oil equivalent	621.5		

Inflation and finance

Consumer price		av. ann. increase 2001–06	
inflation 2008	24.4%	Narrow money (M1)	28.3
Av. ann. inflation 2002–07	11.2%	Broad money	34.6
Treasury bill rate, Oct. 2008	14.15%		

Exchange rates

	end 2008		December 2008
D per $	16,977	Effective rates	2000 = 100
D per SDR	26,149	– nominal	...
D per €	23,632	– real	...

Trade

Principal exports		Principal imports	
	$bn fob		$bn cif
Crude oil	8.1	Machinery & equipment	9.5
Textiles & garments	8.0	Petroleum products	6.8
Footwear	4.0	Steel	4.7
Fisheries products	3.8	Textiles	2.2
Total incl. others	**48.3**	Total incl. others	**60.7**

Main export destinations		Main origins of imports	
	% of total		% of total
United States	21.5	China	20.4
Japan	10.8	Singapore	11.8
Australia	7.0	Japan	9.6
China	5.9	South Korea	7.7
Germany	4.8	Thailand	6.9
Singapore	4.0	Malaysia	4.1
Malaysia	3.4	Hong Kong	4.0

Balance of payments, reserves and debt, $bn

Visible exports fob	48.6	Change in reserves	10.0
Visible imports fob	-58.9	Level of reserves	
Trade balance	-10.4	end Dec.	23.6
Invisibles inflows	7.1	No. months of import cover	4.1
Invisibles outflows	-10.2	Official gold holdings, m oz	0.0
Net transfers	6.4	Foreign debt	24.2
Current account balance	-7.0	– as % of GDP	35
– as % of GDP	-10.2	– as % of total exports	45
Capital balance	17.5	Debt service ratio	2
Overall balance	10.2		

Health and education

Health spending, % of GDP	6.6	Education spending, % of GDP	...
Doctors per 1,000 pop.	0.7	Enrolment, %: primary	...
Hospital beds per 1,000 pop.	1.4	secondary	66
Improved-water source access,		tertiary	...
% of pop.	85		

Society

No. of households	26.3m	Colour TVs per 100 households	76.5
Av. no. per household	3.2	Telephone lines per 100 pop.	32.7
Marriages per 1,000 pop.	12.1	Mobile telephone subscribers	
Divorces per 1,000 pop.	0.5	per 100 pop.	27.2
Cost of living, Feb. 2009		Computers per 100 pop.	9.6
New York = 100	63	Internet hosts per 1,000 pop.	1.8

ZIMBABWE

Area	390,759 sq km	Capital	Harare
Arable as % of total land	8	Currency	Zimbabwe dollar (Z$)

People

Population	13.2m	Life expectancy: men	43.4 yrs
Pop. per sq km	33.8	women	44.3 yrs
Av. ann. growth		Adult literacy	91.2%
in pop. 2010–15	2.08%	Fertility rate (per woman)	3.1
Pop. under 15	39.9%	Urban population	36.8%
Pop. over 60	5.8%		*per 1,000 pop.*
No. of men per 100 women	94	Crude birth rate	31
Human Development Index	...	Crude death rate	16.2

The economy

GDP[a]	Z$76,441bn	GDP per head[a]	$260
GDP[a]	$3.4bn	GDP per head in purchasing	
Av. ann. growth in real		power parity (USA=100)	...
GDP 2002–05	-5.2%	Economic freedom index	22.7

Origins of GDP		**Components of GDP**	
	% of total		*% of total*
Agriculture	19	Private consumption	72
Industry, of which:	24	Public consumption	27
manufacturing	14	Investment	17
Services	57	Exports	57
		Imports	-73

Structure of employment

	% of total		*% of labour force*
Agriculture	...	Unemployed 2002	8.2
Industry	...	Av. ann. rate 1997–2002	7.1
Services	...		

Energy

	m TOE		
Total output	8.8	Net energy imports as %	
Total consumption	9.6	of energy use	9
Consumption per head,			
kg oil equivalent	724		

Inflation and finance

Consumer price		*av. ann. increase 2002–07*	
inflation 2007	24,411%	Narrow money (M1)	1,542%
Av. ann. inflation 2003–07	1,357%	Broad money	1,518%
Deposit rate, 2006	203.4%		

Exchange rates

	end 2008		*December 2008*
Z$ per $	...	Effective rates	2000 = 100
Z$ per SDR	...	– nominal	...
Z$ per €	...	– real	...

Trade

Principal exports[bc]		Principal imports[bc]	
	$m fob		*$m cif*
Gold	306	Machinery & transport equip.	455
Ferro-alloys	210	Fuels	405
Tobacco	206	Manufactured products	255
Platinum	182	Chemicals	235
Total incl. others	**1,582**	Total incl. others	**2,163**

Main export destinations		Main origins of imports	
	% of total		*% of total*
South Africa	19.0	South Africa	38.8
Congo-Kinshasa	13.5	Zambia	28.2
Japan	12.2	China	5.7
Botswana	12.1	United States	3.3
Netherlands	8.9	Botswana	3.0

Balance of payments[b], reserves and debt, $bn

Visible exports fob	1.5	Change in reserves	0.0
Visible imports fob	-2.0	Level of reserves	
Trade balance	-0.5	end Dec.	0.0
Invisibles, net	-0.3	No. months of import cover	0.0
Net transfers	0.3	Official gold holdings, m oz	0.0
Current account balance	-0.5	Foreign debt	5.3
– as % of GDP	-15.0	– as % of GDP	121
Capital balance[d]	-0.4	– as % of total exports	326
Overall balance[d]	-0.4	Debt service ratio[a]	13

Health and education

Health spending, % of GDP	9.3	Education spending, % of GDP	...
Doctors per 1,000 pop.	0.2	Enrolment, %: primary	119
Hospital beds per 1,000 pop.	...	secondary	40
Improved-water source access,		tertiary	...
% of pop.	81		

Society

No. of households	3.4m	Colour TVs per 100 households	...
Av. no. per household	4.0	Telephone lines per 100 pop.	2.6
Marriages per 1,000 pop.	...	Mobile telephone subscribers	
Divorces per 1,000 pop.	...	per 100 pop.	9.2
Cost of living, Feb. 2009		Computers per 100 pop.	6.5
New York = 100	...	Internet hosts per 1,000 pop.	2.1

a 2005
b Estimates.
c 2006
d 2001 estimates.

EURO AREA[a]

Area	2,497,000 sq km	Capital	–
Arable as % of total land	25	Currency	Euro (€)

People

Population	314.4m	Life expectancy: men		77.5 yrs
Pop. per sq km	125.9	women		83.2 yrs
Av. ann. growth		Adult literacy		...
in pop. 2010–15	0.08%	Fertility rate (per woman)		1.5
Pop. under 15	15.4%	Urban population		73.3%
Pop. over 60	24.0%		per 1,000 pop.	
No. of men per 100 women	96	Crude birth rate		9
Human Development Index	94.5	Crude death rate		9.5

The economy

GDP	€8,971bn	GDP per head	$37,870
GDP	$12,278bn	GDP per head in purchasing	
Av. ann. growth in real		power parity (USA=100)	71.8
GDP 2002–2007	2.1%	Economic freedom index	67.5

Origins of GDP		**Components of GDP**	
	% of total		% of total
Agriculture	2	Private consumption	57
Industry, of which:	27	Public consumption	20
manufacturing	18	Investment	22
Services	71	Exports	41
		Imports	-39

Structure of employment

	% of total		% of labour force
Agriculture	4.3	Unemployed 2007	7.5
Industry	27.8	Av. ann. rate 1995–2007	9.2
Services	69.5		

Energy

	m TOE		
Total output	463.1	Net energy imports as %	
Total consumption	1,269.8	of energy use	64
Consumption per head,			
kg oil equivalent	3,936		

Inflation and finance

Consumer price		av. ann. increase 2002–07	
inflation 2008	3.3%	Narrow money (M1)	9.3%
Av. ann. inflation 2003–08	2.4%	Broad money	8.4%
Money market rate, 2008	4.64%	Household saving rate, 2008	10.4%

Exchange rates

	end 2008		December 2008
€ per $	0.72	Effective rates	2000 = 100
€ per SDR	1.11	– nominal	135.63
		– real	131.74

Trade[b]

Principal exports		Principal imports	
	$bn fob		$bn cif
Machinery & transport equip.	743.7	Machinery & transport equip.	527.8
Manufactures	424.2	Manufactures	522.9
Chemicals	270.6	Mineral fuels & lubricants	458.7
Mineral fuels & lubricants	86.9	Chemicals	165.1
Food, drink & tobacco	84.9	Food, drink & tobacco	103.5
Raw materials	41.5	Raw materials	96.4
Total incl. others	**1,699.3**	Total incl. others	**1,962.7**

Main export destinations		Main origins of imports	
	% of total		% of total
United States	21.1	China	16.2
Switzerland	7.5	United States	12.7
Russia	7.2	Russia	10.1
China	5.8	Japan	5.5
Turkey	4.2	Switzerland	5.4
Japan	3.5	Norway	5.3

Balance of payments, reserves and aid, $bn

Visible exports fob	2,073	Overall balance	6
Visible imports fob	-1,990	Change in reserves	81.3
Trade balance	83	Level of reserves	
Invisibles inflows	1,434	end Dec.	510.4
Invisibles outflows	-1,364	No. months of import cover	1.8
Net transfers	-115	Official gold holdings, m oz	353.7
Current account balance	39	Aid given[c]	44.8
– as % of GDP	0.3	– as % of GDP[c]	0.37
Capital balance	138		

Health and education

Health spending, % of GDP	9.8	Education spending, % of GDP	5.3
Doctors per 1,000 pop.	4.0	Enrolment, %: primary	...
Hospital beds per 1,000 pop.	5.7	secondary	...
Improved-water source access,		tertiary	...
% of pop.	100		

Society

No. of households	130.5	Colour TVs per 100 households	97.5
Av. no. per household	2.39	Telephone lines per 100 pop.	52.6
Marriages per 1,000 pop.	4.6	Mobile telephone subscribers	
Divorces per 1,000 pop.	1.9	per 100 pop.	116.7
Cost of living, Feb. 2009		Computers per 100 pop.	52.8
New York = 100	...	Internet hosts per 1,000 pop.	283.0

a Data generally refer to the 13 EU members that had adopted the euro before December 31 2007: Austria, Belgium, France, Finland, Germany, Greece, Ireland, Italy, Luxembourg, Netherlands, Portugal, Slovenia and Spain.

b EU27, excluding intra-trade.

c Excluding Slovenia.

WORLD

Area	148,698,382 sq km	Capital	...
Arable as % of total land	11	Currency	...

People

Population	6,615.9m	Life expectancy: men	65.4 yrs
Pop. per sq km	44.5	women	69.8 yrs
Av. ann. growth		Adult literacy	82.4%
in pop. 2010–15	1.11%	Fertility rate (per woman)	2.5
Pop. under 15	27.2%	Urban population	49.4%
Pop. over 60	10.8%		per 1,000 pop.
No. of men per 100 women	102	Crude birth rate	21
Human Development Index	74.7	Crude death rate	8.5

The economy

GDP	$54.6trn	GDP per head	$8,260
Av. ann. growth in real		GDP per head in purchasing	
GDP 2002–07	3.9%	power parity (USA=100)	21.9
		Economic freedom index	57.4

Origins of GDP		**Components of GDP**	
	% of total		% of total
Agriculture	3	Private consumption	61
Industry, of which:	28	Public consumption	17
manufacturing	18	Investment	22
Services	69	Exports	28
		Imports	-29

Structure of employment[a]

	% of total		% of labour force
Agriculture	...	Unemployed 2007	6.0
Industry	...	Av. ann. rate 1995–2007	6.6
Services	...		

Energy

	m TOE		
Total output	11,786.0	Net energy imports as %	
Total consumption	11,525.2	of energy use	-2
Consumption per head,			
kg oil equivalent	1,820		

Inflation and finance

Consumer price		av. ann. increase 2002–07	
inflation 2008	5.7%	Narrow money (M1)[a]	7.1%
Av. ann. inflation 2003–08	4.0%	Broad money[a]	7.0%
LIBOR $ rate, 3-month, 2008	2.91%	Household saving rate, 2008[a]	4.5%

Trade

World exports

	$bn fob		$bn fob
Manufactures	8,822	Ores & metals	483
Fuels	1,329	Agricultural raw materials	242
Food	725		
		Total incl. others	**12,085**

Main export destinations

	% of total
United States	14.3
Germany	7.5
China	6.8
France	4.4
Japan	4.4
United Kingdom	4.4

Main origins of imports

	% of total
Germany	9.6
China	8.8
United States	8.4
Japan	5.1
France	3.9
United Kingdom	3.2

Balance of payments, reserves and aid, $bn

Visible exports fob	13,867	Overall balance	0
Visible imports fob	-13,656	Change in reserves	1,516
Trade balance	211	Level of reserves	
Invisibles inflows	7,502	end Dec.	7,159
Invisibles outflows	-7,204	No. months of import cover	4
Net transfers	9	Official gold holdings, m oz	853
Current account balance	317	Aid given[b]	108.8
– as % of GDP	0.6	– as % of GDP[b]	0.27
Capital balance	-184		

Health and education

Health spending, % of GDP	9.8	Education spending, % of GDP	4.6
Doctors per 1,000 pop.	1.5	Enrolment, %: primary	106
Hospital beds per 1,000 pop.	...	secondary	65
Improved-water source access,		tertiary	24
% of pop.	83		

Society

No. of households	...	TVs per 100 households	...
Av. no. per household	...	Telephone lines per 100 pop.	19.1
Marriages per 1,000 pop.	...	Mobile telephone subscribers	
Divorces per 1,000 pop.	...	per 100 pop.	50.1
Cost of living, Feb. 2009		Computers per 100 pop.	15.3
New York = 100	...	Internet hosts per 1,000 pop.	94.3

a OECD countries.
b OECD, non-OECD Europe and Middle East countries.

Glossary

Balance of payments The record of a country's transactions with the rest of the world. The **current account** of the balance of payments consists of: visible trade (goods); "invisible" trade (services and income); private transfer payments (eg, remittances from those working abroad); official transfers (eg, payments to international organisations, famine relief). Visible imports and exports are normally compiled on rather different definitions to those used in the trade statistics (shown in principal imports and exports) and therefore the statistics do not match. The **capital account** consists of long- and short-term transactions relating to a country's assets and liabilities (eg, loans and borrowings). The current account and the capital account, plus an errors and omissions item, make up the **overall balance**. In the country pages of this book this item is included in the overall balance. **Changes in reserves** include gold at market prices and are shown without the practice often followed in balance of payments presentations of reversing the sign.

Big Mac index A light-hearted way of looking at exchange rates. If the dollar price of a burger at McDonald's in any country is higher than the price in the United States, converting at market exchange rates, then that country's currency could be thought to be over-valued against the dollar and vice versa.

Body-mass index A measure for assessing obesity – weight in kilograms divided by height in metres squared. An index of 30 or more is regarded as an indicator of obesity; 25 to 29.9 as over-weight. Guidelines vary for men and for women and may be adjusted for age.

CFA Communauté Financière Africaine. Its members, most of the francophone African nations, share a common currency, the CFA franc, which used to be pegged to the French franc but is now pegged to the euro.

Cif/fob Measures of the value of merchandise trade. Imports include the cost of "carriage, insurance and freight" (cif) from the exporting country to the importing. The value of exports does not include these elements and is recorded "free on board" (fob). Balance of payments statistics are generally adjusted so that both exports and imports are shown fob; the cif elements are included in invisibles.

Crude birth rate The number of live births in a year per 1,000 population. The crude rate will automatically be relatively high if a large proportion of the population is of childbearing age.

Crude death rate The number of deaths in a year per 1,000 population. Also affected by the population's age structure.

Debt, foreign Financial obligations owed by a country to the rest of the world and repayable in foreign currency. **The debt service ratio** is debt service (principal repayments plus interest payments) expressed as a percentage of the country's earnings from exports of goods and services.

EU European Union. Members are: Austria, Belgium, Denmark, Finland, France, Germany, Greece, Ireland, Italy, Luxembourg, Netherlands, Portugal, Spain, Sweden and the United Kingdom and, as of May 1 2004, Cyprus, Czech Republic, Estonia, Hungary, Latvia, Lithuania, Malta, Poland, Slovakia and Slovenia and, as of January 1 2007, Bulgaria and Romania.

Effective exchange rate The nominal index measures a currency's depreciation (figures below 100) or appreciation (figures over 100) from a base date against a trade-weighted basket of the currencies of the country's main trading partners. The real effective exchange rate reflects adjustments for relative movements in prices or costs.

Euro area The 16 euro area members of the EU are Austria, Belgium, Finland, France, Germany, Greece, Ireland, Italy, Luxembourg, Netherlands, Portugal and Spain and, from January 1 2007,

Slovenia. Cyprus and Malta joined on January 1 2008. Slovakia joined on January 1 2009. Their common currency is the euro, which came into circulation on January 1 2002.

Fertility rate The average number of children born to a woman who completes her childbearing years.

G7 Group of seven countries: United States, Japan, Germany, United Kingdom, France, Italy and Canada.

GDP Gross domestic product. The sum of all output produced by economic activity within a country. GNP (gross national product) and GNI (gross national income) include net income from abroad eg, rent, profits.

Household saving rate Household savings as % of disposable household income.

Import cover The number of months of imports covered by reserves ie, reserves ÷ $\frac{1}{12}$ annual imports (visibles and invisibles).

Inflation The annual rate at which prices are increasing. The most common measure and the one shown here is the increase in the consumer price index.

Internet hosts Websites and other computers that sit permanently on the internet.

Life expectancy The average length of time a baby born today can expect to live.

Literacy is defined by UNESCO as the ability to read and write a simple sentence, but definitions can vary from country to country.

Median age Divides the age distribution into two halves. Half of the population is above and half below the median age.

Money supply A measure of the "money" available to buy goods and services. Various definitions exist. The measures shown here are based on definitions used by the IMF and may differ from measures

used nationally. Narrow money (M1) consists of cash in circulation and demand deposits (bank deposits that can be withdrawn on demand). "Quasi-money" (time, savings and foreign currency deposits) is added to this to create broad money.

OECD Organisation for Economic Co-operation and Development. The "rich countries" club was established in 1961 to promote economic growth and the expansion of world trade. It is based in Paris and now has 30 members.

Opec Organisation of Petroleum Exporting Countries. Set up in 1960 and based in Vienna, Opec is mainly concerned with oil pricing and production issues. Members are; Algeria, Indonesia, Iran, Iraq, Kuwait, Libya, Nigeria, Qatar, Saudi Arabia, United Arab Emirates and Venezuela.

PPP Purchasing power parity. PPP statistics adjust for cost of living differences by replacing normal exchange rates with rates designed to equalise the prices of a standard "basket" of goods and services. These are used to obtain PPP estimates of GDP per head. PPP estimates are shown on an index, taking the United States as 100.

Real terms Figures adjusted to exclude the effect of inflation.

Reserves The stock of gold and foreign currency held by a country to finance any calls that may be made for the settlement of foreign debt.

SDR Special drawing right. The reserve currency, introduced by the IMF in 1970, was intended to replace gold and national currencies in settling international transactions. The IMF uses SDRs for book-keeping purposes and issues them to member countries. Their value is based on a basket of the US dollar (with a weight of 44%), the euro (34%), the Japanese yen (11%) and the pound sterling (11%).

List of countries

Whenever data is available, the world rankings consider 189 countries: all those which had (in 2007) or have recently had a population of at least 1m or a GDP of at least $1bn. Here is a list of them.

	Population	GDP	GDP per head	Area '000 sq	Median age
	m, 2007	$bn, 2007	$PPP, 2007	km	yrs, 2009
Afghanistan	32.3	8.4[b]	700[a]	652	16.8
Albania	3.2	10.8	7,040	29	29.7
Algeria	33.9	135.3	7,740	2,382	25.8
Andorra	0.1	3.7[a]	42,500[a]	0.4	39.0
Angola	16.9	61.4	5,390	1,247	17.3
Argentina	39.5	262.5	13,240	2,767	30.2
Armenia	3.0	9.2	5,690	30	31.8
Aruba	0.1	2.3[ab]	21,800[ab]	0.2	38.2
Australia	20.6	821.0	34,920	7,682	37.5
Austria	8.2	373.2	37,370	84	41.4
Azerbaijan	8.5	31.2	7,850	87	28.2
Bahamas	0.3	6.6	28,300[a]	14	29.4
Bahrain	0.7	15.8[b]	28,070[b]	1	28.0
Bangladesh	147.1	68.4	1,240	144	24.1
Barbados	0.3	3.0[b]	16,960[b]	0.4	37.3
Belarus	9.6	44.8	10,840	208	38.0
Belgium	10.5	452.8	34,940	31	41.1
Belize	0.3	1.3	6,730	23	21.9
Benin	9.0	5.4	1,310	113	18.3
Bermuda	0.1	5.9	69,900[ab]	1	40.0
Bhutan	2.3	1.1	4,840	47	23.8
Bolivia	9.5	13.1	4,210	1,099	21.7
Bosnia	3.9	15.1	7,760	51	38.9
Botswana	1.8	12.3	13,600	581	22.5
Brazil	191.3	1,313.4	9,570	8,512	28.6
Brunei	0.4	11.5[b]	50,200	6	27.5
Bulgaria	7.6	39.5	11,220	111	41.5
Burkina Faso	14.0	6.8	1,120	274	16.7
Burundi	8.1	1.0	340	28	19.9
Cambodia	14.6	8.4	1,800	181	21.9
Cameroon	16.9	20.7	2,130	475	19.1
Canada	32.9	1,329.9	35,810	9,971	39.6
Cape Verde	0.4	1.4	3,040	4	20.9
Cayman Islands	0.1	1.9[ab]	43,800[ab]	0.3	35.6
Central African Rep	4.2	1.7	410	622	19.4
Chad	10.3	7.1	1,480	1,284	17.0
Channel Islands	0.2	11.5	49,790	0.2	41.7
Chile	16.6	163.9	13,880	757	31.8
China	1,331.4	3,205.5	5,380	9,561	33.8
Colombia	47.0	207.8	8,590	1,142	26.5

	Population	GDP	GDP per head	Area '000 sq	Median age
	m, 2007	$bn, 2007	$PPP, 2007	km	yrs, 2009
Congo-Brazzaville	4.2	7.6	300	342	19.4
Congo-Kinshasa	61.2	9.0	3,510	2,345	16.5
Costa Rica	4.5	26.3	10,840	51	27.8
Côte d'Ivoire	18.8	19.8	1,690	322	19.4
Croatia	4.6	51.3	16,030	57	41.3
Cuba	11.3	45.5[a]	9,100[a]	111	37.7
Cyprus	0.8	21.3	24,790	9	36.3
Czech Republic	10.2	175.0	24,140	79	39.4
Denmark	5.5	311.6	36,130	43	40.5
Dominican Republic	9.1	36.7	6,710	48	24.8
Ecuador	13.6	44.5	7,450	272	25.2
Egypt	76.9	130.5	5,350	1,000	23.6
El Salvador	7.1	20.4	5,800	21	23.7
Equatorial Guinea	0.6	9.9	30,630	28	19.1
Eritrea	4.7	1.4	630	117	19.0
Estonia	1.3	20.9	20,360	45	39.5
Ethiopia	81.2	19.4	780	1,134	17.9
Faroe Islands	0.1	1.7[ab]	31,000[ab]	1	36.6
Fiji	0.9	3.4	4,300	18	24.7
Finland	5.3	244.7	34,530	338	41.8
France	60.9	2,589.8[c]	33,670	544	39.9
French Guiana	0.2	3.4[b]	14,550[b]	90	23.9
French Polynesia	0.3	4.7[ab]	18,000[ab]	3	28.2
Gabon	1.4	11.6	15,170	268	21.3
Gambia, The	1.6	0.6	1,230	11	18.8
Georgia	4.4	10.2	4,660	70	37.2
Germany	82.7	3,317.4	34,400	358	43.9
Ghana	23.0	15.1	1,330	239	20.4
Greece	11.2	313.4	28,520	132	41.3
Greenland	0.1	1.7[ab]	20,000[ab]	2,176	34.0
Guadeloupe	0.5	9.8[b]	20,320[b]	2	36.3
Guam	0.2	2.5[ab]	15,000[ab]	1	29.0
Guatemala	13.2	33.9	4,560	109	18.7
Guinea	9.8	4.6	1,140	246	18.4
Guinea-Bissau	1.7	0.4	480	36	18.7
Guyana	0.8	1.1	2,780	215	27.1
Haiti	8.8	6.7	1,160	28	21.3
Honduras	7.5	12.2	3,800	112	20.7
Hong Kong	7.2	207.2	42,310	1	41.3
Hungary	10.0	138.4	18,760	93	39.7
Iceland	0.3	20.0	35,740	103	34.9

	Population	GDP	GDP per head	Area '000 sq	Median age
	m, 2007	$bn, 2007	$PPP, 2007	km	yrs, 2009
India	1,135.6	1,176.9	2,750	3,287	24.7
Indonesia	228.1	432.8	3,710	1,904	27.9
Iran	71.2	286.1	10,960	1,648	26.3
Iraq	30.3	60.1[a]	3,800[a]	438	19.2
Ireland	4.3	259.0	44,610	70	34.3
Israel	7.0	164.0	26,320	21	29.5
Italy	58.2	2,101.6	30,350	301	43.0
Jamaica	2.7	11.4	6,080	11	26.1
Japan	128.3	4,384.3	33,630	378	44.4
Jordan	6.0	15.8	4,900	89	22.4
Kazakhstan	14.8	104.9	10,860	2,717	29.3
Kenya	36.0	24.2	1,540	583	18.3
Kuwait	2.8	112.1	46,570[b]	18	30.3
Kyrgyzstan	5.4	3.7	2,010	199	24.8
Laos	6.2	4.1	2,170	237	20.4
Latvia	2.3	27.2	16,380	64	39.9
Lebanon	3.7	24.4	10,110	10	28.8
Lesotho	1.8	1.6	1,540	30	19.6
Liberia	3.5	0.7	360	111	18.4
Libya	6.1	58.3	14,360	1,760	25.8
Lithuania	3.4	38.3	17,580	65	39.4
Luxembourg	0.5	49.5	79,490	3	39.1
Macau	0.5	14.2[b]	44,100[b]	0.02	37.9
Macedonia	2.0	7.7	9,100	26	35.7
Madagascar	19.6	7.4	930	587	18.3
Malawi	13.5	3.6	760	118	16.8
Malaysia	26.2	186.7	13,520	333	26.0
Maldives	0.3	1.1	5,200	0.3	23.8
Mali	14.3	6.9	1,080	1,240	17.6
Malta	0.4	7.4	23,080	0.3	38.7
Martinique	0.4	9.6[b]	22,260[b]	1	38.3
Mauritania	3.2	2.6	1,930	1,031	19.9
Mauritius	1.3	6.8	11,300	2	32.2
Mexico	109.6	1,022.8	14,100	1,973	27.2
Moldova	4.2	4.4	2,550	34	35.0
Mongolia	2.7	3.9	3,240	1,565	25.9
Montenegro	0.7	3.5	11,700	14	35.6
Morocco	32.4	75.1	4,110	447	25.8
Mozambique	20.5	7.8	800	799	17.9
Myanmar	51.5	19.6[a]	850[b]	677	27.6
Namibia	2.1	7.0	5,160	824	20.8
Nepal	28.2	10.3	1,050	147	21.3

	Population	GDP	GDP per head	Area '000 sq	Median age
	m, 2007	$bn, 2007	$PPP, 2007	km	yrs, 2009
Netherlands	16.4	765.8	38,690	42	40.5
Netherlands Antilles	0.2	2.8[ab]	16,000[ab]	1	37.9
New Caledonia	0.2	3.2[ab]	15,000[ab]	19	30.0
New Zealand	4.1	135.7	27,340	271	36.4
Nicaragua	5.7	5.7	2,570	130	21.7
Niger	14.9	4.2	630	1,267	15.1
Nigeria	137.2	165.5	1,970	924	18.5
North Korea	22.7	40.0[a]	1,700[ab]	121	33.6
Norway	4.7	388.4	53,430	324	38.7
Oman	2.7	35.7[b]	22,230[b]	310	24.0
Pakistan	164.6	142.9	2,500	804	21.0
Panama	3.3	19.5	11,390	77	27.1
Papua New Guinea	6.1	6.3	2,080	463	19.9
Paraguay	6.4	12.2	4,430	407	22.8
Peru	28.8	107.3	7,840	1,285	25.3
Philippines	85.9	144.1	3,410	300	23.0
Poland	38.5	422.1	15,990	313	37.9
Portugal	10.6	222.8	22,770	89	40.6
Puerto Rico	4.0	77.4[a]	18,300[a]	9	35.7
Qatar	0.8	52.7[b]	70,720[b]	11	30.1
Réunion	0.8	15.8[b]	18,320[b]	3	30.1
Romania	21.5	166.0	12,370	238	38.1
Russia	141.9	1,290.1	14,690	17,075	37.9
Rwanda	9.4	3.3	870	26	18.5
Saudi Arabia	25.8	382.7	22,940	2,200	24.3
Senegal	12.2	11.2	1,670	197	17.9
Serbia	9.9	40.1	10,250	88	37.4
Sierra Leone	5.8	1.7	680	72	18.3
Singapore	4.4	161.3	49,700	1	40.0
Slovakia	5.4	75.0	20,080	49	36.8
Slovenia	2.0	47.2	26,750	20	41.4
Somalia	8.8	2.5[a]	600[a]	638	17.6
South Africa	47.7	283.0	9,760	1,226	24.7
South Korea	48.1	969.8	24,800	99	37.3
Spain	43.6	1,435.9	31,560	505	39.9
Sri Lanka	21.1	32.3	4,240	66	30.3
Sudan	37.8	46.2	2,090	2,506	20.1
Suriname	0.5	2.2	7,810	164	27.3
Swaziland	1.0	2.9	4,790	17	19.1
Sweden	9.1	464.3	34,710	450	40.7
Switzerland	7.3	424.4	40,660	41	41.6
Syria	20.0	37.7	4,510	185	22.1

	Population	GDP	GDP per head	Area	Median age
	m, 2007	$bn, 2007	$PPP, 2007	'000 sq km	yrs, 2009
Taiwan	22.9	383.3	34,390	36	37.0
Tajikistan	6.7	3.7	1,750	143	20.4
Tanzania	39.7	16.2	1,210	945	17.5
Thailand	65.3	245.4	8,040	513	32.8
Timor-Leste	1.1	0.4	720	15	17.2
Togo	6.5	2.5	790	57	19.6
Trinidad & Tobago	1.3	20.9	23,510	5	30.4
Tunisia	10.3	35.0	7,520	164	28.6
Turkey	75.2	655.9	12,960	779	28.0
Turkmenistan	5.0	12.9	4,680[b]	488	24.4
Uganda	30.9	11.8	1,060	241	15.5
Ukraine	45.5	141.2	6,910	604	39.4
United Arab Emirates	4.8	163.3[b]	53,210[b]	84	31.2
United Kingdom	60.0	2,772.0	35,130	243	39.7
United States	303.9	13,751.4	45,590	9,373	36.5
Uruguay	3.5	23.1	11,220	176	33.5
Uzbekistan	27.4	22.3	2,430	447	24.2
Venezuela	27.7	228.1	12,160	912	25.8
Vietnam	86.4	68.6	2,600	331	27.9
Virgin Islands (US)	0.1	1.6[ab]	14,500[ab]	0.4	38.1
West Bank and Gaza	3.9	5.3[b]	2,900[ab]	6	17.4
Yemen	22.3	22.5	2,340	528	17.6
Zambia	12.1	11.4	1,360	753	16.8
Zimbabwe	13.2	3.4[b]	200[a]	391	18.9
Euro area (13)	314.4	12,173.9	32,740	2,497	40.6
World	6,615.9	54,583.8	9,980	148,698	28.9

a Estimate.
b Latest available year.
c Including French Guiana, Guadeloupe, Martinique and Réunion.

Sources

Academy of Motion Picture Arts
 and Sciences
Airports Council International,
 Worldwide Airport Traffic Report
ASEAN, Asian Development
 Report

Bloomberg
BP, *Statistical Review of World
 Energy*
British Mountaineering Council
Business Software Alliance

CB Richard Ellis, *Global
 MarketView Office Occupancy
 Costs*
Central banks
Central Intelligence Agency, *The
 World Factbook*
CIRFS
Confederation of Swedish
 Enterprise
Corporate Resources Group,
 Quality of Living Report
Council of Europe

The Economist
 www.economist.com
Economist Intelligence Unit, *Cost
 of Living Survey*; *Country
 Forecasts*; *Country Reports*; *E-
 readiness rankings*; *Global
 Outlook – Business Environment
 Rankings*
ERC Statistics International,
 World Cigarette Report
Euromonitor, *International
 Marketing Data and Statistics*;
 *European Marketing Data and
 Statistics*
Europa Publications, *The Europa
 World Yearbook*
Eurostat, *Statistics in Focus*

Financial Times Business
 Information,
 The Banker

Food and Agriculture
 Organisation

The Heritage Foundation, *Index
 of Economic Freedom*
Human Rights Research

IFPI
IMD, *World Competitiveness
 Yearbook*
IMF, *Direction of Trade*;
 *International Financial
 Statistics*; *World Economic
 Outlook*
International Centre for Prison
 Studies, *World Prison Brief*
International Cocoa
 Organisation, *Quarterly
 Bulletin of Cocoa Statistics*
International Coffee
 Organisation
International Cotton Advisory
 Committee, *Bulletin*
International Diabetes
 Federation, *Diabetes Atlas*
International Grains Council, *The
 Grain Market Report*
International Institute for
 Strategic Studies, *Military
 Balance*
International Labour
 Organisation
International Obesity Task Force
International Road Federation,
 World Road Statistics
International Rubber Study
 Group, *Rubber Statistical
 Bulletin*
International Sugar
 Organisation, *Statistical
 Bulletin*
International Tea Committee,
 Annual Bulletin of Statistics
International
 Telecommunication Union,
 ITU Indicators
International Union of Railways

International Wool Trade Organisation

ISTA Mielke, *Oil World*

Johnson Matthey

Mercer, *Quality of Living Survey*

Morgan Stanley Research

National statistics offices

Network Wizards

Nobel Foundation

OECD, *Development Assistance Committee Report; Economic Outlook; Environmental Data; Programme for International Student Assessment; Society at a Glance*

www.olympic.org

Population Reference Bureau

Reporters Without Borders, *Press Freedom Index*

Space.com

Standard & Poor's *Emerging Stock Markets Factbook*

Taiwan Statistical Data Book

The Times, *Atlas of the World*

Thomson Datastream

Time Inc Magazines, *Fortune International*

Transparency International

UN, *Demographic Yearbook; Global Refugee Trends; Review of Maritime Transport; State of World Population Report; Survey on Crime Trends; World Contraceptive Use; World Population Database; World Population Prospects; World Urbanisation Prospects*

UNAIDS, *Report on the Global AIDS Epidemic*

UNCTAD, *Review of Maritime Transport; World Investment Report*

UNCTAD/WTO International Trade Centre

UN Development Programme, *Human Development Report*

UNESCO, website: unescostat. unesco.org

Unicef, *Child Poverty in Perspective*

Union Internationale des Chemins de Fer, *Statistiques Internationales des Chemins de Fer*

US Census Bureau

US Department of Agriculture

University of Michigan, Windows to the Universe website

WHO, *Global Tuberculosis Report; Immunisation Summary; World Health Statistics Annual; World Report on Violence and Health*

World Bank, *Doing Business; Global Development Finance; World Development Indicators; World Development Report*

World Bureau of Metal Statistics, *World Metal Statistics*

World Economic Forum/Harvard University, *Global Competitiveness Report*

World Resources Institute, *World Resources*

World Tourism Organisation, *Yearbook of Tourism Statistics*

World Trade Organisation, *Annual Report*